IMAGES
of America

ALEXANDRIA

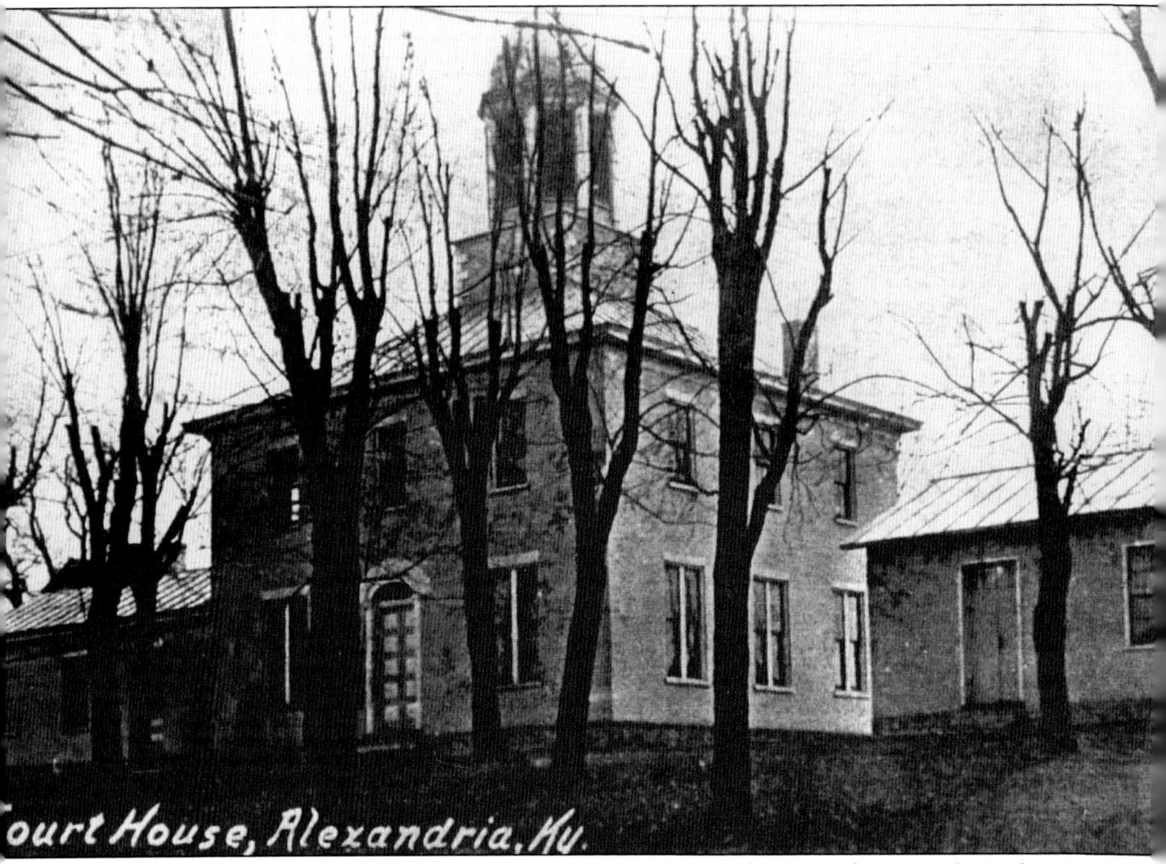

CAMPBELL COUNTY COURTHOUSE, 1840–1842. Construction began on the original courthouse in the early 1840s. The red brick used for the structure was burned at the kiln owned by the Spilman family. Stonemason and bricklayer Rev. James Jolly, who was the minister of the Alexandria Baptist Church at the time, is credited with building the courthouse. The first court was held on December 26, 1842. On November 14, 1845, the heirs of Frank and Rebecca Erskine Spilman deeded the property to the Town of Alexandria.

ON THE COVER: In 1948, Bess Lemon had this diner, the Betsy Ann, built at the fork of U.S. 27 and Washington Street. The establishment offered lunch, ice cream, soda, pie, and cake, along with a daily special. On weekends and holidays, it was the place to stop when traveling south. Manager Madeline "Maggie" Rembus is pictured at the fountain.

IMAGES
of America

ALEXANDRIA

Campbell County Historical
and Genealogical Society

ARCADIA
PUBLISHING

ISBN 978-0-7385-5392-4

Published by Arcadia Publishing
Charleston, South Carolina

Printed in the United States of America

Library of Congress Catalog Card Number: 2007942779

For all general information contact Arcadia Publishing at:
Telephone 843-853-2070
Fax 843-853-0044
E-mail sales@arcadiapublishing.com
For customer service and orders:
Toll-Free 1-888-313-2665

Visit us on the Internet at www.arcadiapublishing.com

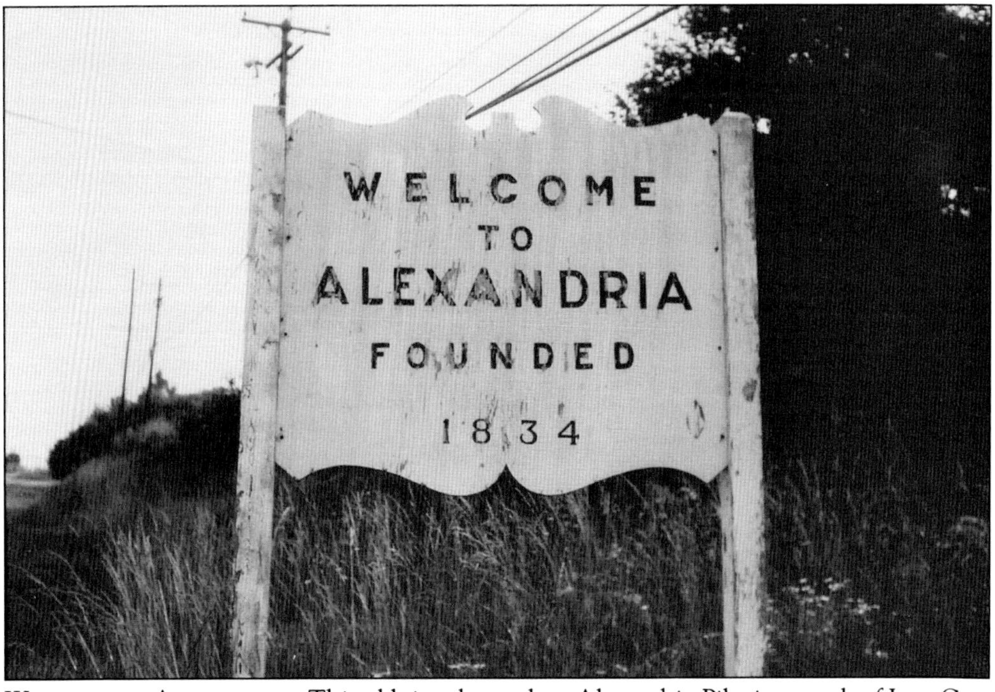

WELCOME TO ALEXANDRIA. This old sign, located on Alexandria Pike just south of Low Gap, greeted visitors as they drove south along the pike. A new sign and small flower garden replaced this sign after the road was widened. It is fitting for the Campbell County Historical and Genealogical Society to dedicate this book to the citizens of Alexandria—past, present, and future.

Contents

ACKNOWLEDGMENTS

The Campbell County Historical and Genealogical Society would like to thank the individuals who have donated photographs, family histories, and historical items over the years. Their contributions have made this book possible. All photographs appearing in this book were donated to, and appear courtesy of, the Campbell County Historical and Genealogical Society. We would also like to recognize the late Elizabeth Morrow Cooley, who devoted her time to the booklet *Early Days of Alexandria, Kentucky* for the society, and to Elizabeth Thatcher Clough, who made additions to the booklet in 1946. The booklet *Campbell County Kentucky 200 years 1794–1994*, written by society members, also served as a good resource as we prepared *Alexandria.*

We also wish to thank the contributors to this book, namely the society's members: Kenneth A. Reis, president; Jim Reis, vice president; Herman "Buck" Seibert, director; Elizabeth Thatcher Klem; and Pamela Ciafardini Casebolt. This project required a team effort, including countless hours of writing and gathering the images for layout. All of the proceeds will go directly to the Campbell County Historical and Genealogical Society, thus enabling the society to continue to preserve the history of not only the city of Alexandria, but all cities within Campbell County, Kentucky.

INTRODUCTION

Early settlers, most of them Revolutionary War veterans, traveled to Kentucky to build a new home from various parts of Virginia as early as 1793. Frank Spilman, whose previous home was Alexandria, Virginia, is credited with naming the settlement. On February 22, 1834, the town was incorporated on 12 acres of land donated by Frank and his wife, Rebecca Erskine Spilman. Some of the first to arrive were the Spilman, Thatcher, Reiley, White, Morin, Shaw, Beall, Baker, and Griffey families.

Alexandria is located 15 miles from Cincinnati, Ohio, and about 8 miles from Newport, Kentucky. In 1797, the Thatcher Tavern became one of the first businesses established in the town. The first post office opened in 1819, and area churches were built as early as 1820. Alexandria served as the original county seat in 1840 and remains one of two county seats in Campbell County. Citizens formed the Agricultural Society of Campbell County in 1856 to aid area farmers in selling their produce, livestock, and handmade items to the general public. Transportation in the early years involved traveling on dirt roads by horse and buggy, followed by buses and finally automobiles. The city began building its infrastructure of electricity in 1916 and telephone and gas lines in the 1920s. The first fair was held from October 14 to 17, 1856. The fair continues to be an annual event, with the exception of the Civil War years.

Today the city of Alexandria is home to more than 8,286 individuals representing 2,275 families, as of the 2000 census. It is no longer the agricultural community it once was, although some families still farm on a smaller level and participate in local farmers' markets. Much of the farmland has been sold, and new residential communities are being developed. Where rolling hills once stood, commercial developments are rising up to provide residents with shopping centers, drugstores, food markets, and highways.

As progress continues in the area, it is a good time to survey the past to see how it all began. *Alexandria* will guide you through the rolling hills, valleys, and meadows of this upper Bluegrass city.

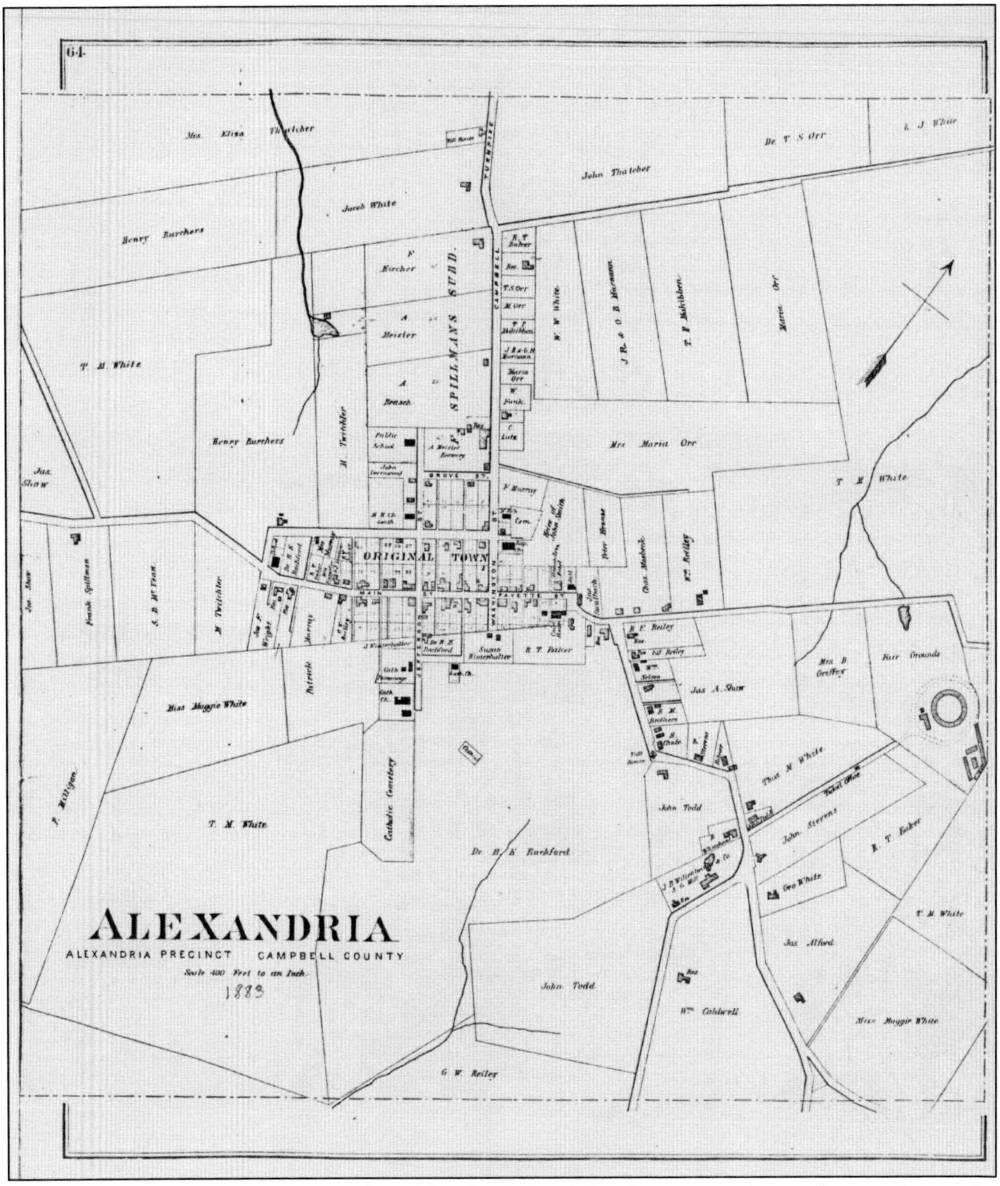

MAP OF ALEXANDRIA, 1883. Produced by the Lake Atlas Company, this early map shows the layout of family lots in the town of Alexandria. Early settlers, in order to define their property, cut trees from the wilderness, built their log cabin, and staked the land they claimed to be theirs. As time went on, the property was eventually registered in the county deed book.

One

FIRST FAMILIES

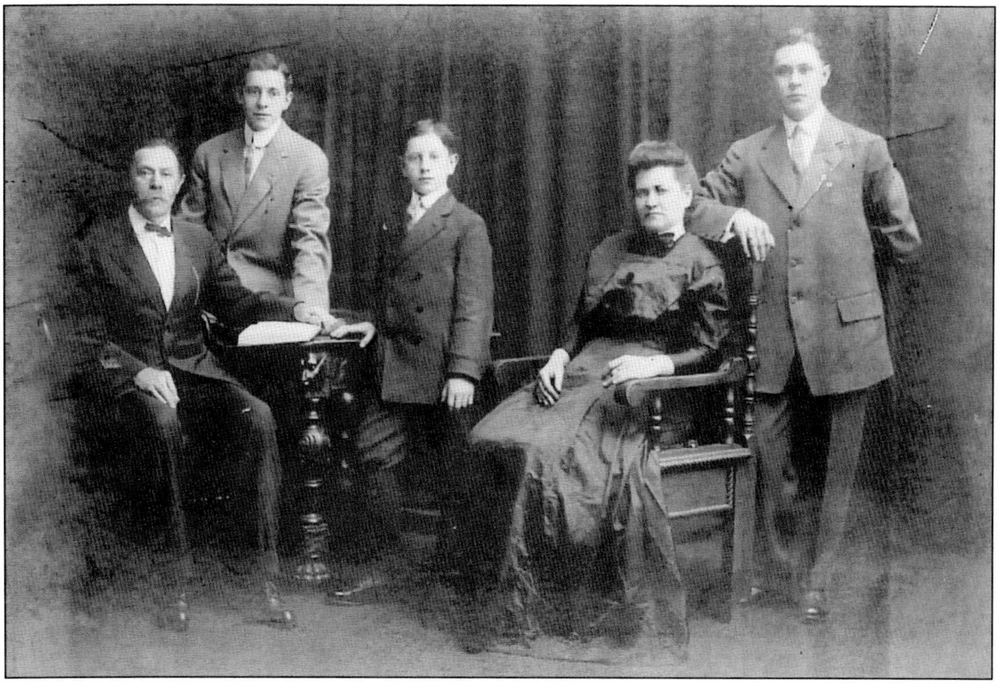

THE JOHN AND HARRIET "HATTIE" REBECCA MOORE SHAW FAMILY, 1911. John and Hattie were married on December 25, 1890, and had three sons: Ennis (left), Joseph Peter (center), and John Willis "J. W." Ennis wed Eula Harris on October 24, 1931, and lived at the original home. In 1917, Joe married Inez McPeak of Wisconsin. He moved out of the area after his father's death. J. W., who married Henrietta Schub on October 8, 1913, operated a real estate and insurance business in Newport. The couple had two children: Virginia Allene and Gordon William.

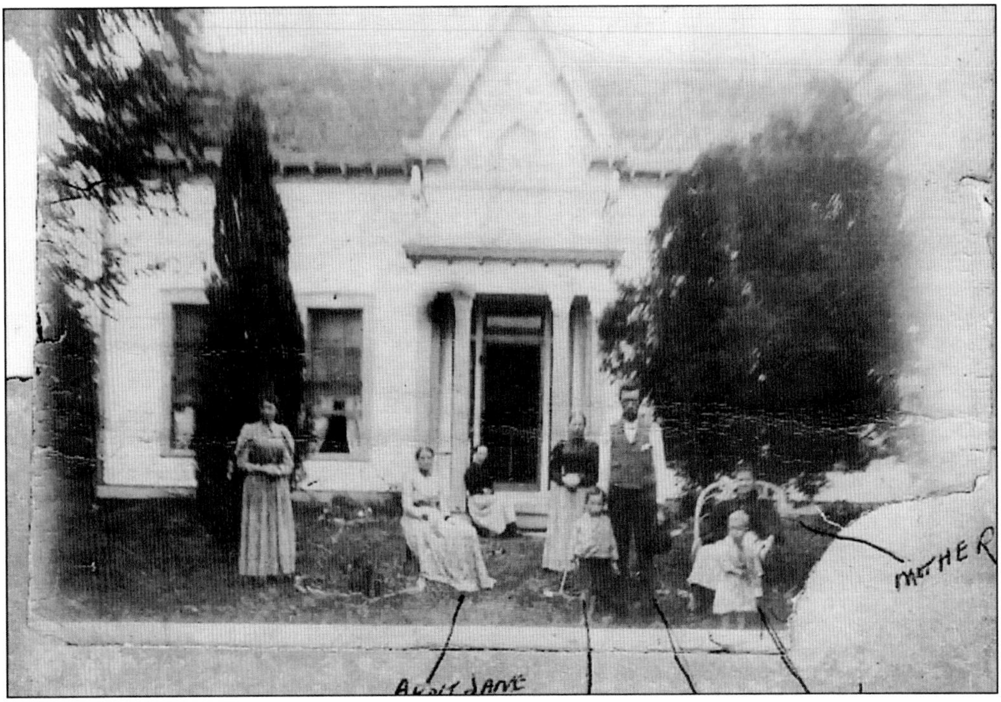

THE JOHN AND HATTIE SHAW HOME, c. 1896. This house is located on Persimmon Grove Pike. Above, John Shaw's sister Jane Alford sits in the left forefront, accompanied by John's family. The photograph below shows the original house as it looks today.

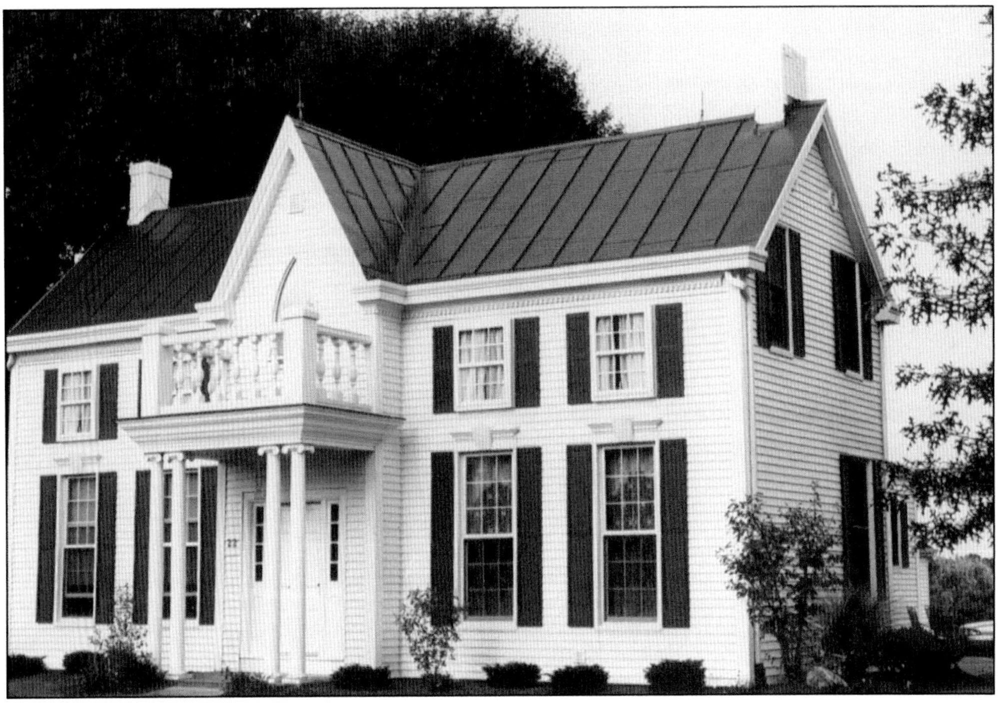

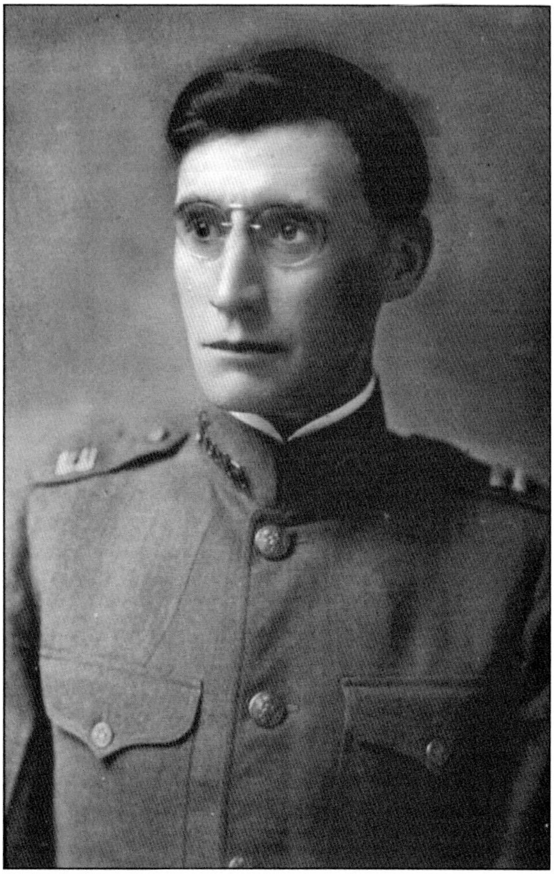

DR. CLAYTON W. SHAW, c. 1918. Clayton Whitemore Shaw (pictured right) was born on August 10, 1871, to James and Laura Reed Shaw. Dr. Shaw married Fay Fern, the daughter of Theodore M. Hill and Mary Isophene White; together they raised three sons, Hill McDonald, Roy Raymond, and Harold. In addition to running an office in Alexandria, Dr. Shaw practiced medicine during World War I. He is shown below with two of his nurses (unidentified). Dr. Shaw died on September 11, 1944.

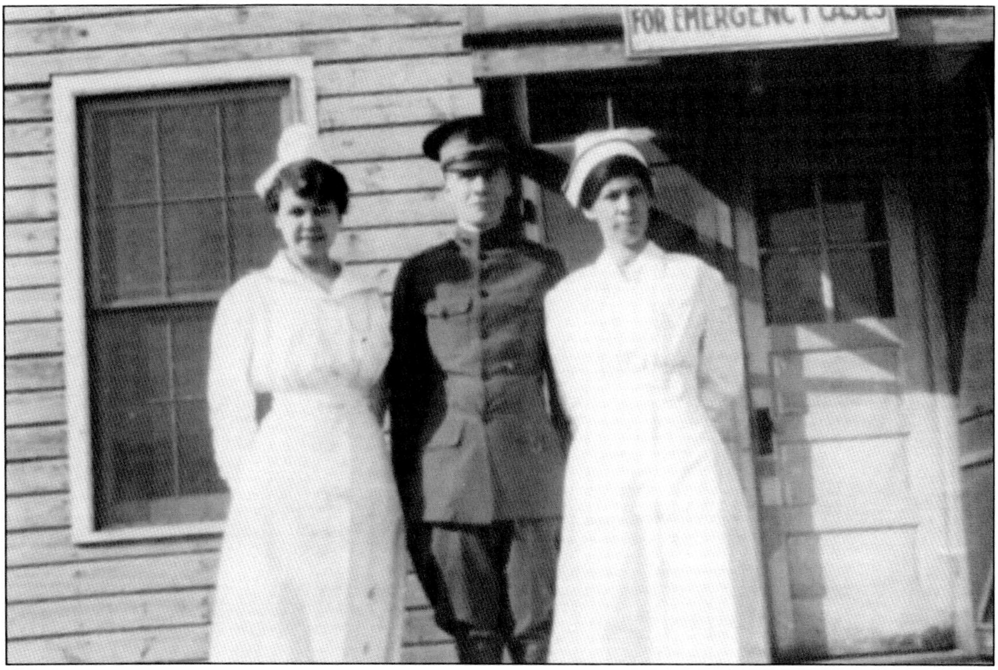

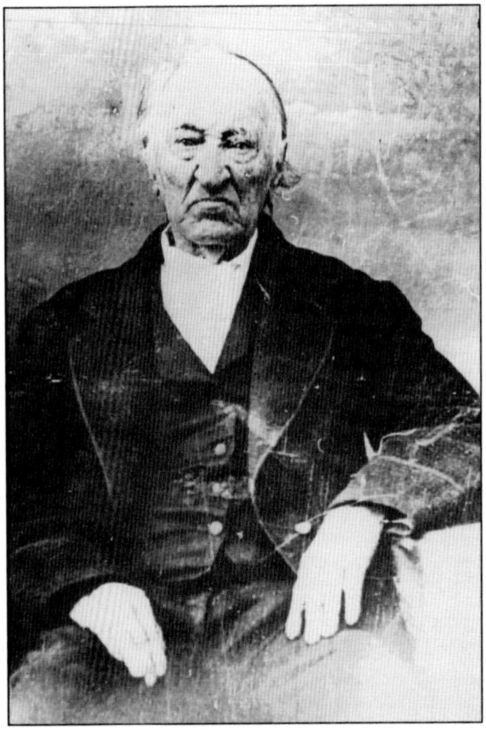

William Reiley. Born on October 21, 1786, William Reiley was best known for building the first Catholic church in Cincinnati, Ohio, in 1821. Known as Christ Church, it was located on the northwest corner of Liberty and Vine Streets. He cut logs from Carmen Drive in Alexandria and floated them across the Ohio River to aid construction. The congregation was organized under Dominican Fr. Edward Fenwick in 1818.

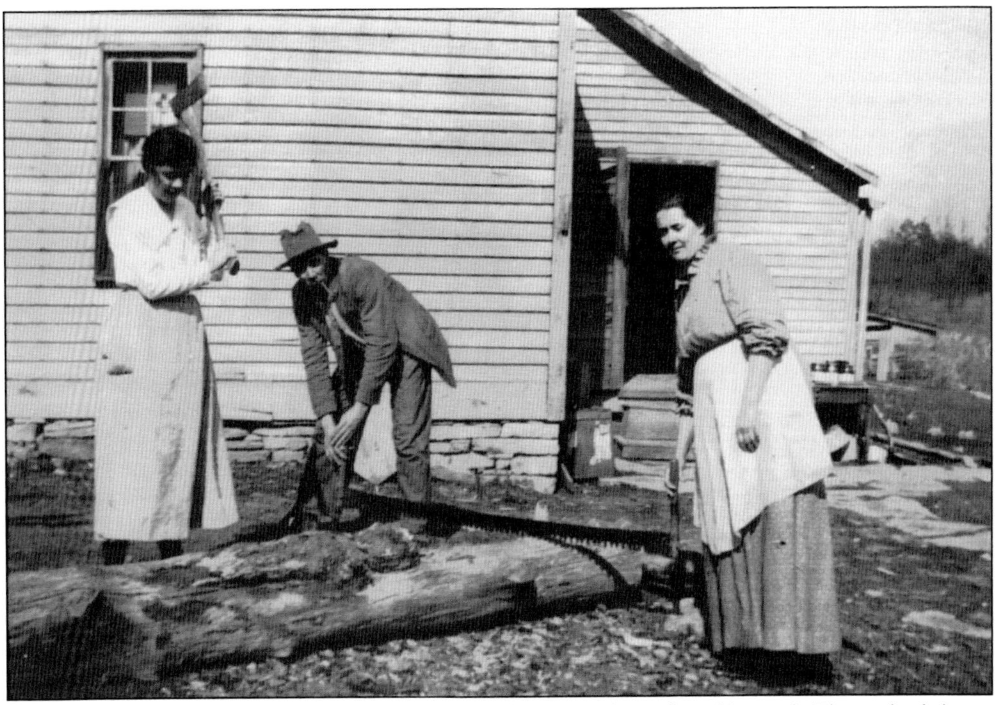

Crosscut Saw. Here Verner Reiley (center, with the corncob pipe) and his wife, Flossie (right), cut wood with a crosscut saw. Two people could make quick work of a log with this type of equipment, but they had to work in unison. After the invention of the chain saw, this labor-intensive job became much faster and easier. The Reileys' daughter Alta (left) is wielding the ax.

THE NELSON FAMILY. Seen from left to right are the following: (first row) Ada Reiley Nelson and Thomas G. Nelson; (second row) Cora Pearl Nelson Tarvin and her daughter Ada Tarvin. On this day, the family went to the zoo all dressed up and wearing hats.

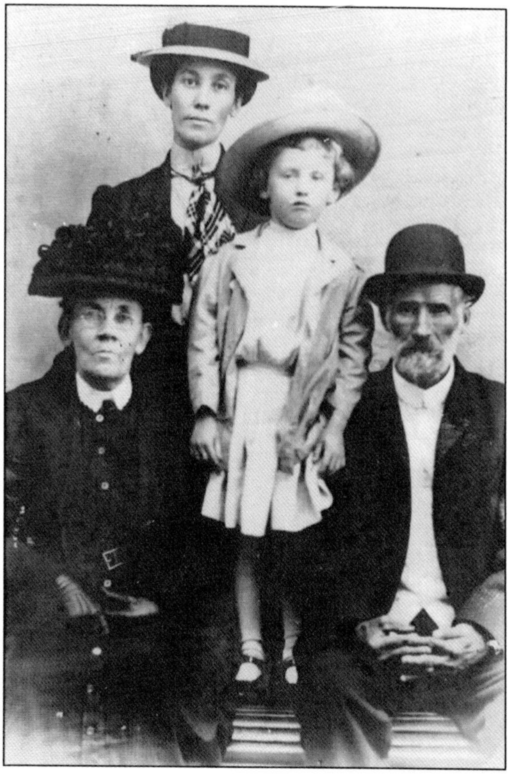

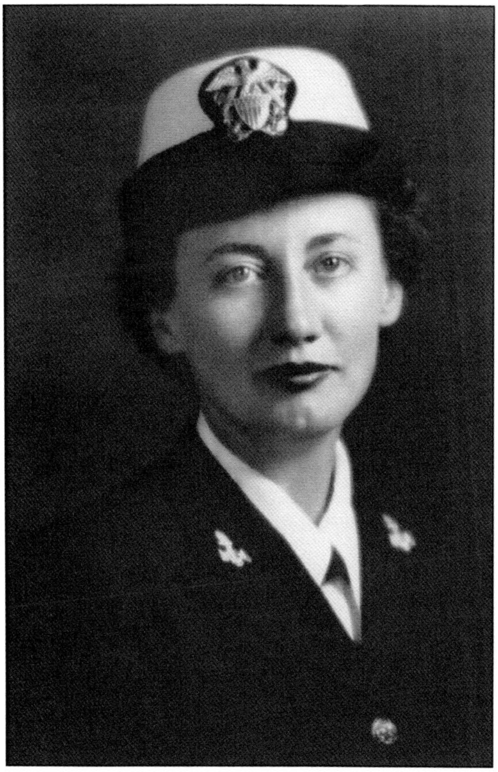

ADA TARVIN. Ada Tarvin graduated from Georgetown University when she was only 18 years old and then returned to Campbell County, where she taught local schoolchildren. She became the first Spanish and English teacher at Dixie Heights High School when it opened in 1939. Ada joined the U.S. Navy during World War II.

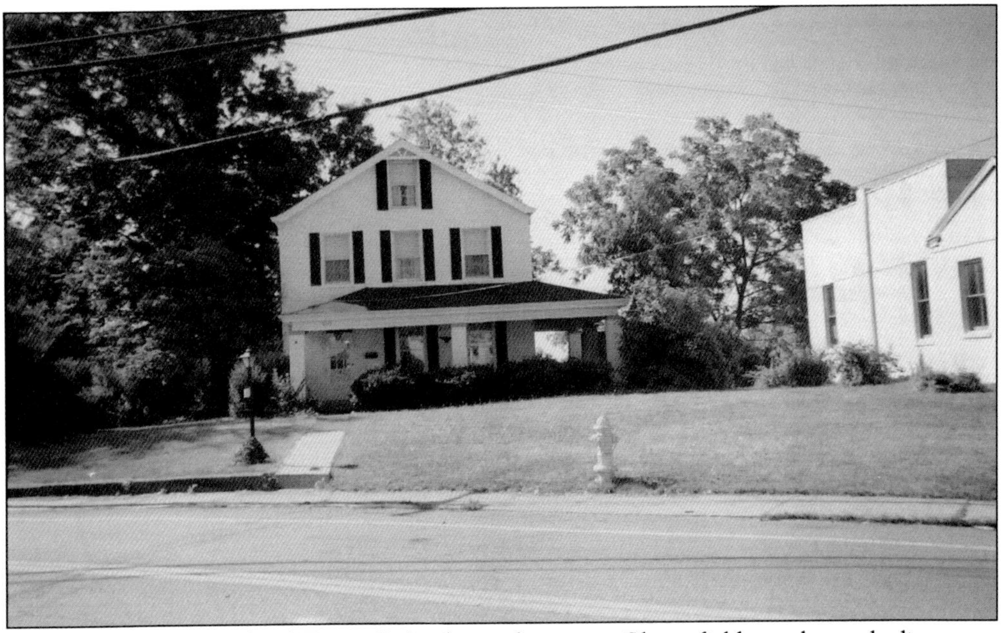

CHERRYFIELD. The Richard Tarvin Baker home, known as Cherryfield, was located adjacent to the courthouse on Main Street. Richard Tarvin Baker was born in Alexandria in 1816 and died there in 1891. He was married twice—first to Sarah K. Beall in 1846 and then to Maria J. Orr, the daughter of Dr. John Orr, in 1854. Baker graduated from the Cincinnati Law School in 1844. Samuel Clemens visited the home before he became known as Mark Twain.

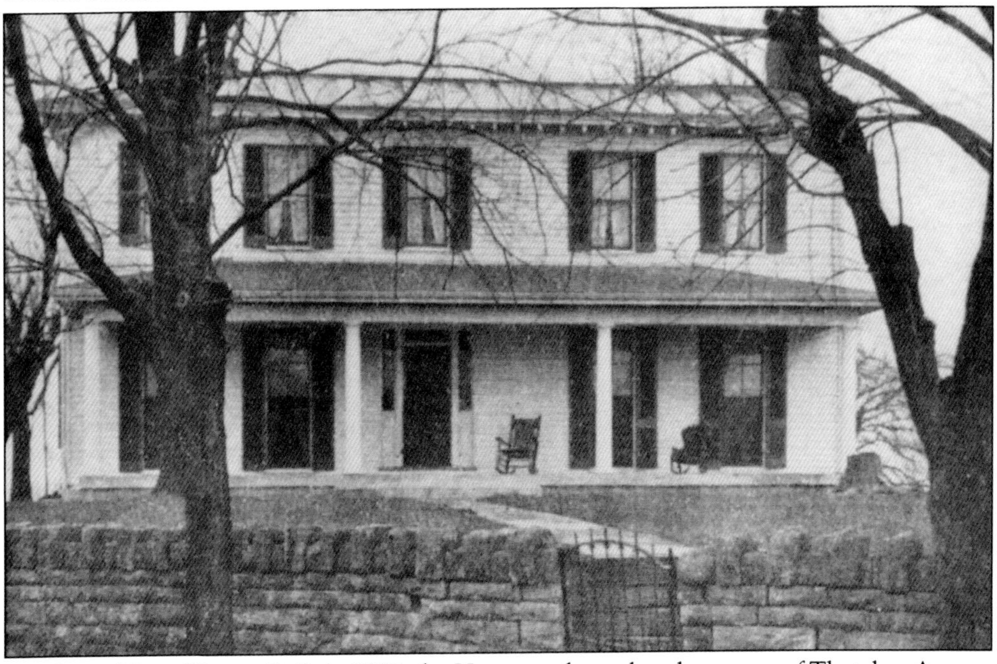

THE JOHN TODD HOME. Built in 1862, the Homestead stood at the corner of Thatcher Avenue and Main Street, adjoining a 100-acre farm. John Todd and Maria Shaw were married on July 7, 1860, and had five children. Operating the general store and the farm, John was also appointed the first postmaster of Alexandria.

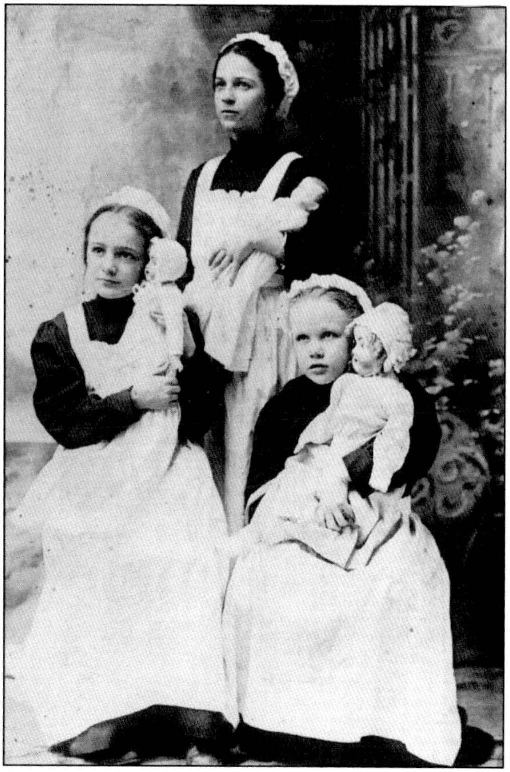

LITTLE GIRLS AT PLAY. Wearing pinafore dresses, the little girls pictured on the right play with their dolls. The girl shown below is enjoying a fruit barrel ring that looks much like the present-day hula hoop.

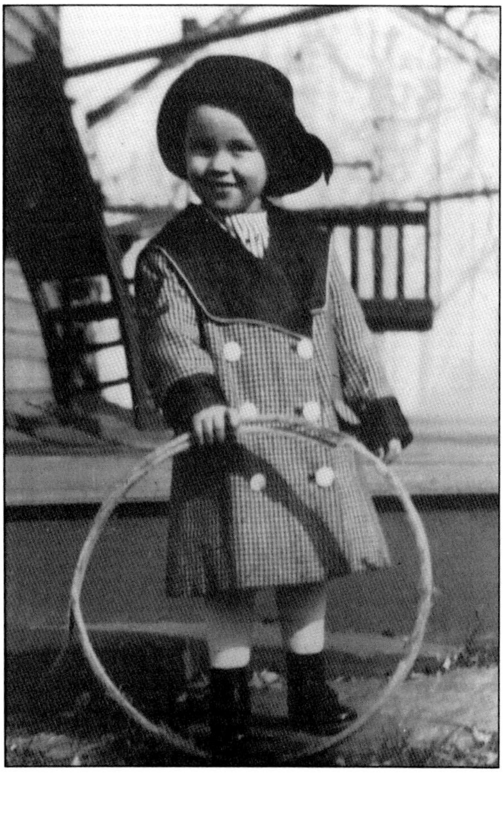

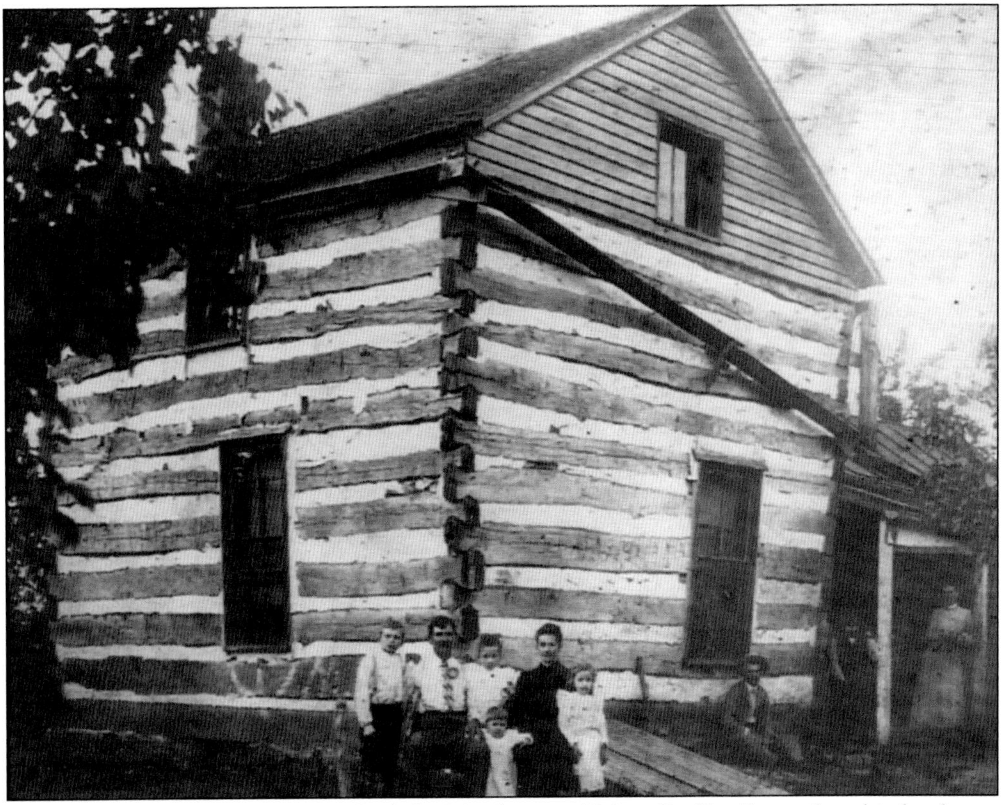

ORIGINAL LOG HOME, c. 1903. Built by Matthew and Mary Steffen Enzweiler, this log home was situated on Enzweiler Road (named after the family surname) in Alexandria. Shown above from left to right are Clem, Matthew, Frances Enzweiler Koeninger, Mary, and Susan Enzweiler Bauman. John is in front. Those at the far right are unidentified. The Enzweiler house (pictured below) was built right next to the original log structure in 1911. Once the new one was completed, the old log home was torn down.

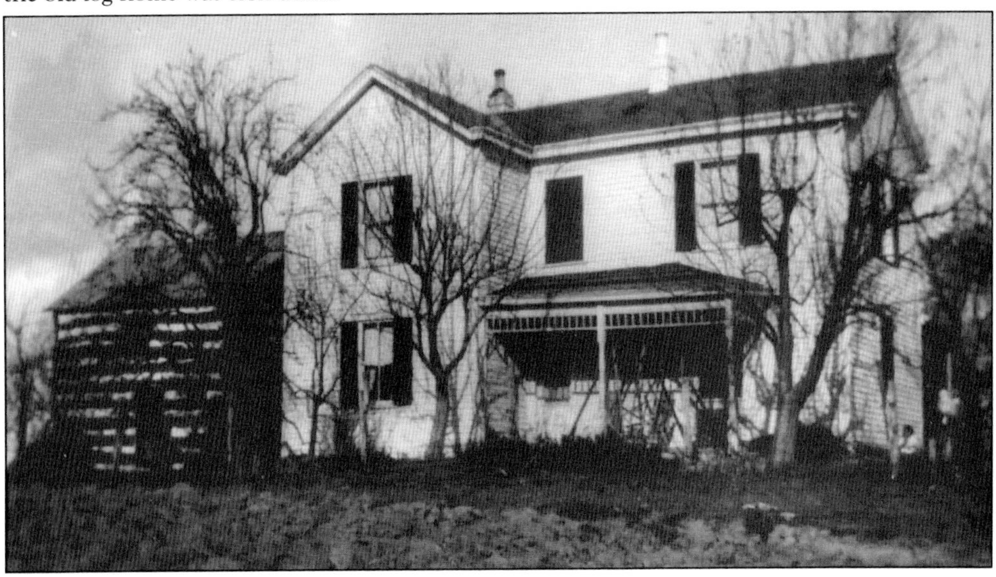

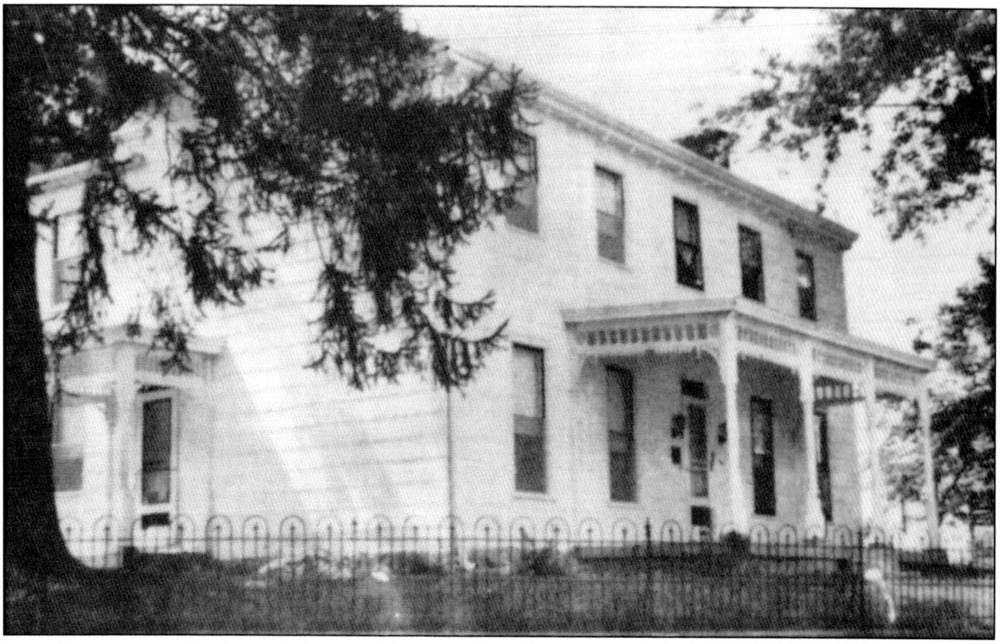

THE BENJAMIN D. BEALL HOME. This stately old home still stands at the bend of East Main Street on the southwest side. In 1834, Benjamin D. Beall met with John R. Purcell, Benjamin Smith, John J. Thomas, and Dr. John Orr at his residence to discuss legislation to incorporate the community as a town named Alexandria. The first court was held in the Beall home until the courthouse was built.

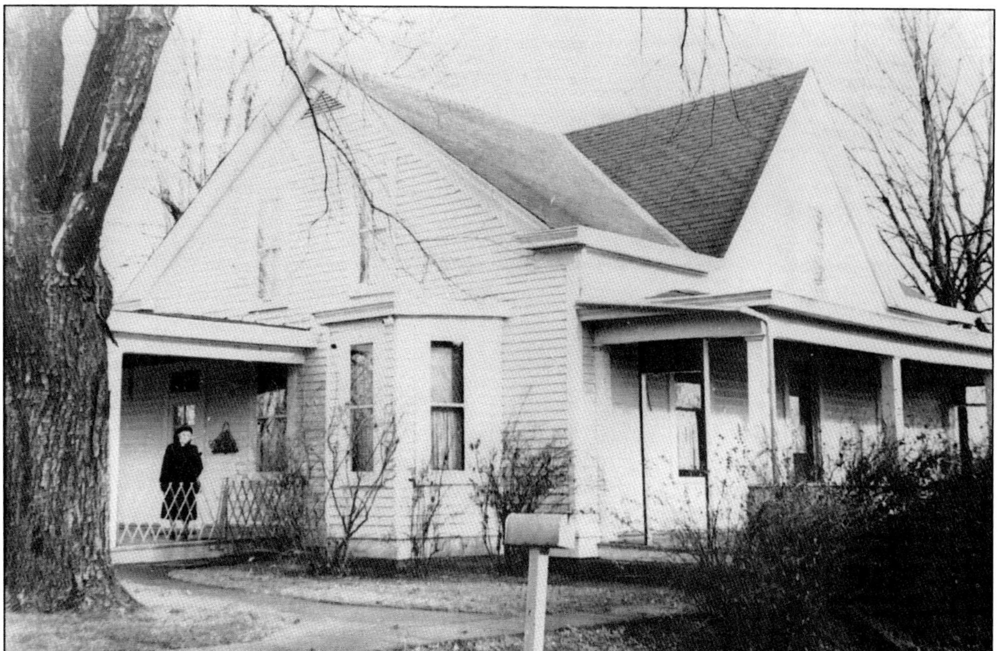

LUCY DAVIS WILLIAMS'S BOARDINGHOUSE. Long before Alexandria had a motel or restaurant, Lucy Williams took in travelers for the night and fixed meals for others who were just passing by. The home was located on Reiley Road.

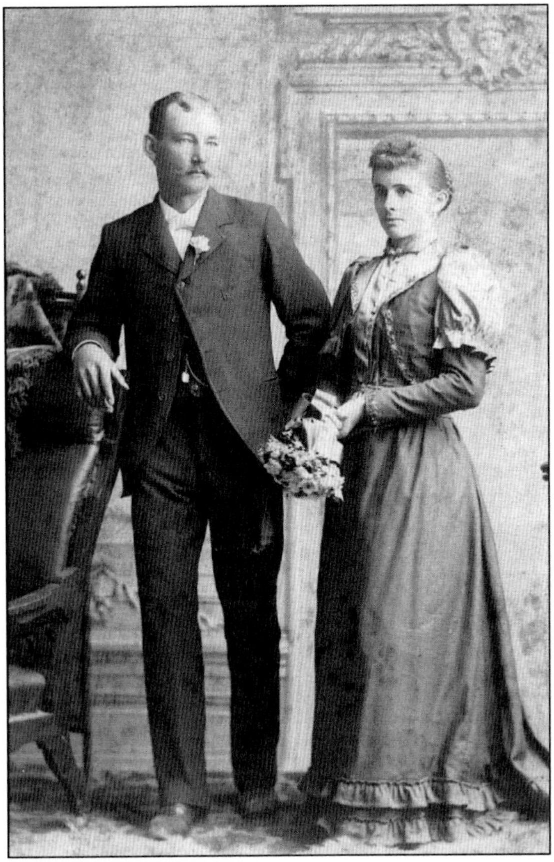

WILLIAM AND KATHERINE YUNG LOOS, APRIL 26, 1893. William Loos was born on April 29, 1862, the son of Conrad Loos, who had emigrated from Mittelrusselbach, Grafenberg, Bavaria, Germany, and Anna Margaret Deuerlein Loos, originally from Ober-russelbach, Grafenberg, Bavaria, Germany. Pictured at left, William, a farmer, married Katherine Yung, who was born in Melbourne, Kentucky, in 1871. Katherine died in 1928 and William in 1935. Both are buried in the Alexandria Cemetery. Shown below are unidentified members of the Loos family.

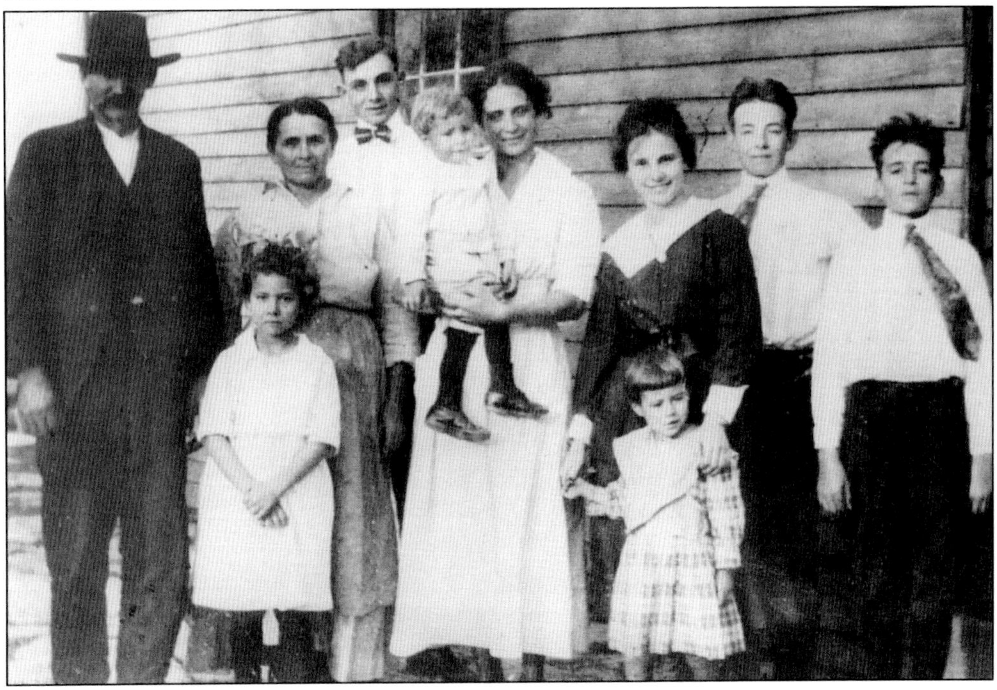

GENEVA LOOS, WITH HER DAUGHTER HELEN, c. 1928. Standing on the woodpile is Helen Loos, the daughter of William and Geneva Stubbs Loos. She graduated from Campbell County High School in 1943.

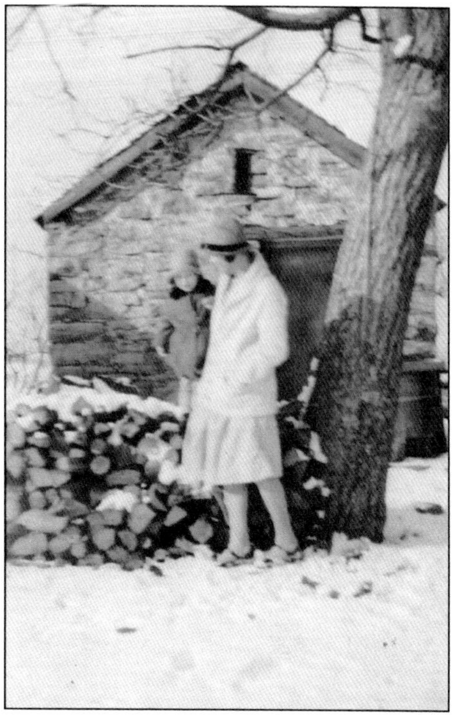

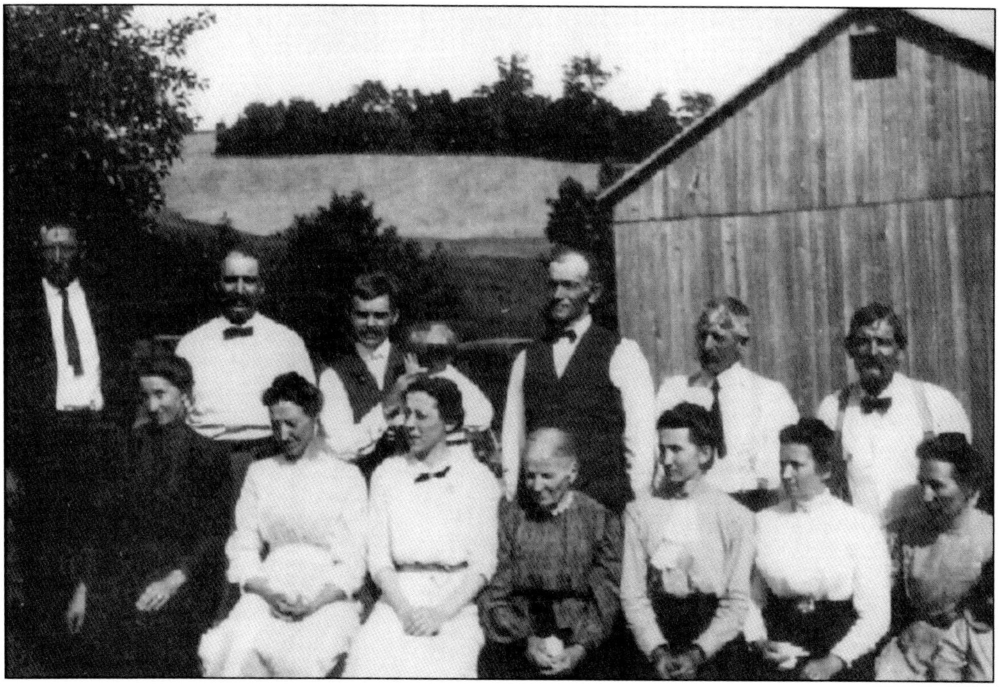

THE JOHN AND JOSEPHA GREIS STEFFEN FAMILY. Shown from left to right are: (first row) Sophia Schneider Steffen, Susan Steffen Bathalter, Anna Steffen Averbeck, Josepha Greis Steffen, Kate Steffen Schultz, Mary Steffen Enzweiler, and an unidentified woman and child; (second row) Edward Bathalter, John Steffen, Henry Averbeck, unidentified, John Steffen, Edward Schultz, and Matthew Enzweiler.

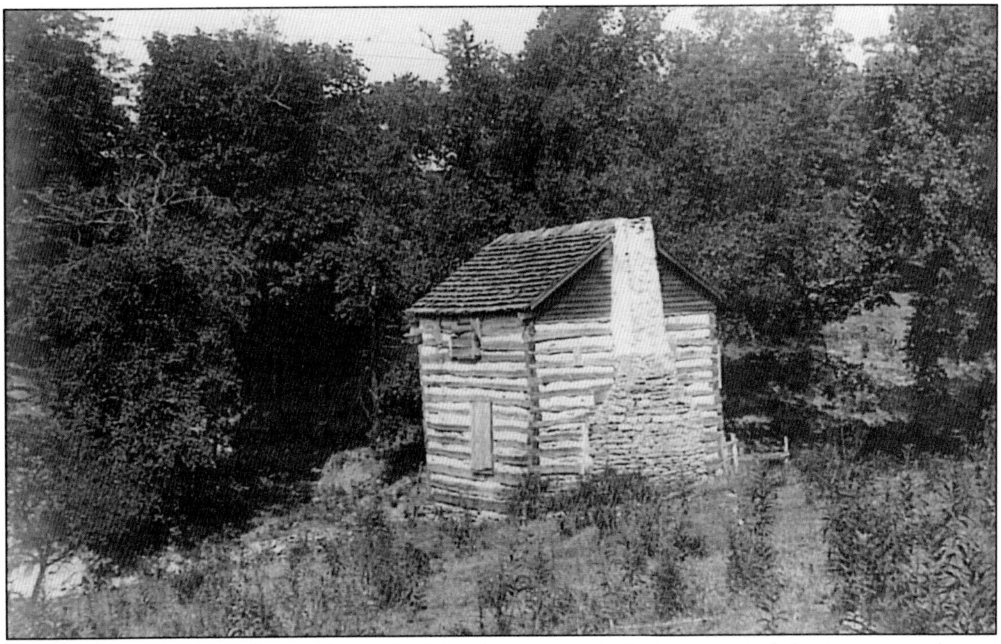

THE STUBBS CABIN. This early settlers' log home was built in a typical, basic square design using trees from the area. The logs were notched at both ends and laid one upon another. The spaces between the logs were filled with chinking, which consisted of a mixture of straw, grass, horsehair, and mud or clay. The split-shingle roof sported a chimney built of stone with a mud and wood top.

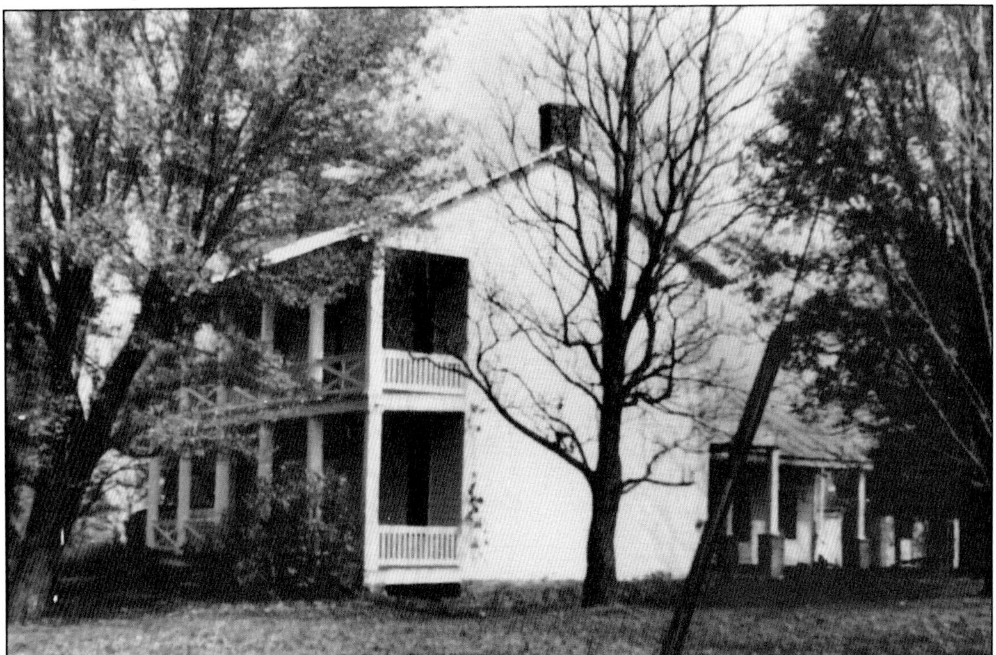

THE GEORGE SR. AND FRAN KEES HOME. As was common for many first-generation homes, logs were the primary building material for this residence. At a later date, the logs were covered by wood siding. This Southern-designed home is still located on Popular Ridge Road.

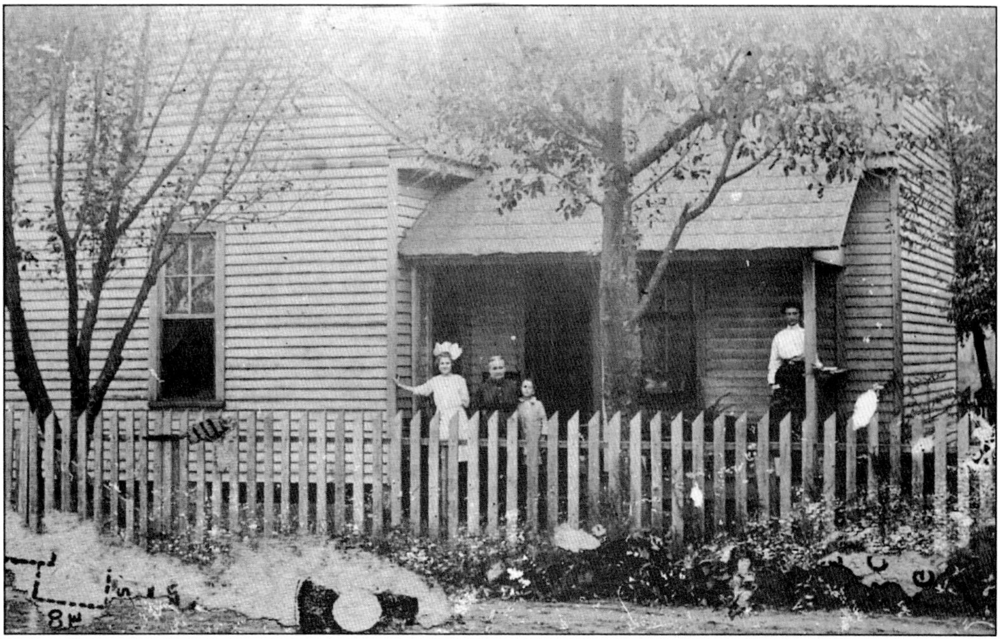

THE BROWN FAMILY HOME. Surrounded by a rail fence, this clapboard frame house stood on Popular Ridge Road in the 1930s. Clapboard homes have been popular since the beginning of Colonial settlements. The wood used in construction was usually oak or yellow pine, which was applied horizontally to the frame while overlapping to the next board. Today it is often referred to as siding.

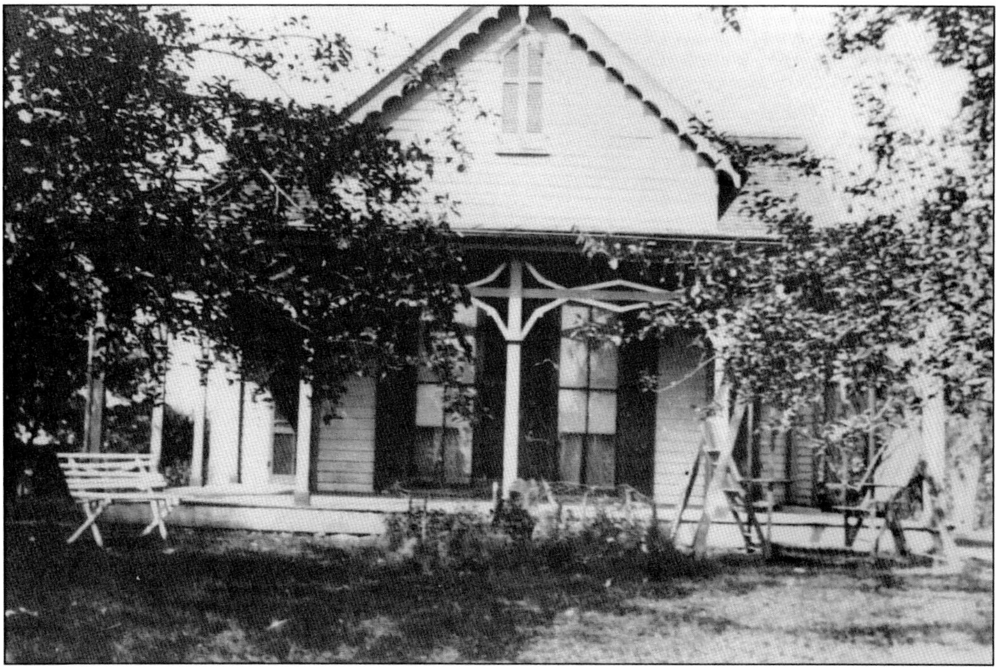

THE EDGAR THATCHER HOME. This house was once located at the current site of the Alexandria Fire Department on U.S. 27. The cottage-style home included a big porch, with the popular gingerbread trim introduced in the mid- to late 19th century. Construction costs totaled $585.

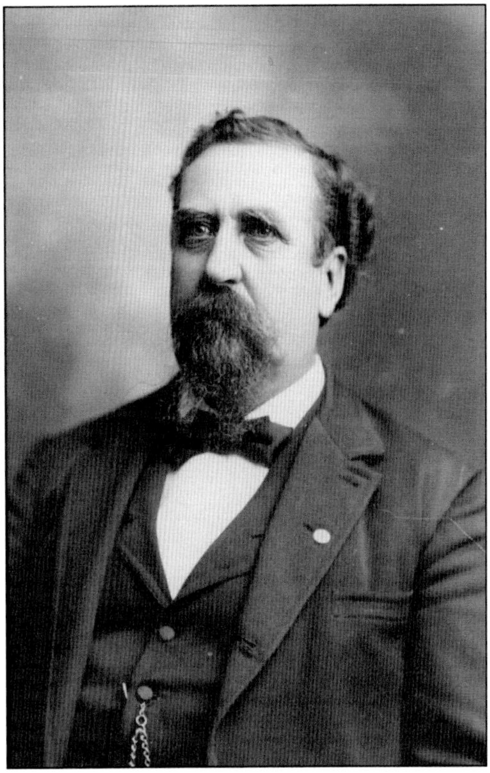

WILLIAM SAMUEL GRANT. William (pictured left) was born on April 9, 1807, to Capt. Squire Boone Grant and Susannah Haan Grant. His father, Squire, was the son of William and Elizabeth Boone Grant. Elizabeth was the sister of the famous woodsman and pioneer Daniel Boone. Placed in the same regiment, Squire Boone Grant fought alongside Col. Daniel Boone in the Battle of Blue Licks on August 19, 1782, the last battle of the Revolutionary War fought in Kentucky. Grants Bend on the Licking River was named after Squire Boone Grant, and the Grant County name honors the family. William Samuel Grant married Lydia Ann Grant (pictured below), the daughter of Elijah and Kitturah Grant of Walnut Ridge, Boone County, Kentucky, on February 12, 1839. Together they raised eight children. The community of Grants Lick was named after John Grant, the brother of Squire Grant.

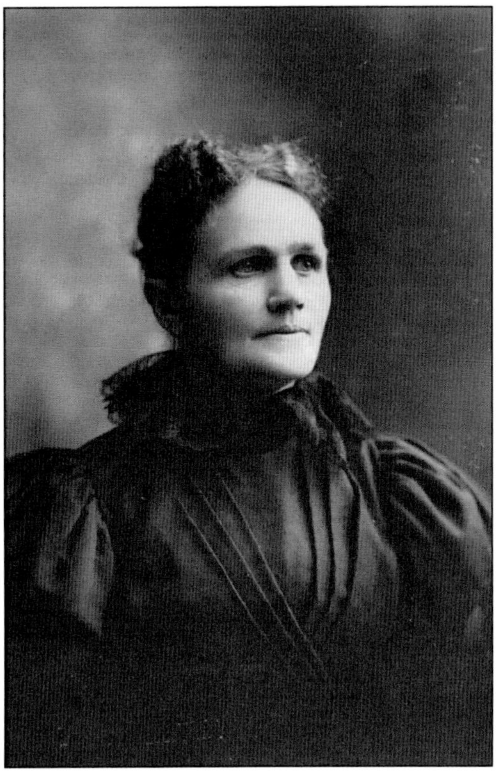

Mary Elizabeth "Bessie" Grant Thatcher. The daughter of William Samuel and Lydia Ann Grant, Mary Elizabeth, was born at her parents' Grants Bend home, Errondale, on December 23, 1857. She wed Frank Spilman Thatcher at the family residence on April 27, 1882. Bessie was a homemaker who raised six children. She died in 1929.

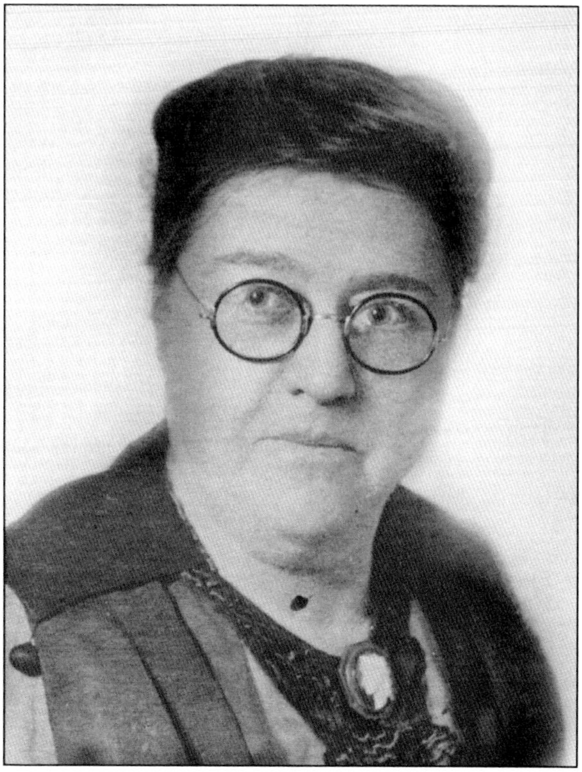

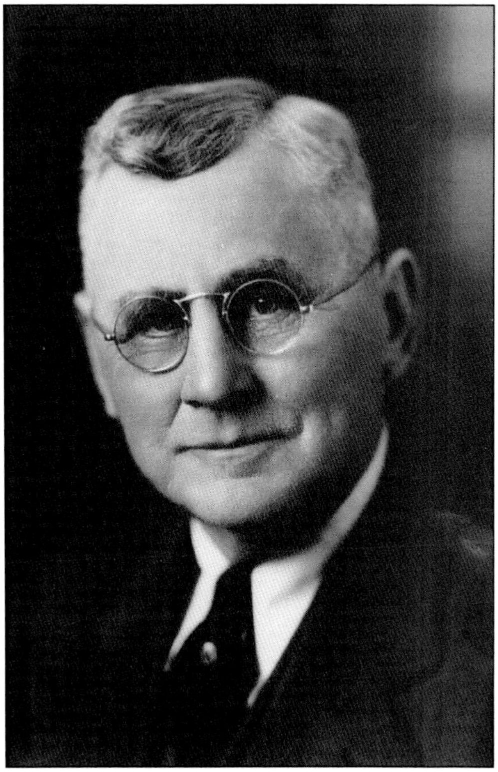

Frank Spilman Thatcher. Born on High View Farm on April 28, 1856, Frank was a farmer and fruit grower who spent his entire life in Campbell County. He helped to organize the Campbell County Fire Insurance Company in 1901 and to create the Bank of Alexandria. Frank acted as the bank director in 1903, and prior to his death on August 6, 1939, he was serving as bank president. He also sat on the Alexandria Cemetery Board.

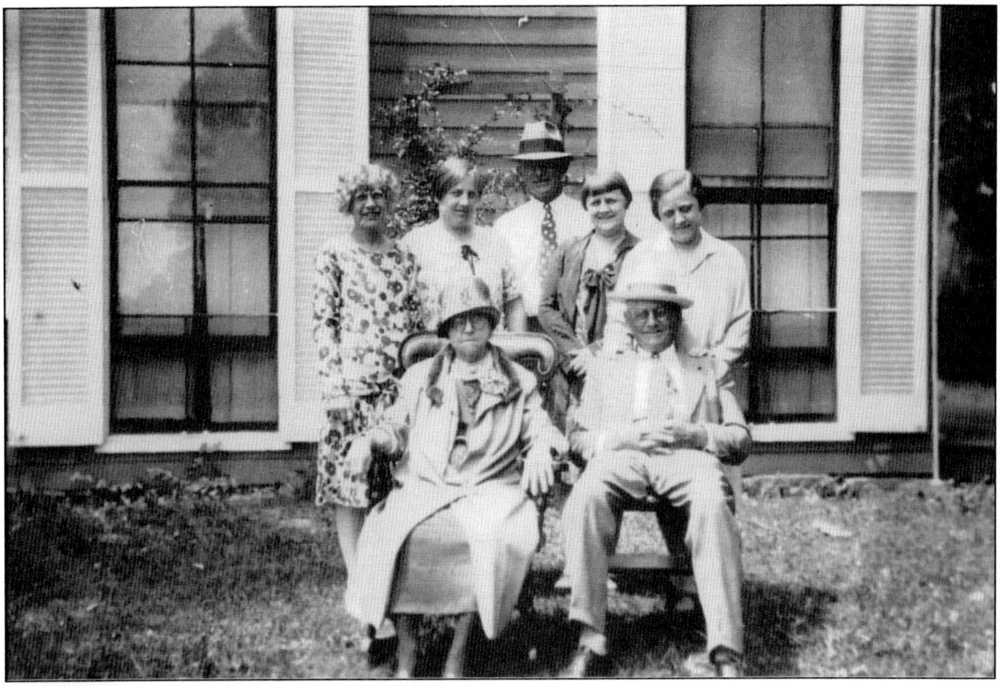

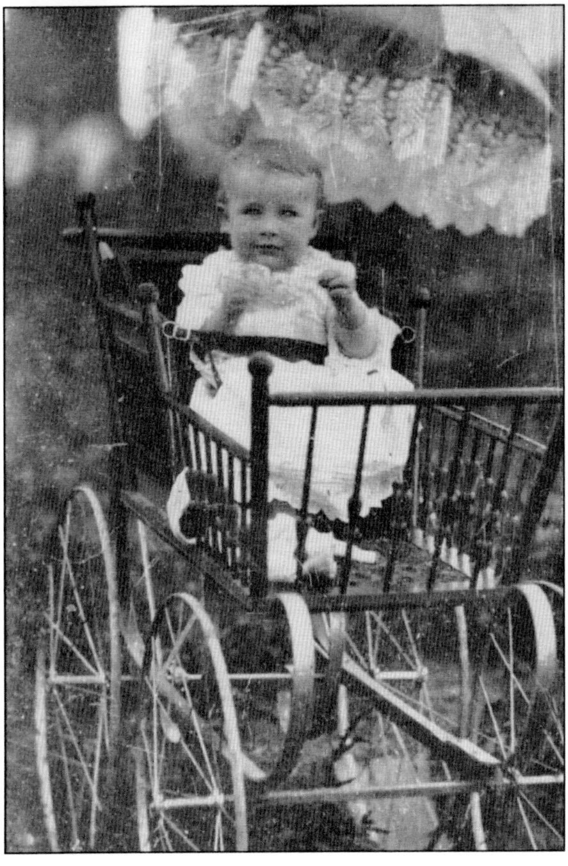

THE FRANK SPILMAN THATCHER FAMILY. Frank and Mary Elizabeth Grant Thatcher are seated above with their grown children. Standing from left to right are Ruth Cleveland Thatcher, Frances, Jack, Bessie Julia, and Edith Elnora. This photograph was taken at the McVean House, which was owned by Jack Thatcher and was located at the south end of the family farm, which stood at 7940 Alexandria Pike. Pictured to the left, Jack H. Thatcher is sitting in his baby buggy in 1893.

Two

FARM LIFE

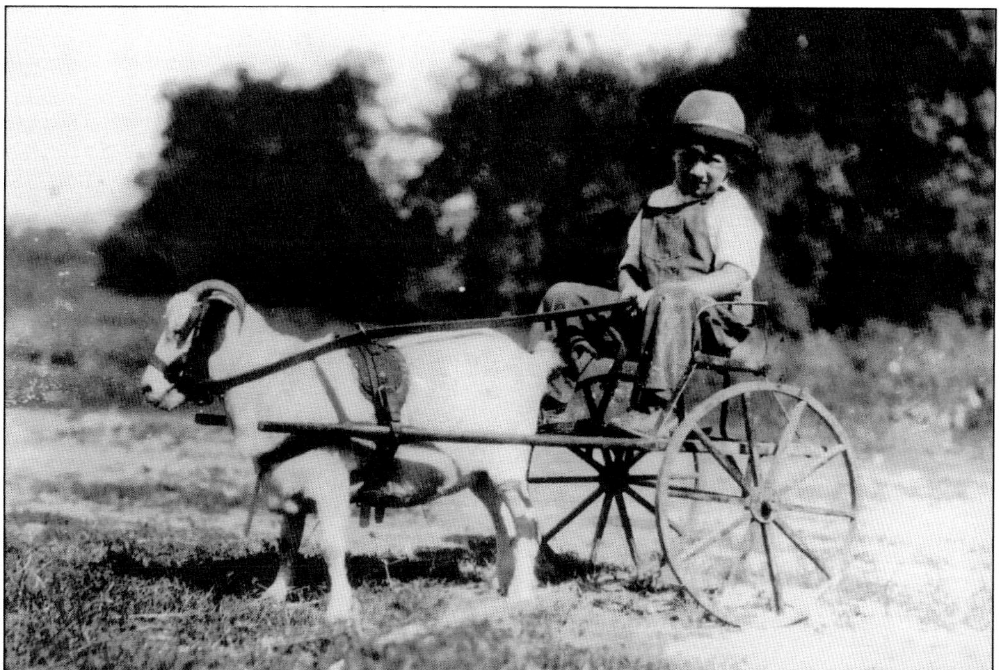

JACK KEES AND THE GOAT CART. Jack Kees (1921–1968) is seated in a cart made by his uncle Jack Thatcher. Kees was a businessman, an entrepreneur, and eventually a mayor of Alexandria. One of his business ventures was the Brass Key Restaurant and Swimming Pool. He died in an automobile accident on Alexandria Pike just south of the city limits of Cold Spring, Kentucky.

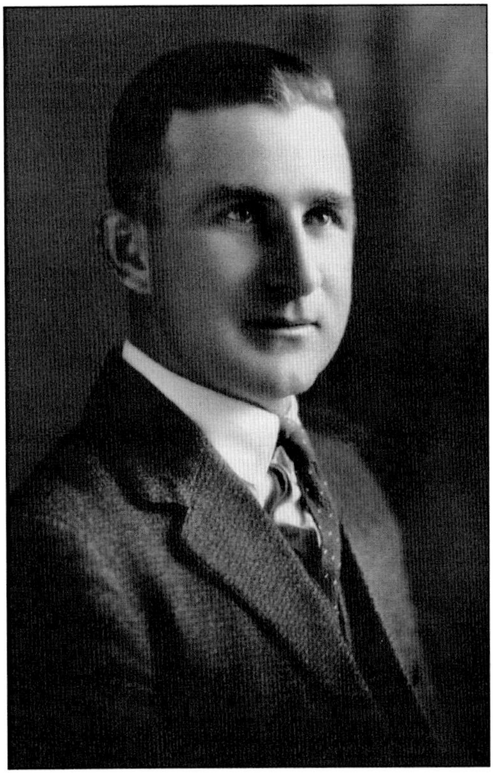

JACK H. THATCHER, 1921. Jack Henry Thatcher (pictured left) was born at the family homestead on High View Farm on July 31, 1893. At the age of 14, he started trading cattle and horses. In addition to farming, Jack served as the director and later the president of the Bank of Alexandria. On May 5, 1925, in Winston-Salem, North Carolina, he wed Lillian Cole (pictured below), the daughter of Dr. James E. and Annie E. Cole. Lillian was the first home demonstration agent in Campbell County. She made the dress she is wearing in this photograph, complete with hand-detailed embroidery. She and Jack Thatcher raised three girls: twins Elizabeth Thatcher Klem and Edith Thatcher Bedford, and Lillian Thatcher Shaw.

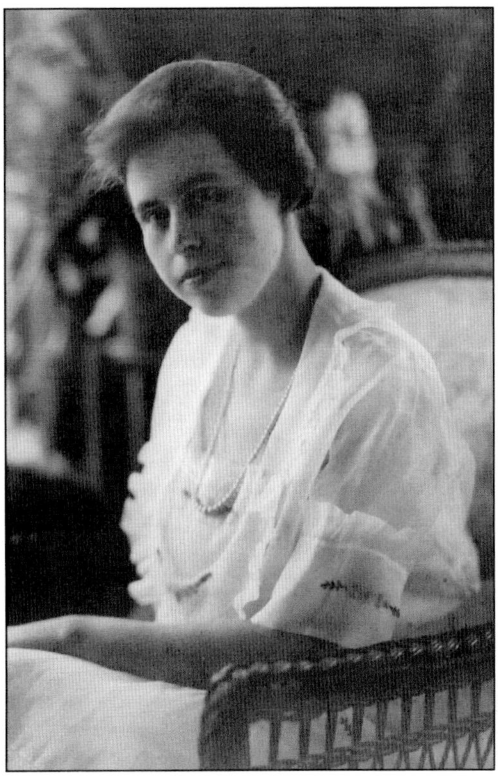

THE FRANCIS "FRANK" SPILMAN HOME. This log home with a flat face stood in front of the old cemetery adjacent to the First Baptist Church on Alexandria Pike, which at the time was the center of town. Baby Jimmy Gray is in the carriage.

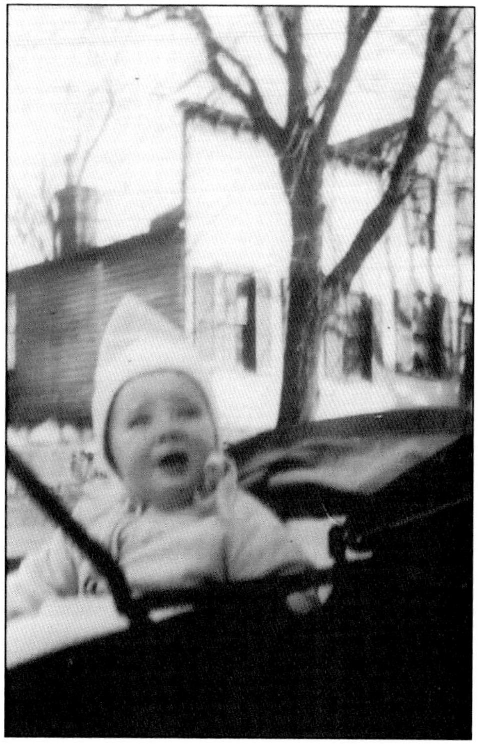

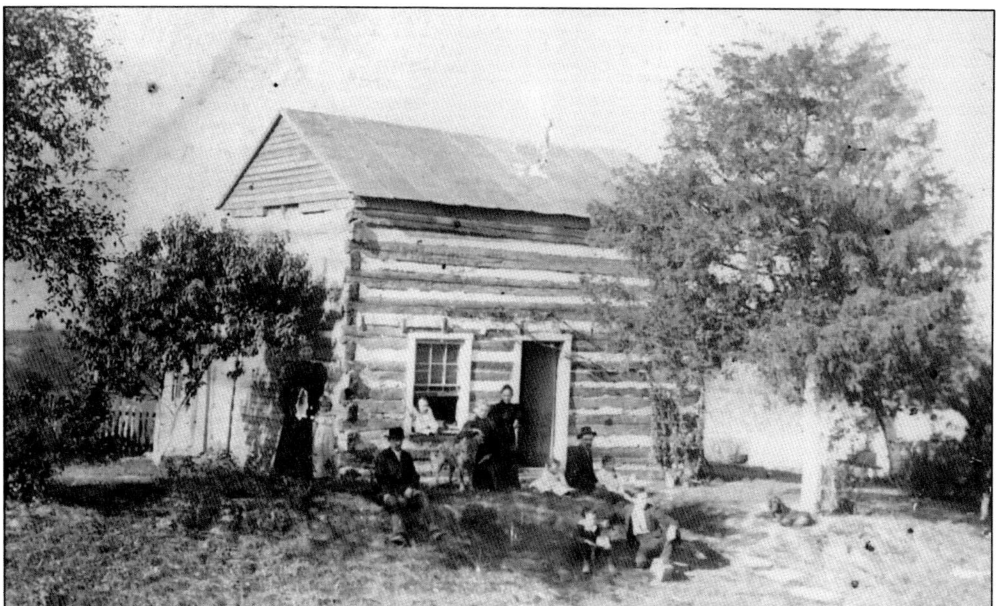

THE SPILMAN LOG CABIN. Edward Kendall Spilman constructed this log cabin for his family. Pictured from left to right are Lizzy Perry, Edith Spilman Perry, Benjamin Perry, Allen Spilman, Bertha Perry, Ella Burr, Margaret Lucille Spilman, Charles Henry Spilman, William E. Spilman, and William Harrison Burr. The dog Jack is under the window, while Carlo is lying under the tree. The home was destroyed by fire about 1940.

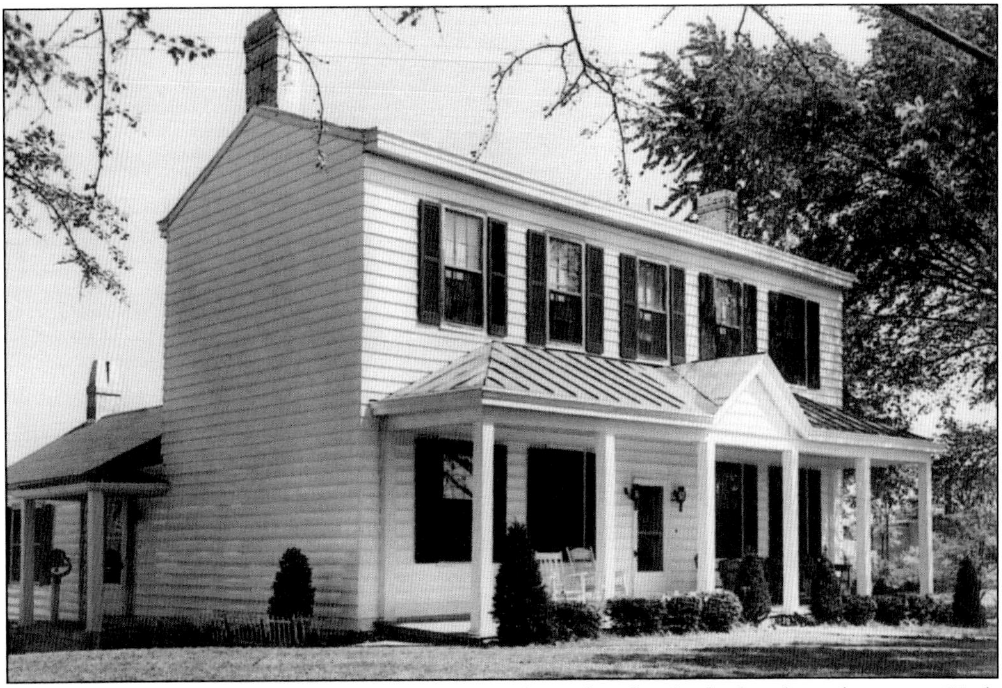

The Thatcher Home and Underpass. Daniel E. Thatcher built the above house on High View Farm in 1806, and the Jack H. Thatcher family has resided there from 1940 to the present. Though now covered with siding, it is one of the oldest standing log cabins in Campbell County. The underpass, shown below with gates beside the driveway of the Thatcher home, was used to move dairy cows on High View Farm to the other pasture, located across U.S. 27. It was wide enough for two cows to maneuver side by side and tall enough for the cow driver to ride through on a horse.

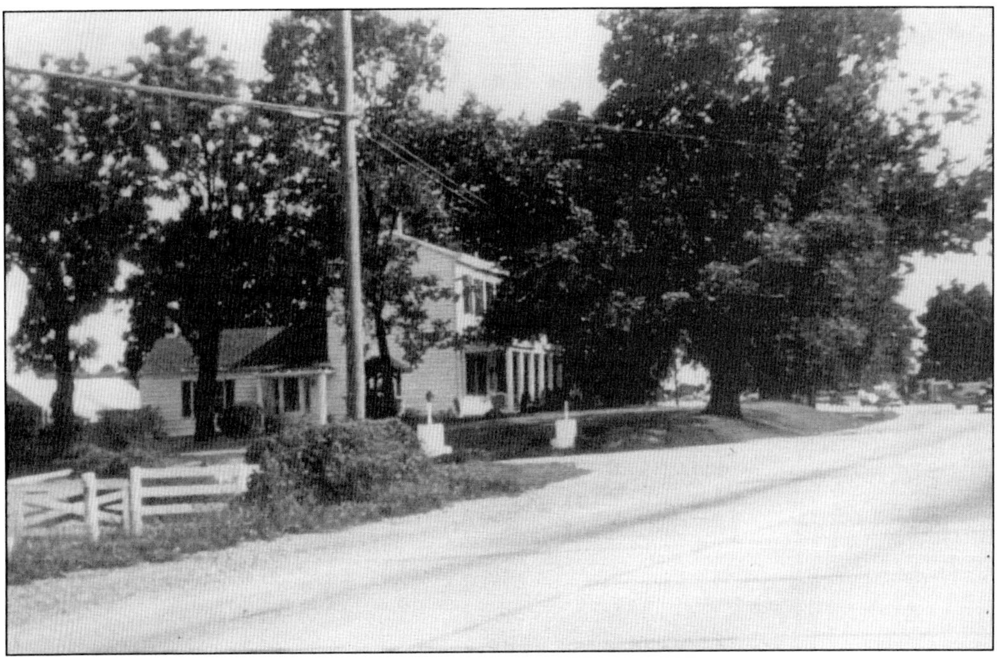

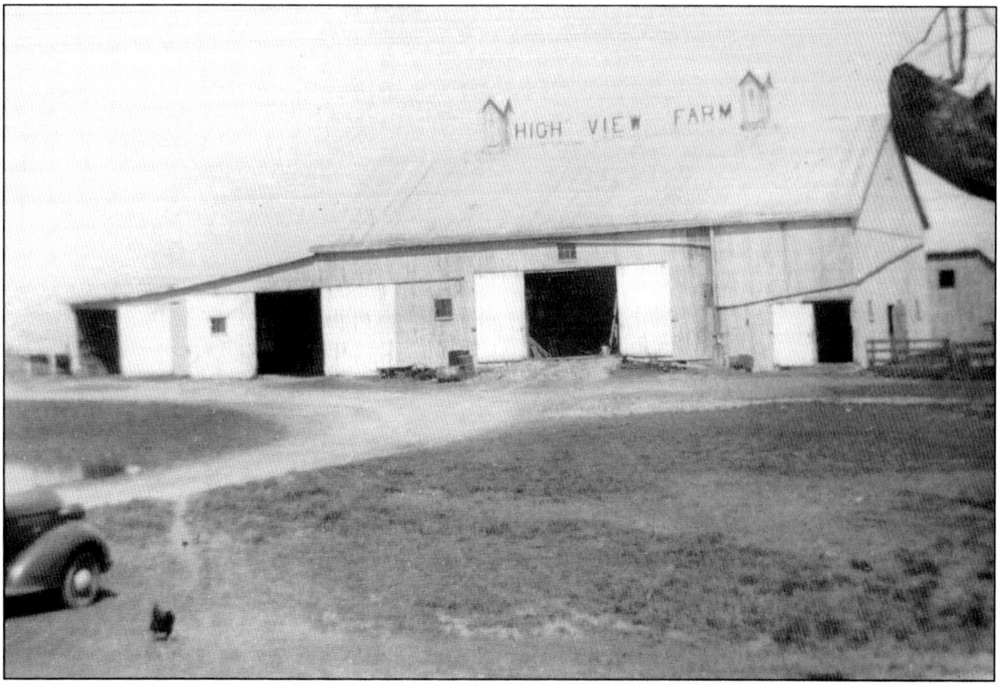

HIGH VIEW FARM AND BARNYARD, 1950S. High View Farm (above) was established in 1805 as a fruit, vegetable, cattle, and horse farm. The family also had a distillery from which the mash was fed to the cattle and pigs. In 1940, a dairy was started, and within 20 years, Black Angus cattle were roaming the pastures (below). Frank Spilman Thatcher built the barn.

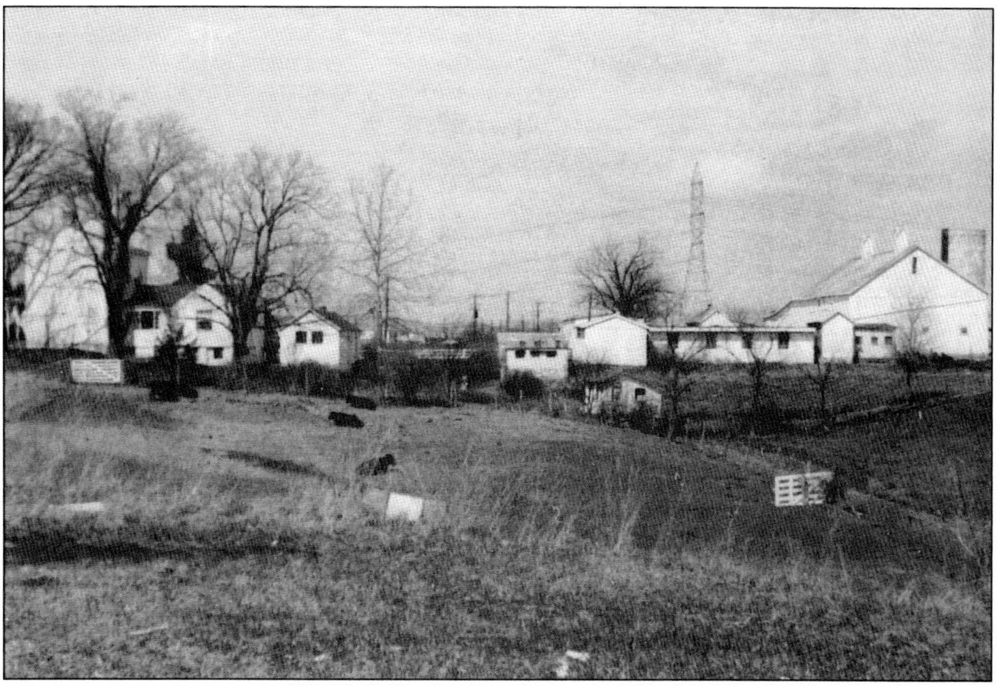

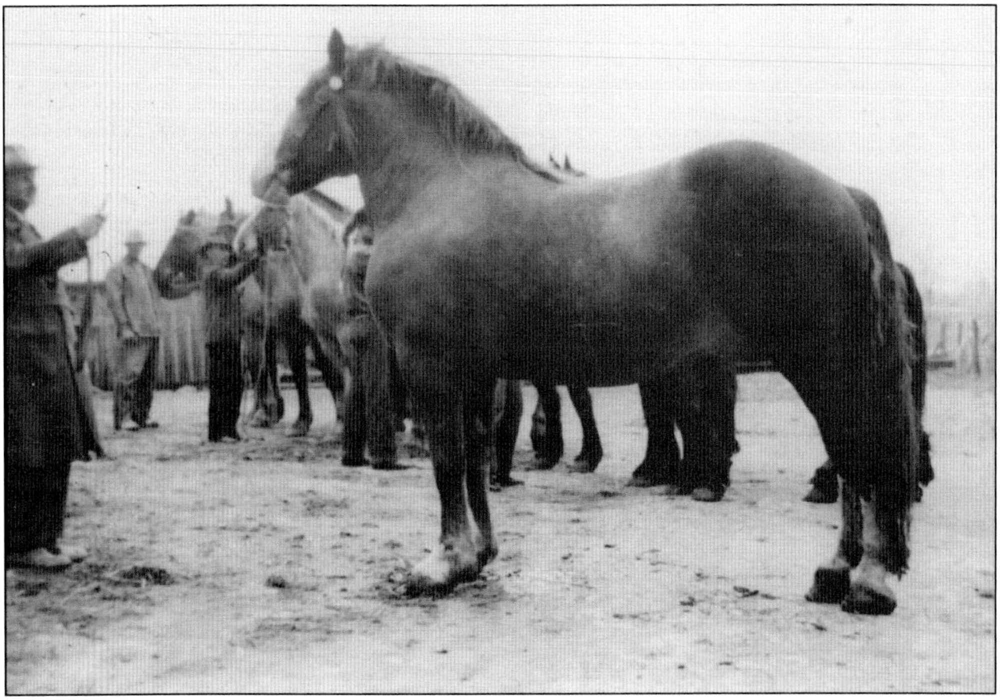

King Gordon, 1940s. King Gordon was a chestnut-colored Belgian draft horse with the distinguishing features of the breed: a small head, a thick and muscular neck, powerful shoulders and quarters, and short legs with a small amount of feathering. Originating in Belgium, the breed is one of the heaviest, weighing in at slightly over one ton, or 2,000 pounds.

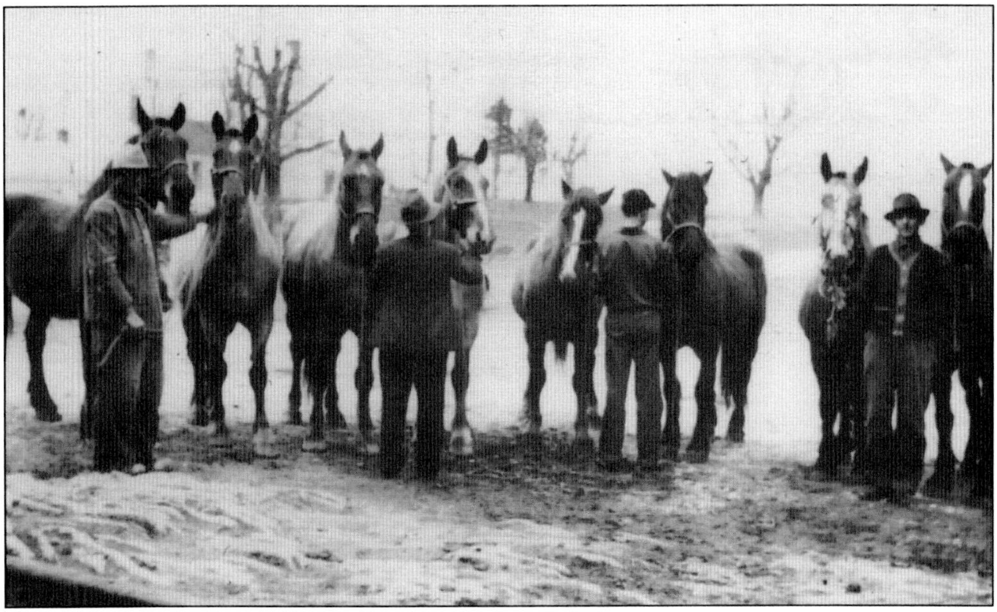

Draft Horses. From left to right, Reiley Rahe, Frank Spilman, T. Rahe, and Fred Warners hold the teams of Belgian draft horses sired by King Gordon at High View Farm. These colts, strawberry roan in color, operated strictly as farm horses. King Gordon was often used as a good middle horse when a three-hitch team was needed for a heavy job.

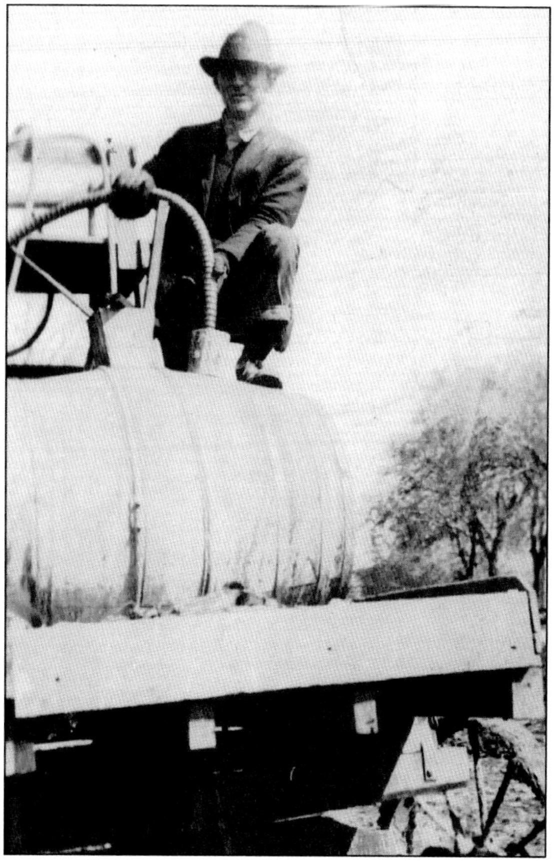

PROTECTING HIS ORCHARD. Jack Thatcher (pictured right) fills the spray barrel for the apple orchards. Grandpa Frank Spilman Thatcher (below) sits in his buggy holding a gun after making the rounds of his orchard. People from town were known to stop and help themselves to the crops when they had the chance. Frank was determined to stop this from happening. Also shown below are Frank's horse Titus and his young son Jack. Pete (left) and Johnny Neiser (right) look on. Notice the split-rail fence in the background.

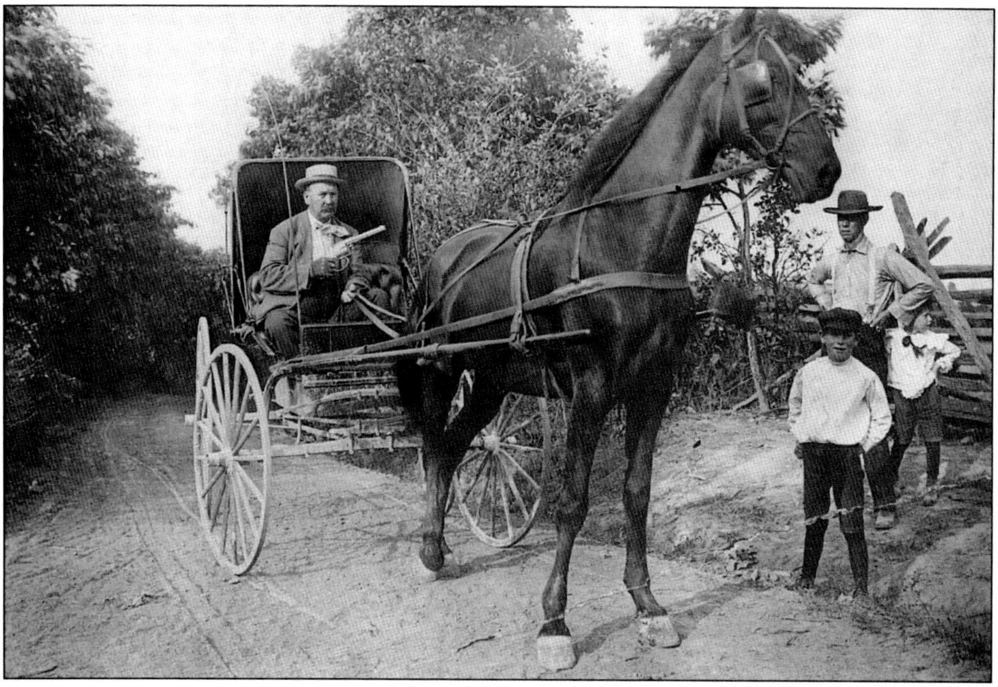

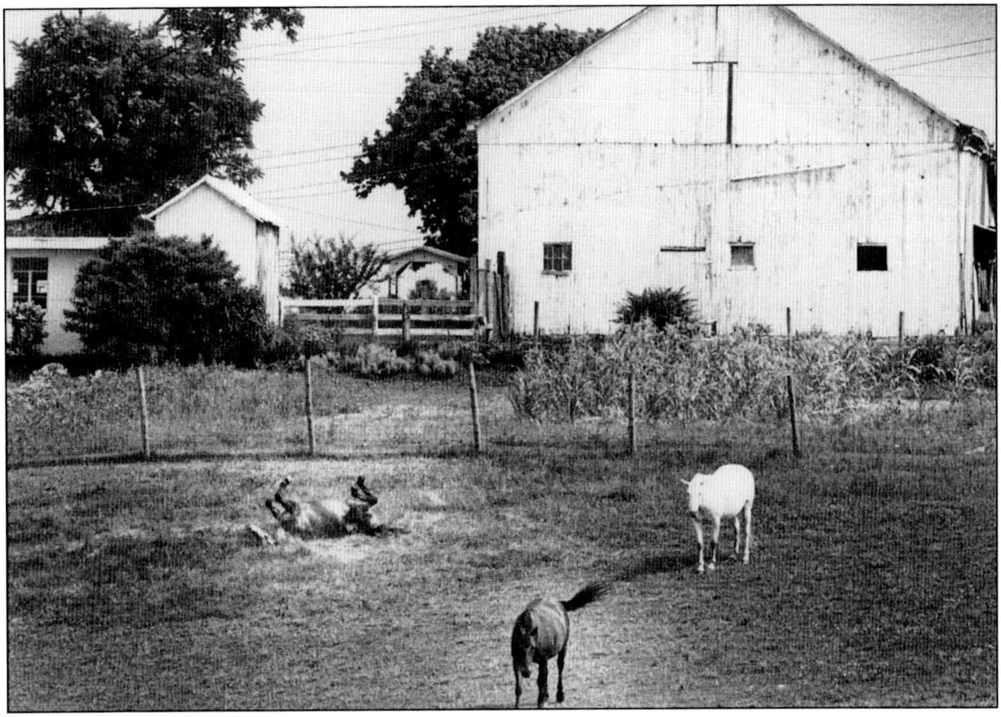

JAKE, JUDY, AND REASON. As quarter horses, these three High View Farm horses were strictly for riding pleasure and could run a quarter of a mile faster than any other breed in the world. The breed is usually brown, reddish brown, chestnut, or black in color. Jake is rolling around in the grass while Reason (white) and Judy (bay) walk along.

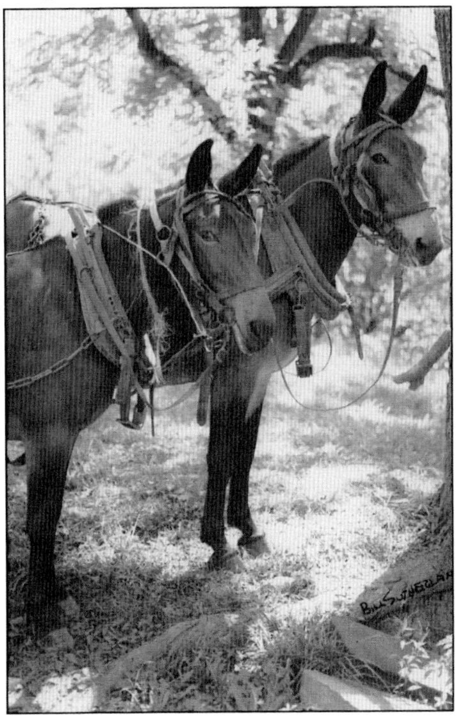

JACK AND JERRY. Mules, the offspring of a female horse and a male donkey, typically have long ears such as Jack (left) and Jerry (right), but they are slightly shorter than a donkey's ears. This team is harnessed and ready to work. Mules are great farm animals because they can carry a heavy weight and tend not to panic as easily as horses.

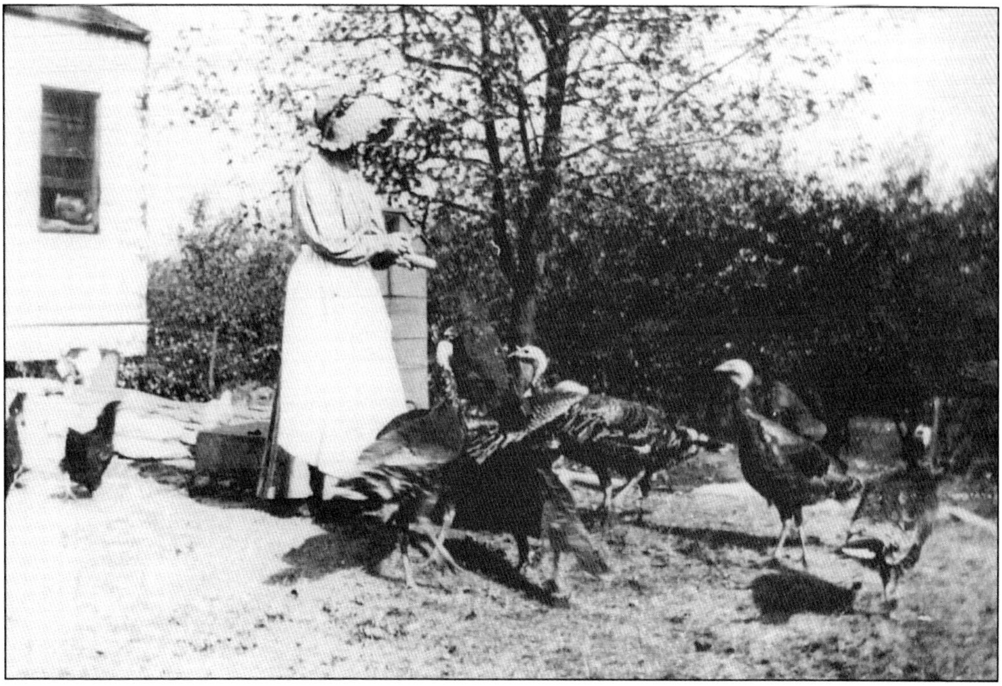

FEEDING TIME. Wearing a prairie dress and bonnet, Lizzie Thatcher (above) feeds her domestic turkeys on the farm. Below, an unidentified gentleman feeds his chickens. Both types of fowl were commonly fed wheat. A farmer's life was a hard one; therefore, they raised animals, grains, and vegetables to feed the family.

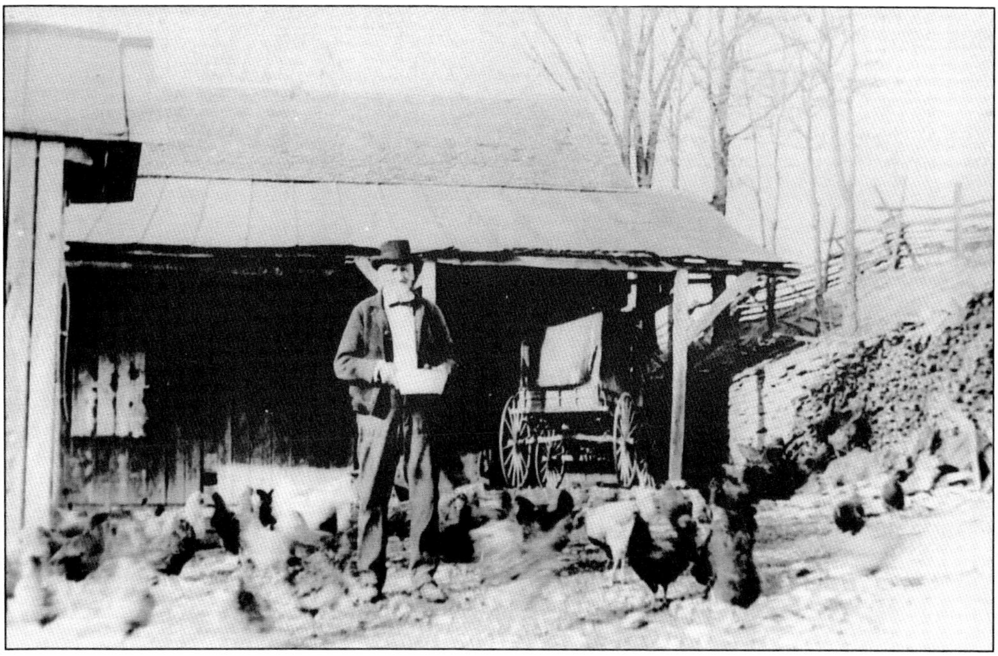

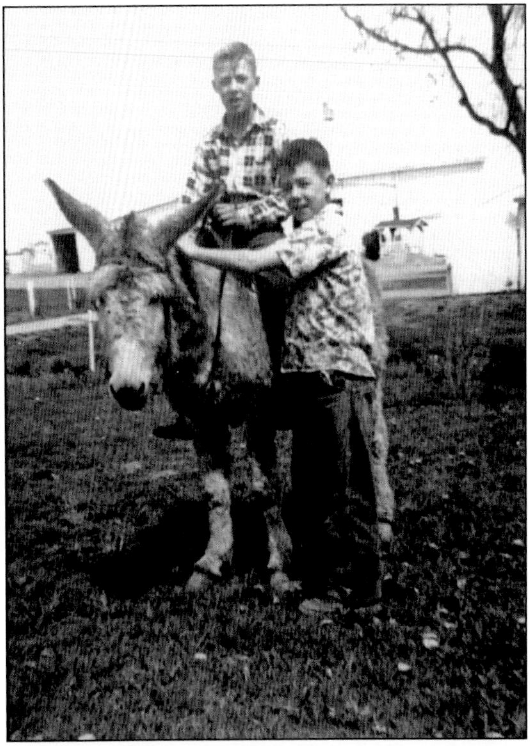

Snow Ball. Visiting High View Farm, John Burt sits on Snow Ball while his brother Jim stands. Donkeys are considered beasts of burden because they can carry a heavy weight on their backs. They usually have large ears and small feet, and though normally brownish gray, they can be other colors as well.

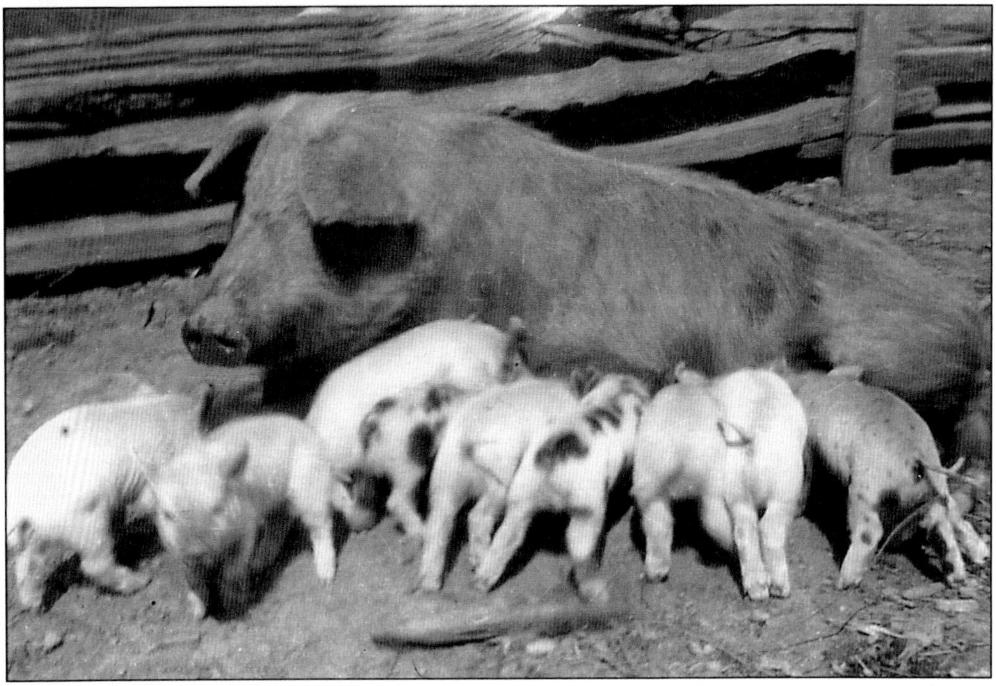

Dinnertime. All but one of the little piglets line up for dinner. The mama pig is identified as Mary on the back of this photograph. Mother pigs, called sows, usually birth 8 to 12 piglets at a time. When it is time for slaughter, virtually every part of the pig is used for different cuts of pork, ribs, sausage, pickled pigs feet, and lard.

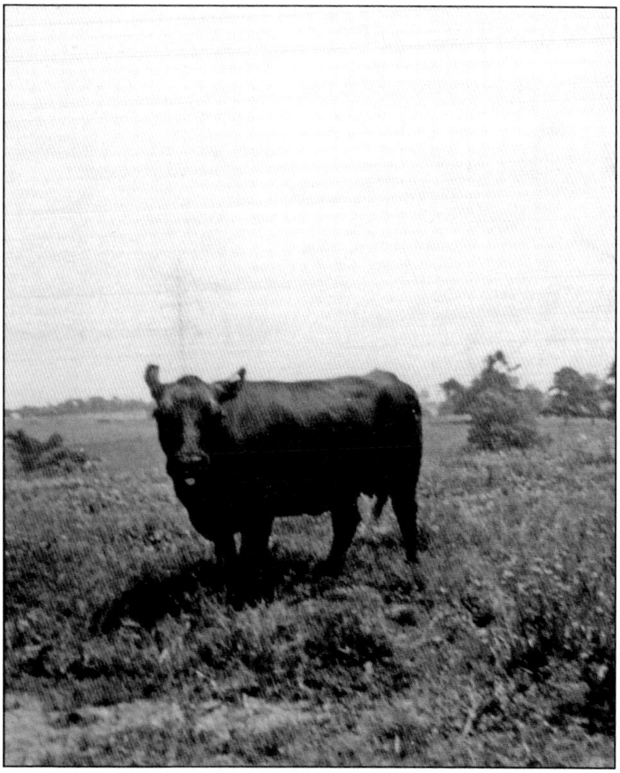

BLACK ANGUS. A Black Angus roams the back pasture at High View Farm. Aberdeen Angus is the original name of this breed, which is usually referred to simply as Angus or Black Angus. First imported in 1873, Black Angus is considered the most popular beef breed in the country.

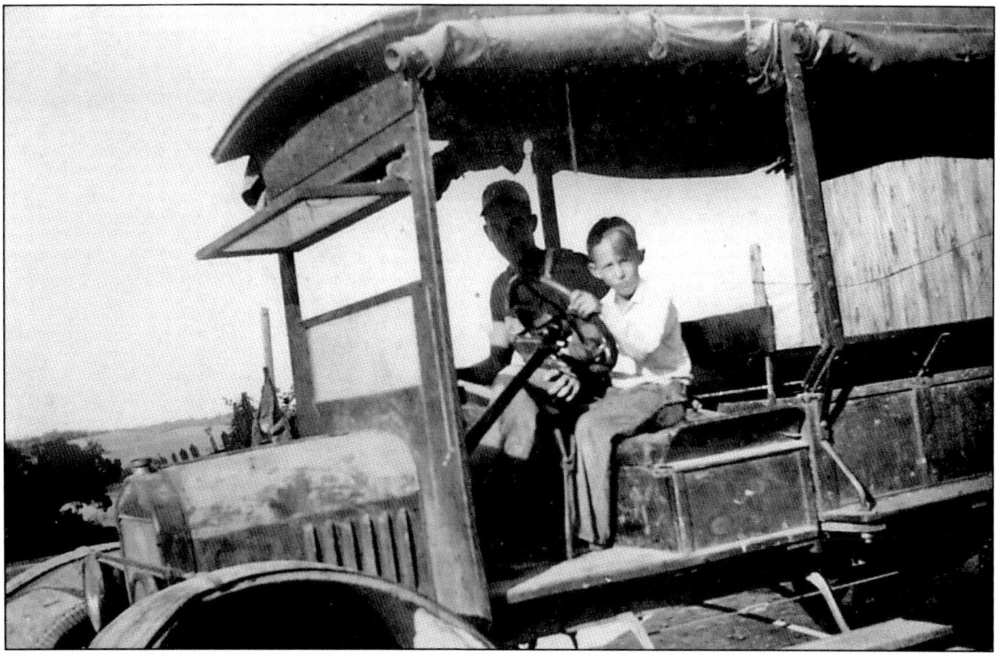

THE FARM TRUCK. The railroad and riverboats do not directly serve Alexandria; therefore, horse-drawn wagons and then motorized trucks were used to take produce to markets in Newport, Kentucky, and Cincinnati, Ohio. Many farmers in the area owned trucks for this purpose. Here young Bill Loos sits at the wheel of an old farm truck. Beside him is a man named Ralph.

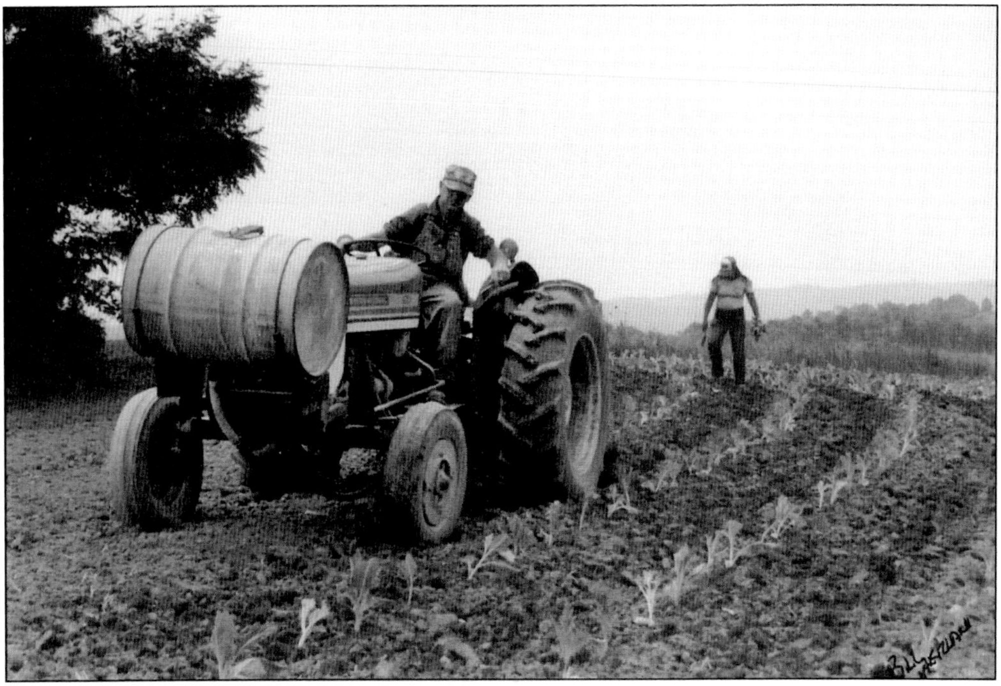

TOBACCO PLANTING. For Campbell County as well as Alexandria, agriculture was the most important means of living for the first 150 years. Shown are two photographs of growing tobacco, the cash crop of area farmers. Tobacco was first raised in a hot bed frame and then transplanted by horse-drawn, and later tractor-drawn, setters (pictured above). The crop was planted in long rows (as shown below), usually in May. It was carefully cultivated all summer until it began turning a golden yellow in August and September.

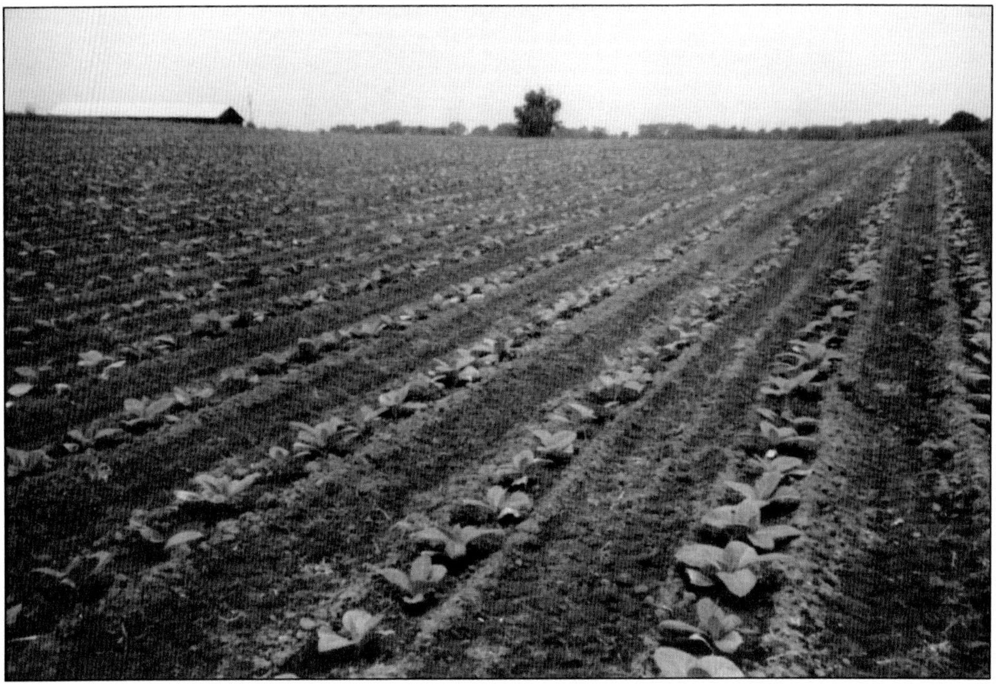

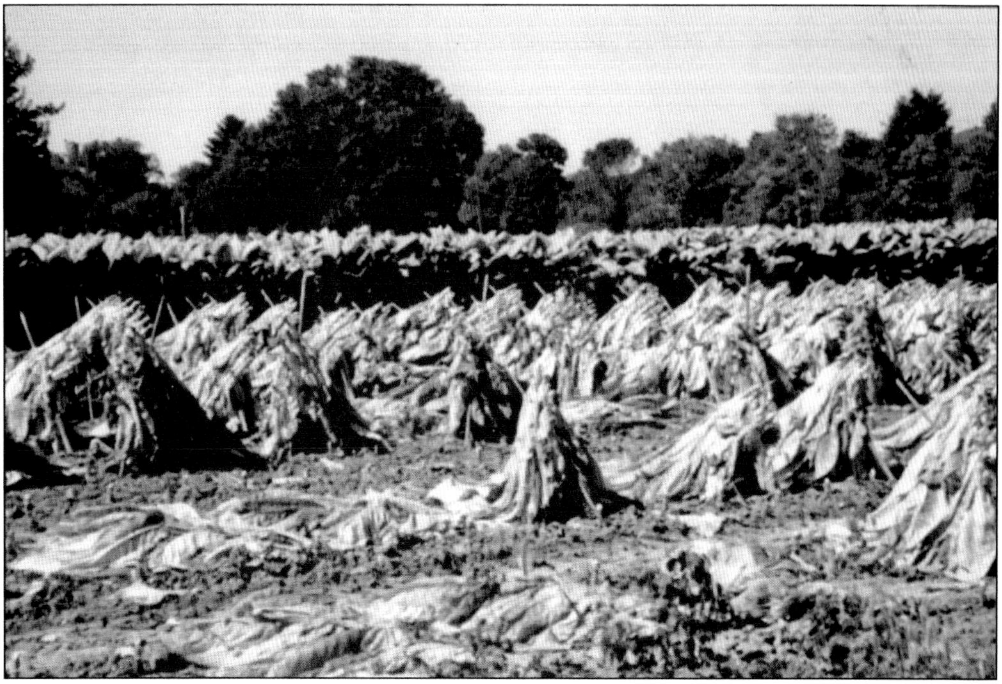

Tobacco Cutting and Hanging. Tobacco was cut as it turned yellow. It was first cut off at the ground with a sharp, hatchet-like cutter. Then the stalk was split with a pointed spear sitting atop a pointed stick (above). This splitting action continued until the stick was full. It was then loaded on a wagon and hung in a barn until early winter. At that time, the dried leaves (below) were stripped off and made into bundles, which were sold to tobacco warehouses. Tobacco farming was a labor-intensive and dirty process that required the participation of all members of the family.

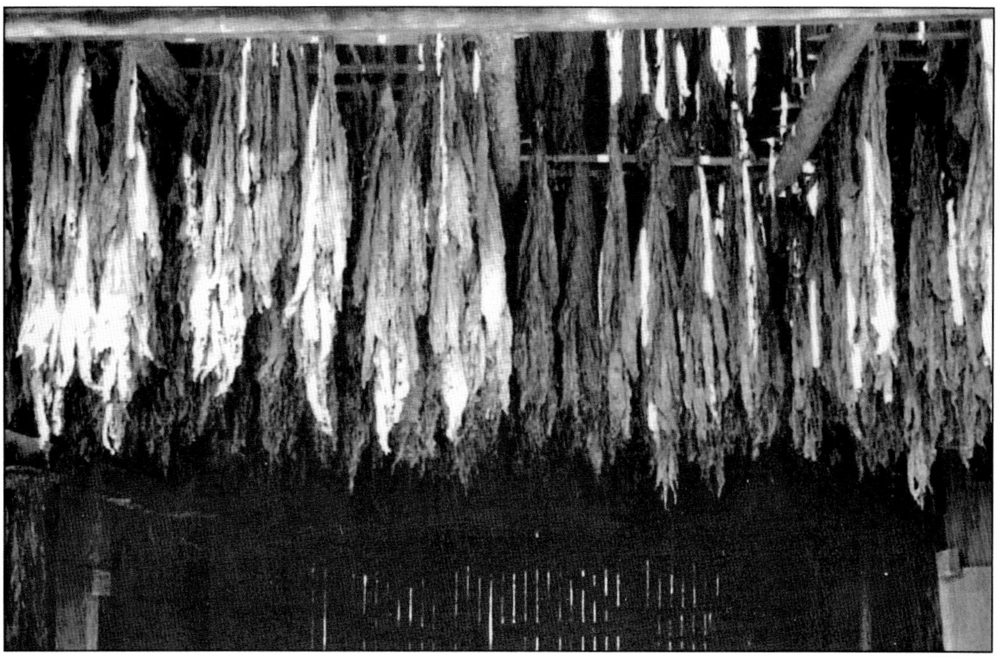

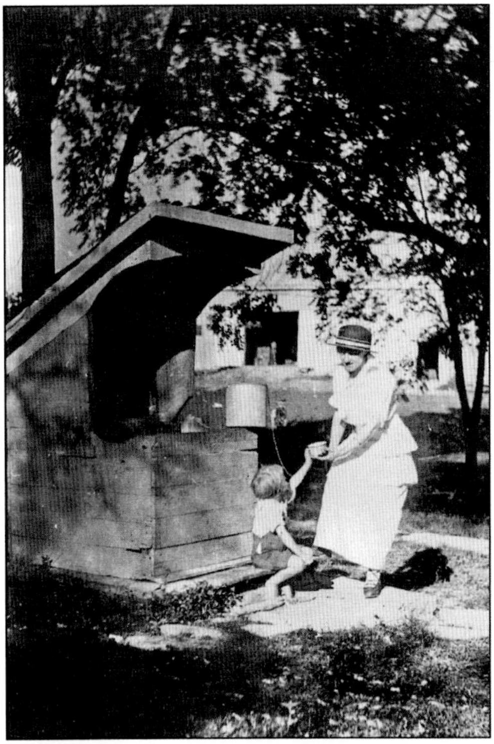

MARY ELIZABETH THATCHER. Mary Elizabeth is shown at the High View Farm well with an unidentified child. Well water was the main water supply until the city provided it in the late 1940s.

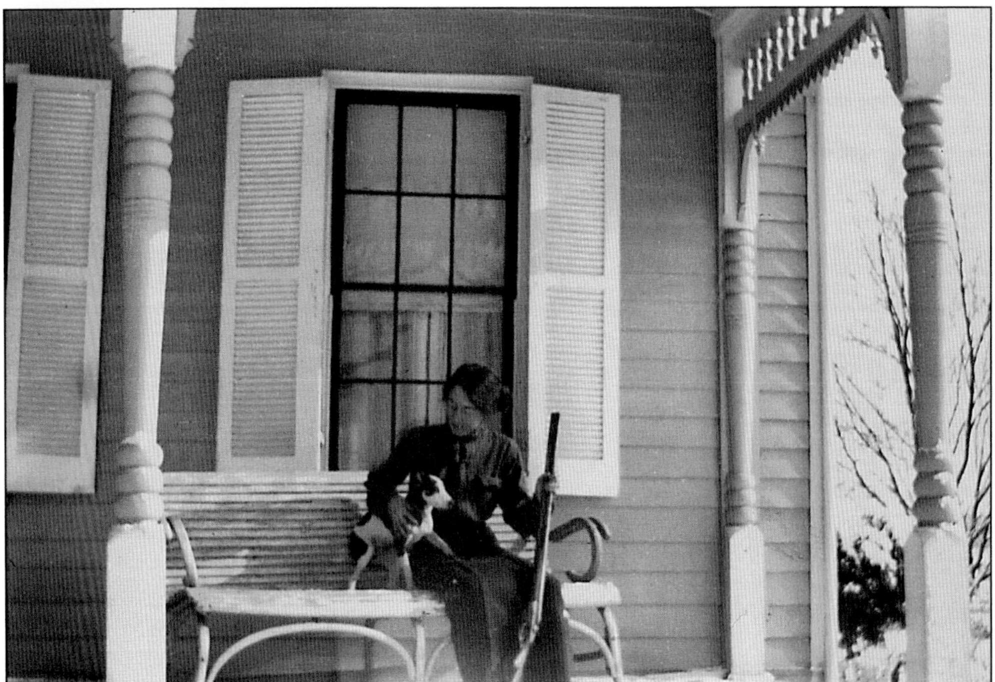

MARGIE HORNER. Born on June 3, 1887, Margie Horner married William Pratt Scott of Fort Thomas on June 21, 1911. Here she visits on the front porch of the Thatcher home on Alexandria Turnpike. It is unknown why she is holding a double-barrel shotgun.

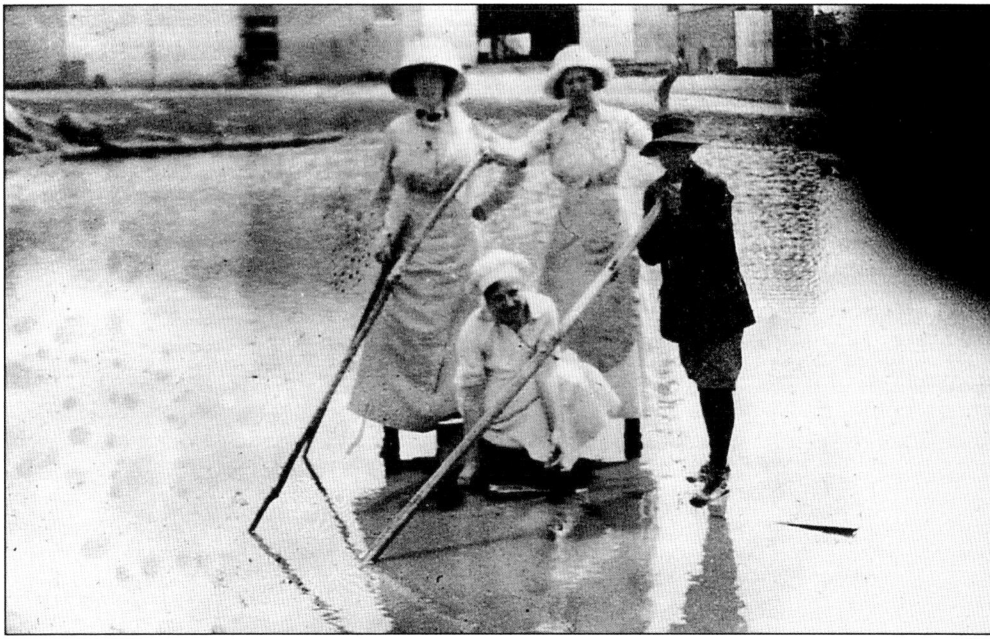

ICE-SKATING, c. 1905. When the High View Farm pond froze, it was time to skate. Poles were used to steady skaters on the ice. Standing from left to right are Ethel Horner, Margie Horner, and Ruth Thatcher, and Jack Thatcher is kneeling. Empress Chili now occupies the former site of the pond.

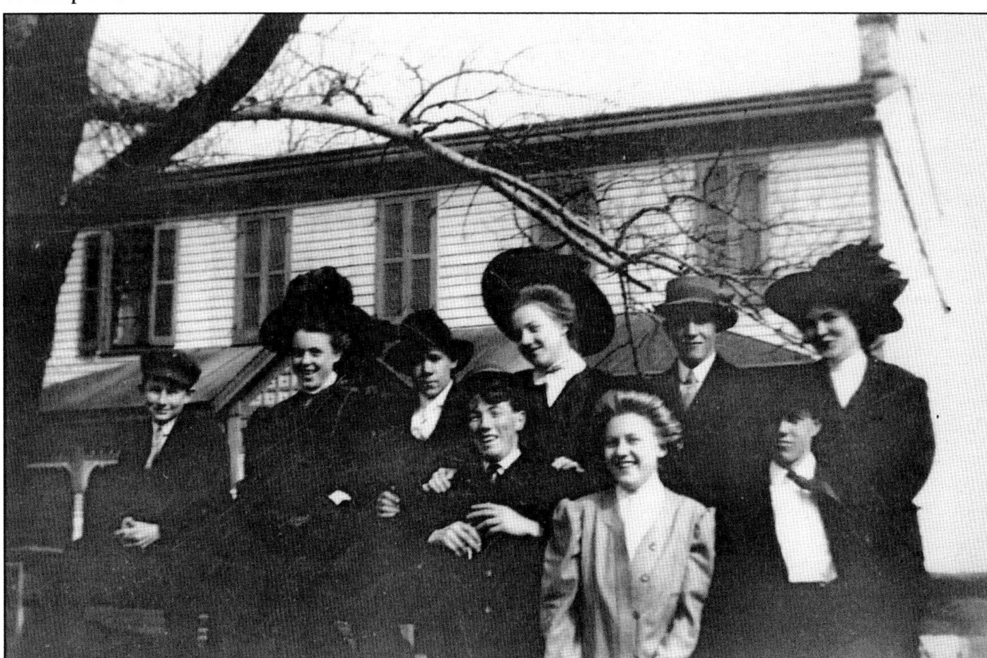

THE WALKING CLUB. The Walking Club gathered on Sunday afternoons and returned home to socialize over hot chocolate and cookies. Members standing in front of the Thatcher home include the following, from left to right: (first row) unidentified, Ruth Thatcher, and unidentified; (second row) Jack Thatcher, Myrtle Neal, Fanney Thatcher, and several unidentified people.

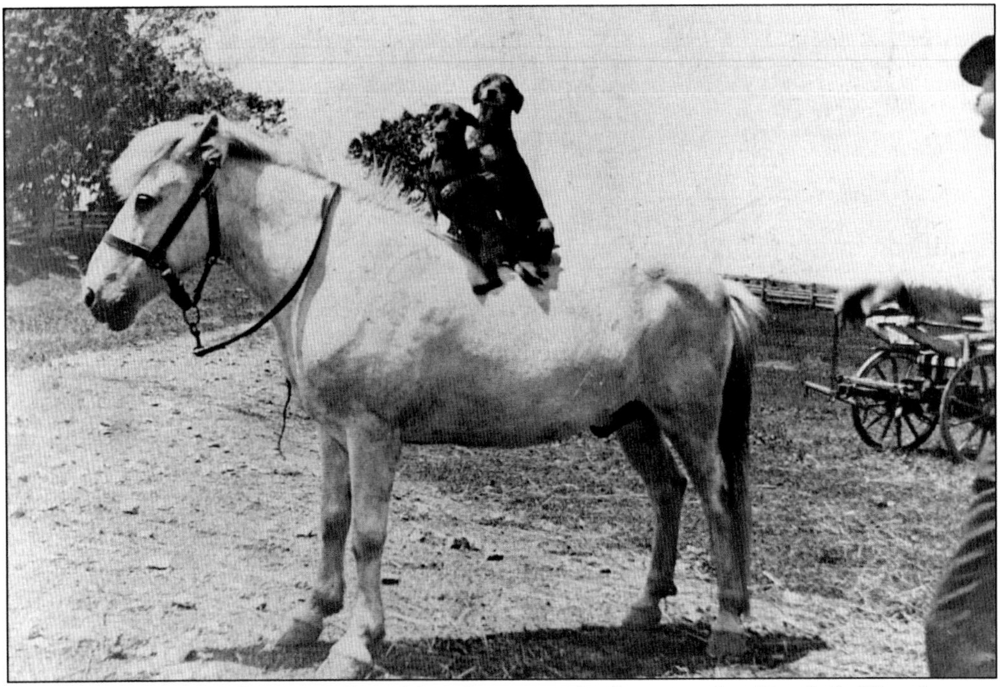

Bareback Riders. These two dogs (above) are astride the pony that Frank S. Thatcher got for his children. Jack Thatcher (below) drives his horse Raven on a snowy winter's day in 1946. Lillian (center) and Elizabeth Thatcher (right) ride in the one-horse, open sleigh one last time. During the snowy Campbell County winters, many families relied on some sort of sleigh or sled to get through the snow. Wagons or buggies pulled by a horse were not much use in the snow. Bells were often added since a sleigh was very quiet.

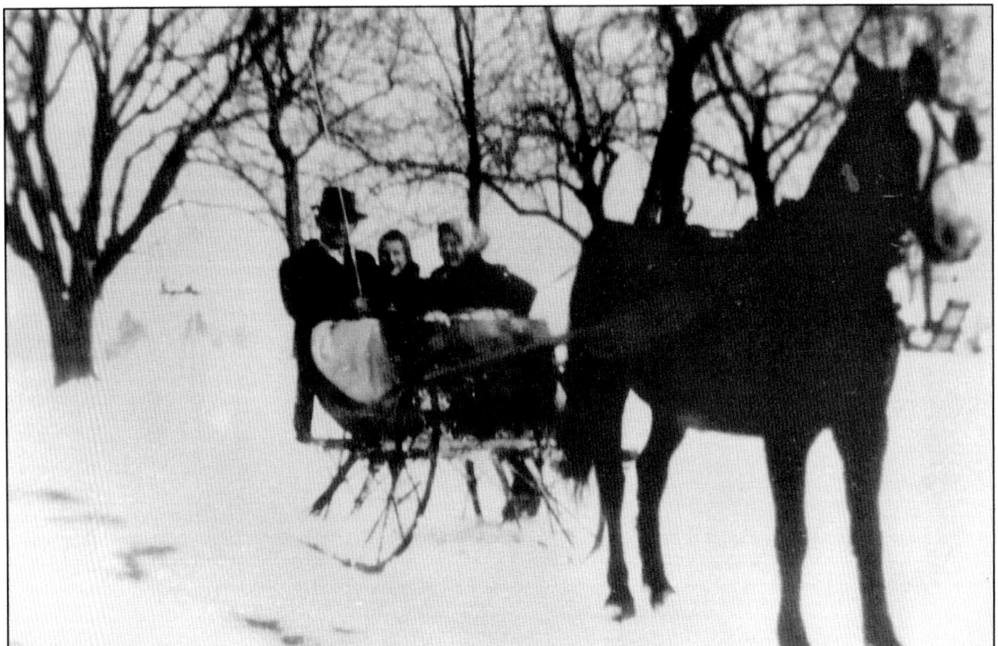

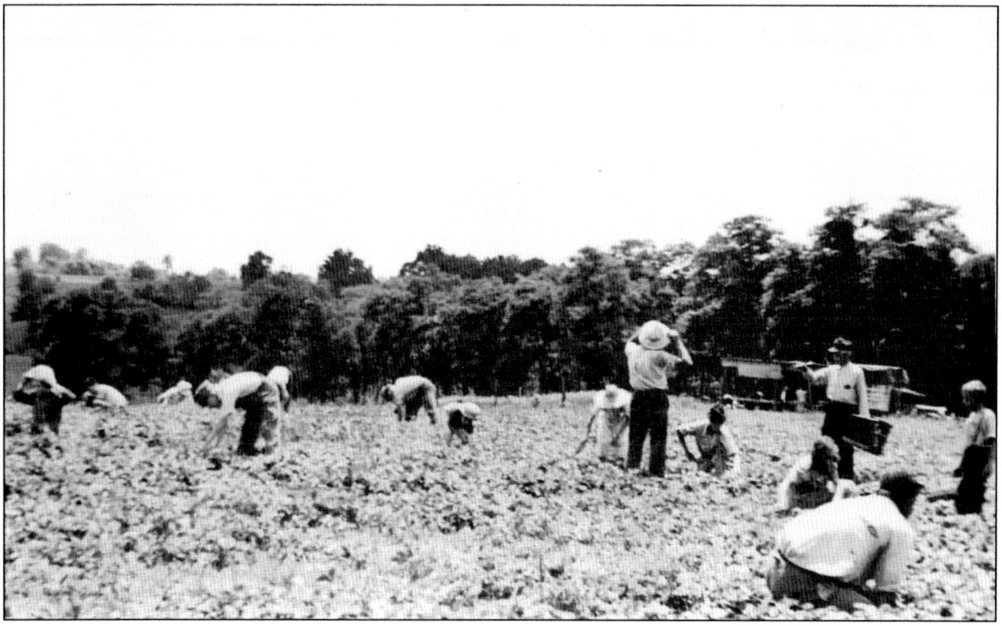

PICKING STRAWBERRIES. This strawberry patch was located on Thatcher Court in Alexandria; the same area is now filled with homes. The berry shed is visible in the right background. The only identified individuals are Edith Thatcher, adjusting her bonnet, and Frank Spilman, holding the carriers. As shown here, people of all ages helped to get the berries to market.

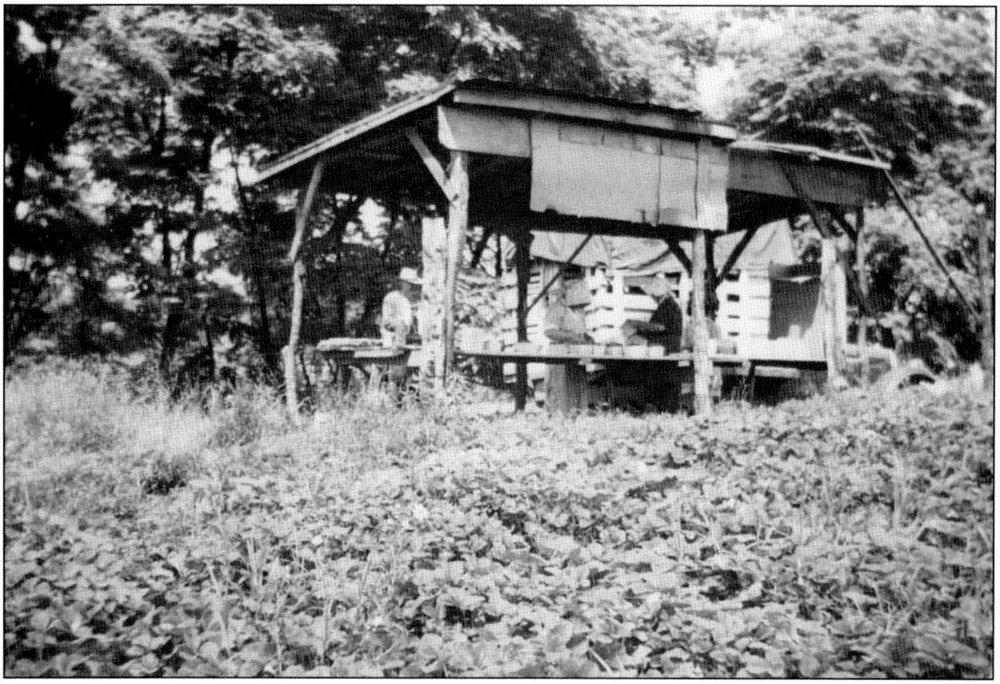

THE BERRY SHED. During harvest, pickers placed the strawberries in a quart-sized box. Four of these boxes went into a carrier. Pickers were paid with a chip or token for each carrier. The carriers were then taken to the shed, pictured here. The workers in the shed inspected the berries and loaded them into crates, which were then packed into the truck for transport to market.

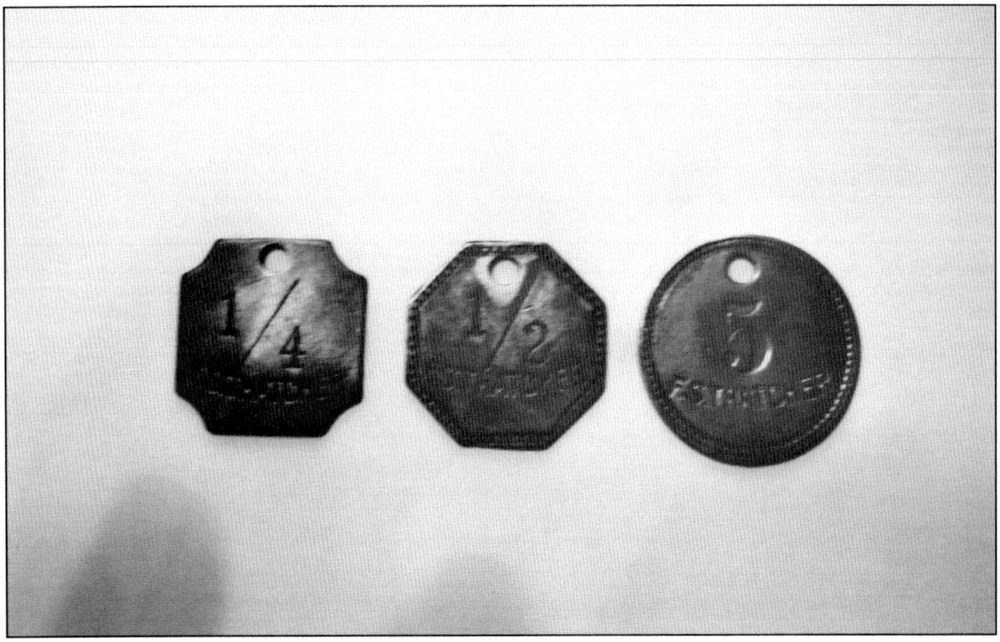

BERRY CHIPS. Frank Spilman Thatcher and his son Jack H. Thatcher had their workers use these berry chips through the 1940s. The strawberry pickers pinned these chips on their clothes until the day's end, when they were turned in for a payment of 5¢ each.

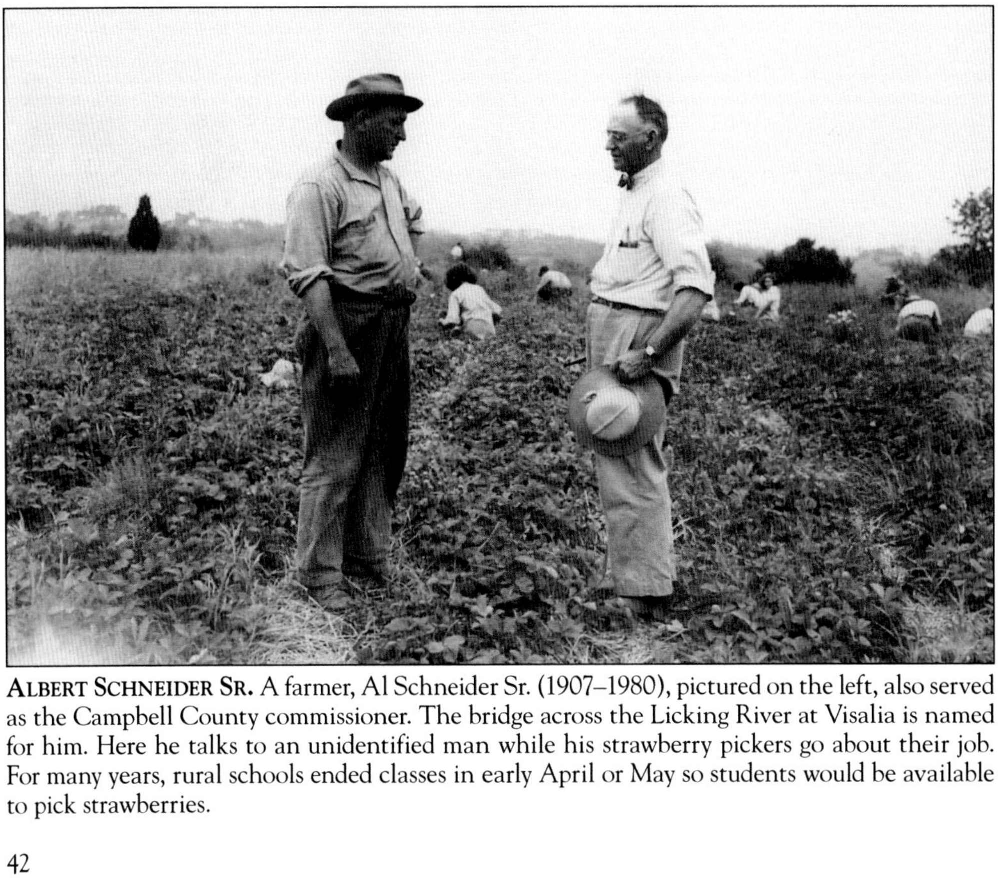

ALBERT SCHNEIDER SR. A farmer, Al Schneider Sr. (1907–1980), pictured on the left, also served as the Campbell County commissioner. The bridge across the Licking River at Visalia is named for him. Here he talks to an unidentified man while his strawberry pickers go about their job. For many years, rural schools ended classes in early April or May so students would be available to pick strawberries.

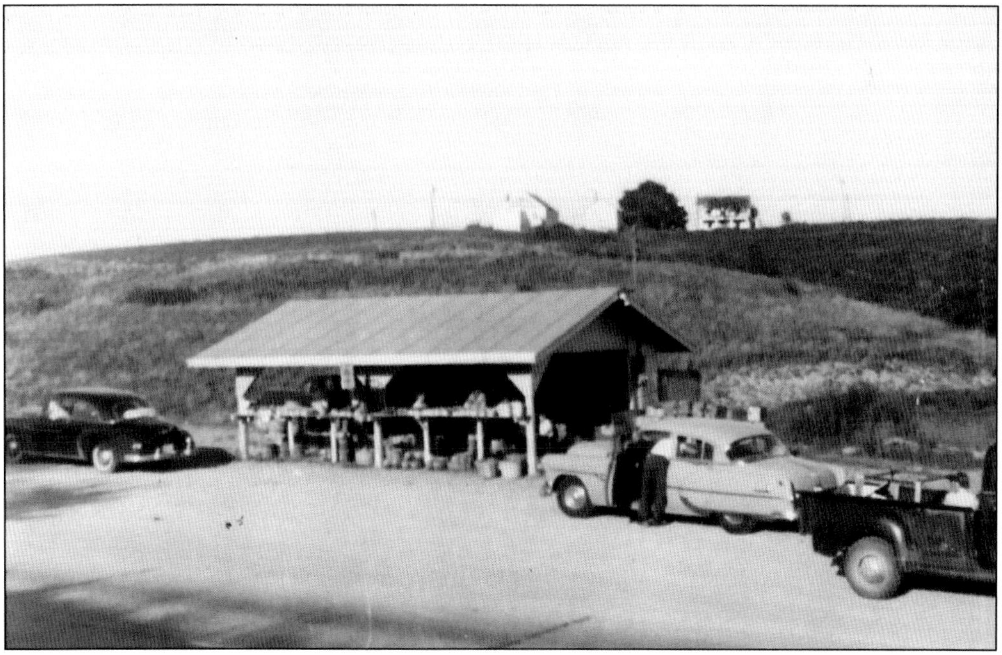

SCHNEIDER'S FRUIT STAND, 1950S. The Schneider family operated a fruit and produce stand on U.S. 27 for many years. Traveling city dwellers and local residents would stop for fresh produce at the roadside market. Visible in the background are the Schneider home (which is shown more clearly below) and farm. Often in the spring, the hills were covered with flowering fruit trees. The stand was torn down with the widening of U.S. 27.

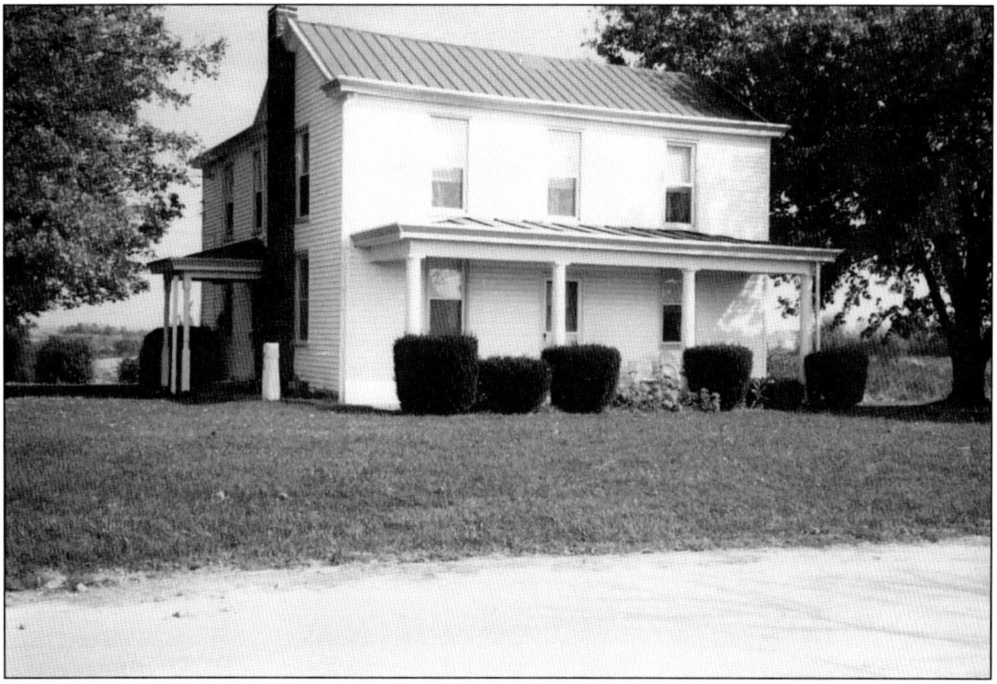

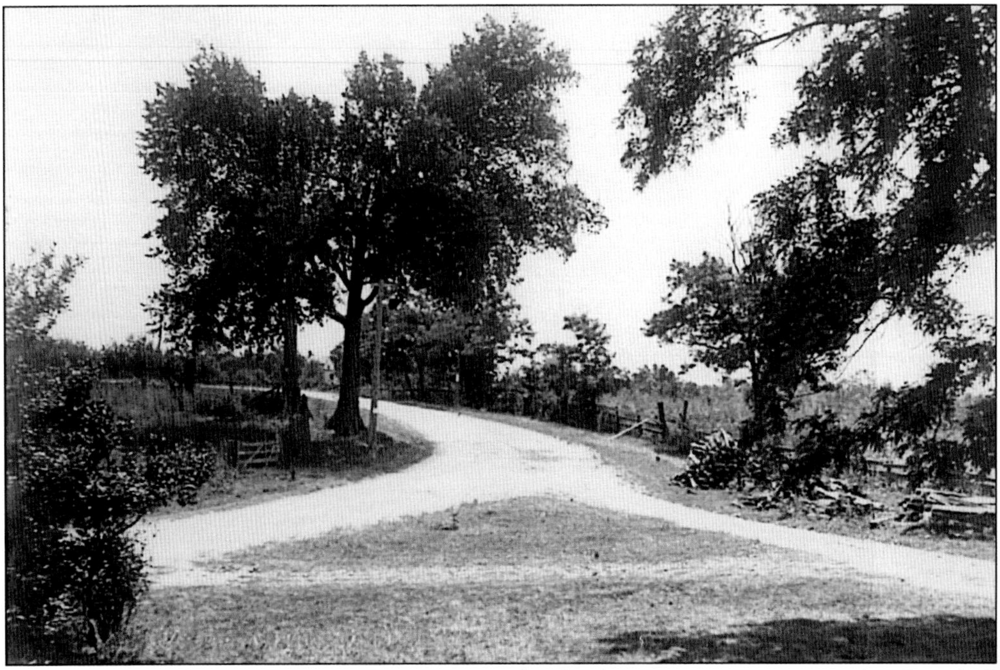

YOUTSEY HILL. John S. Youtsey was from a pioneer family whose ancestors immigrated to Campbell County in the latter part of the 18th century. The Beggs family arrived around the same time, and Youtsey married Elizabeth Beggs in 1842. He owned many acres on what became known as Youtsey Hill (above), the main hill located in the north end of Alexandria behind the current Wal-Mart store in the Village Green Shopping Center. Youtsey built the log home pictured below in the wilderness where they lived.

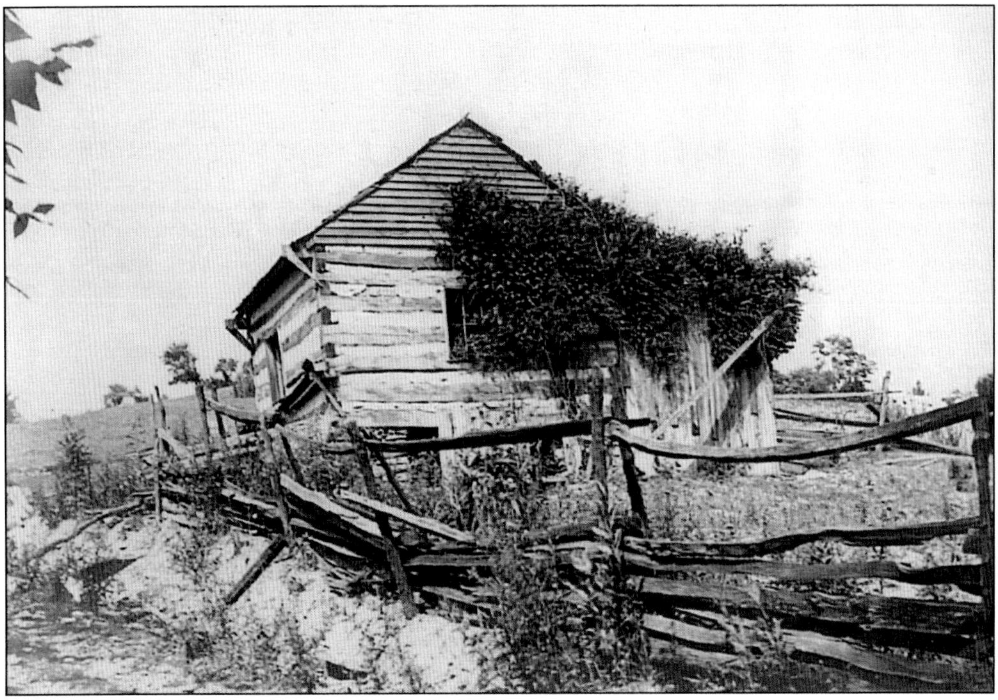

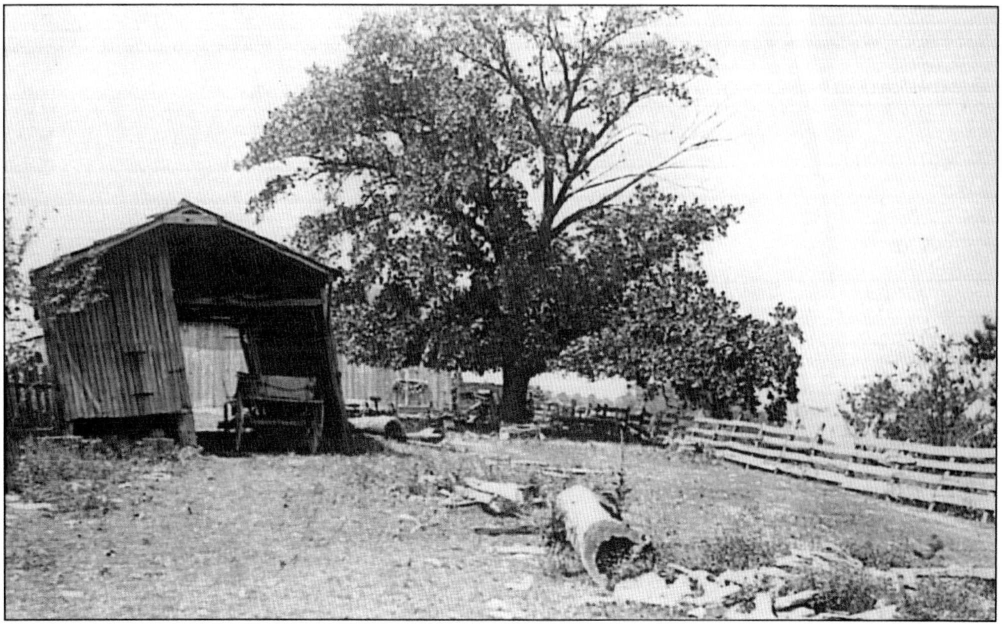

Corncrib. This corncrib was used to store corn while still on the cob. The farmer pulled his wagon into the shed and unloaded the corn, placing it in a crib to air dry. The vertical board construction allowed more air to reach the corn, thus keeping it dry. Corncribs were elevated off the ground to protect the corn from pests and rodents. The idea originated with Native Americans and was adapted by European settlers.

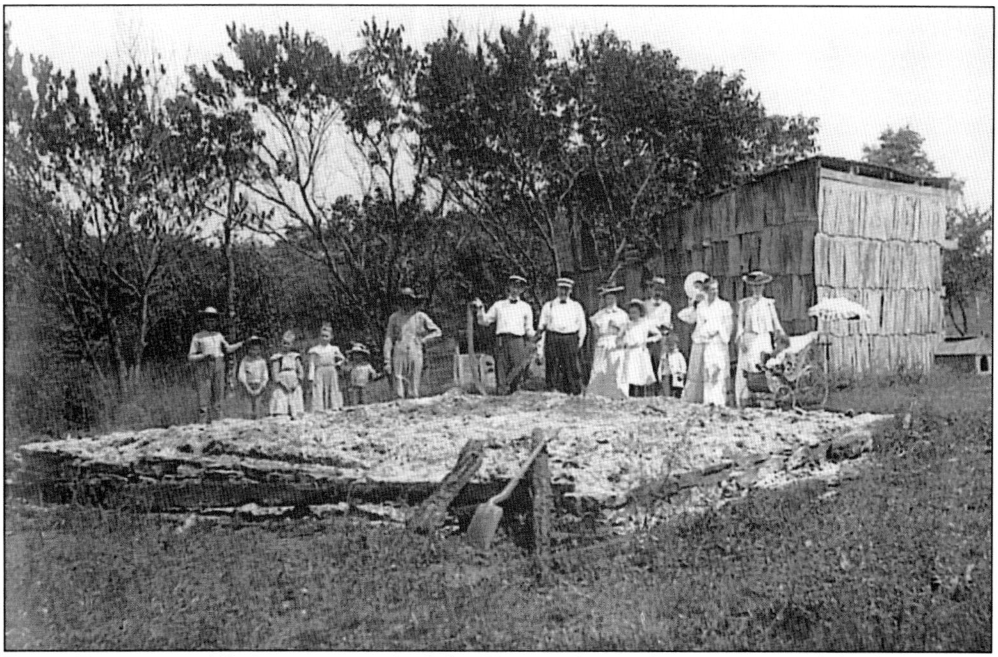

Barn Burning. All that remained of the Youtsey barn after it was struck by lighting on July 21, 1903, was the stone foundation. The very nature of its wood construction, along with the hay stored in the barn, made it burn quickly. The only way to fight a fire was with a brigade of family and neighbors carrying buckets of water.

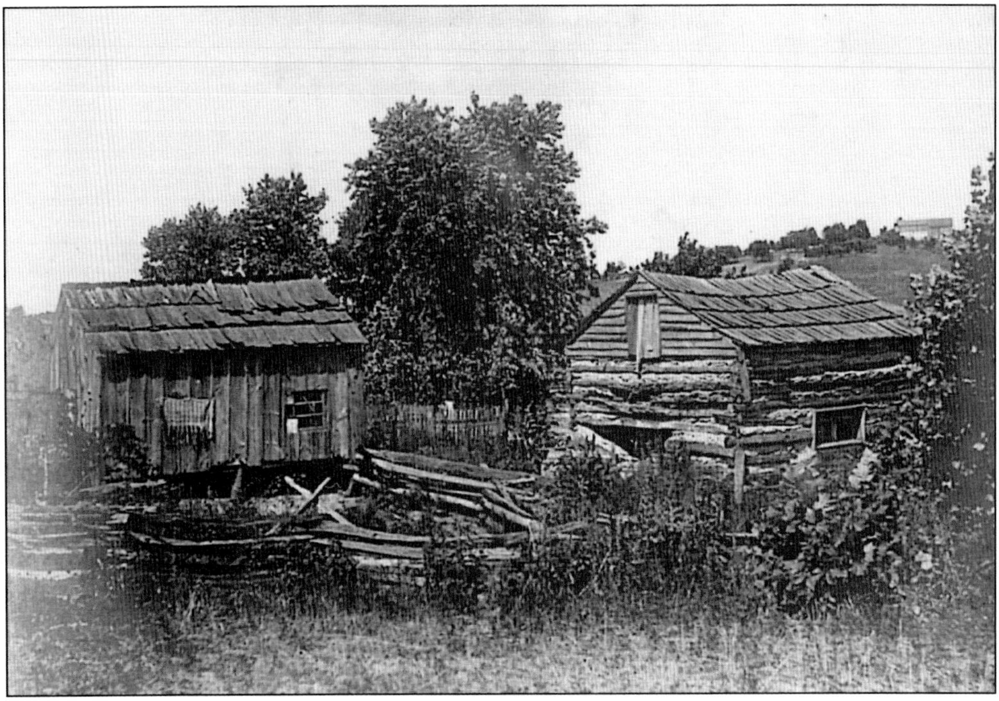

THE STUBBS WORKSHOP. In order to perform repairs on the log cabin or farm equipment, a shelter was needed to keep the wind off the farmer's head and the rain off his neck. This primitive building (left), shown with a split-rail fence, was just enough to do the job.

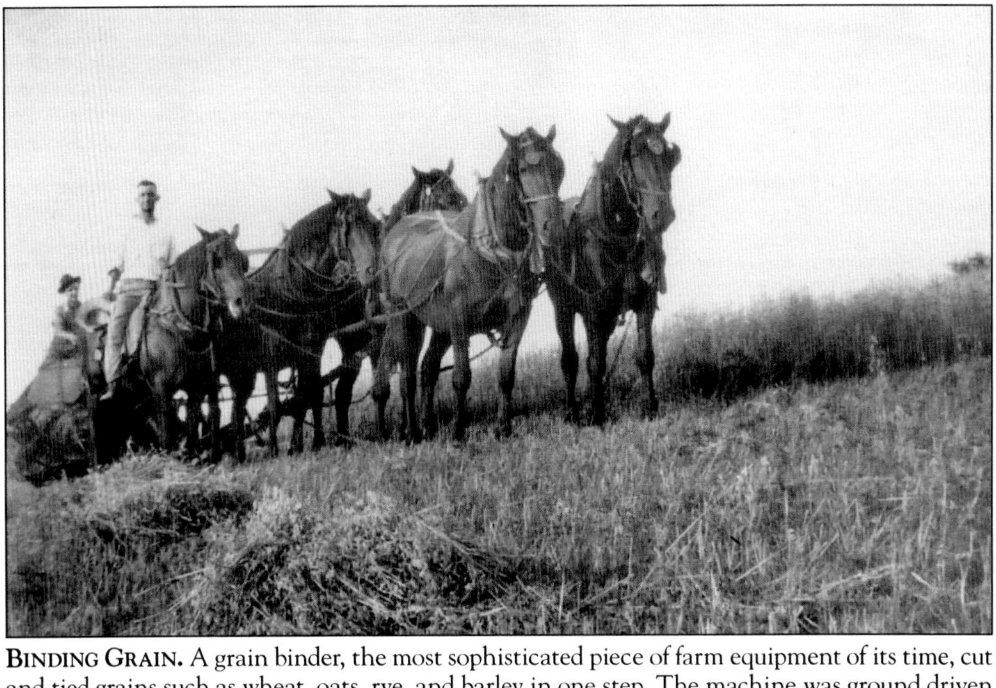

BINDING GRAIN. A grain binder, the most sophisticated piece of farm equipment of its time, cut and tied grains such as wheat, oats, rye, and barley in one step. The machine was ground driven and was pulled by a team of horses. The resulting bundles were then picked up by field-workers and stacked to form a small tepee, called a "shock," allowing the grain to dry.

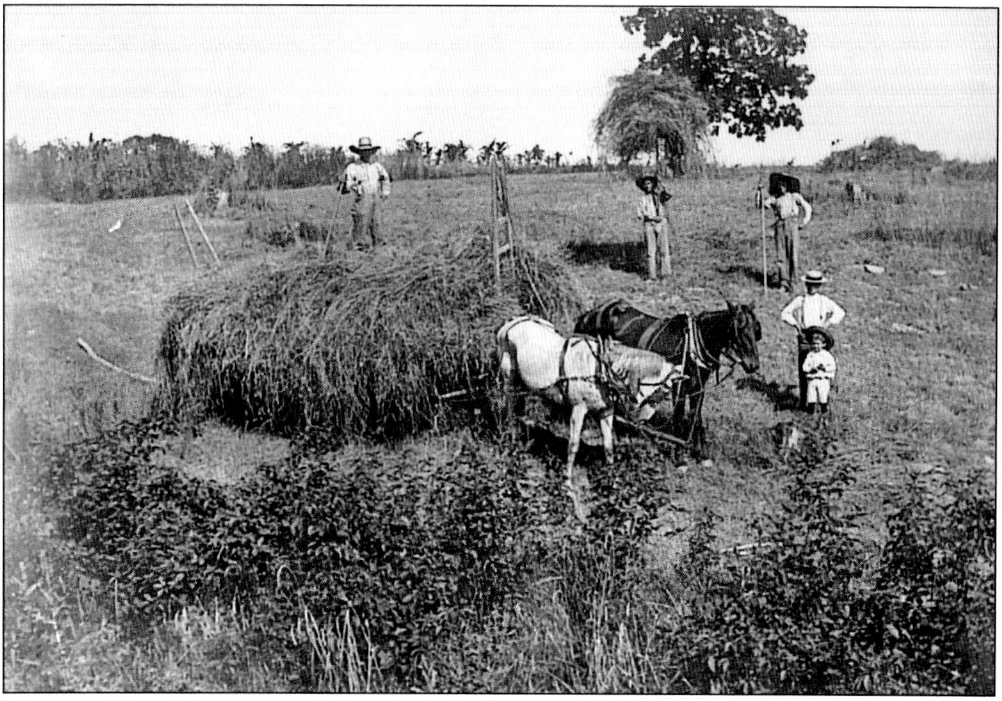

MAKING HAY. Hay was needed to feed the horses and cows over the winter. In the above photograph, several people fork loose hay onto an old wood wagon pulled by a team of horses. "Making hay when the sun shined" was an important part of any farm. Cutting, drying, and hauling hay required two to three days of hot, dry weather, and everyone helped to complete the task. In the below photograph, a new method with round balers speeds up the labor-intensive process of making hay. The bundles are then loaded onto this typical wood-wheeled wagon, pulled by a team of horses known as Andy (left) and Pete (right). John Thomas is standing on the hay.

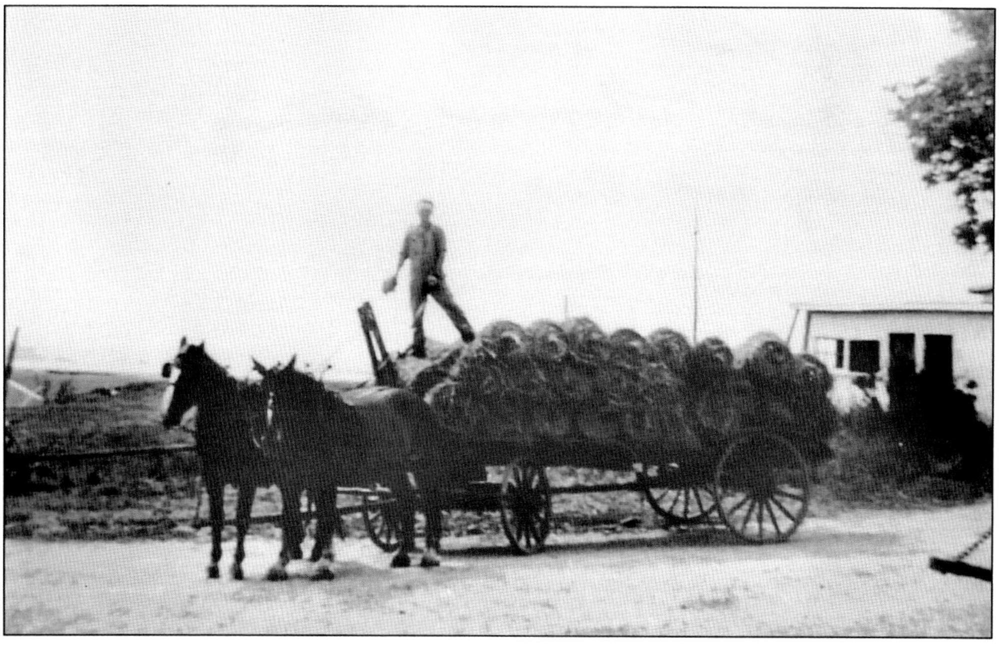

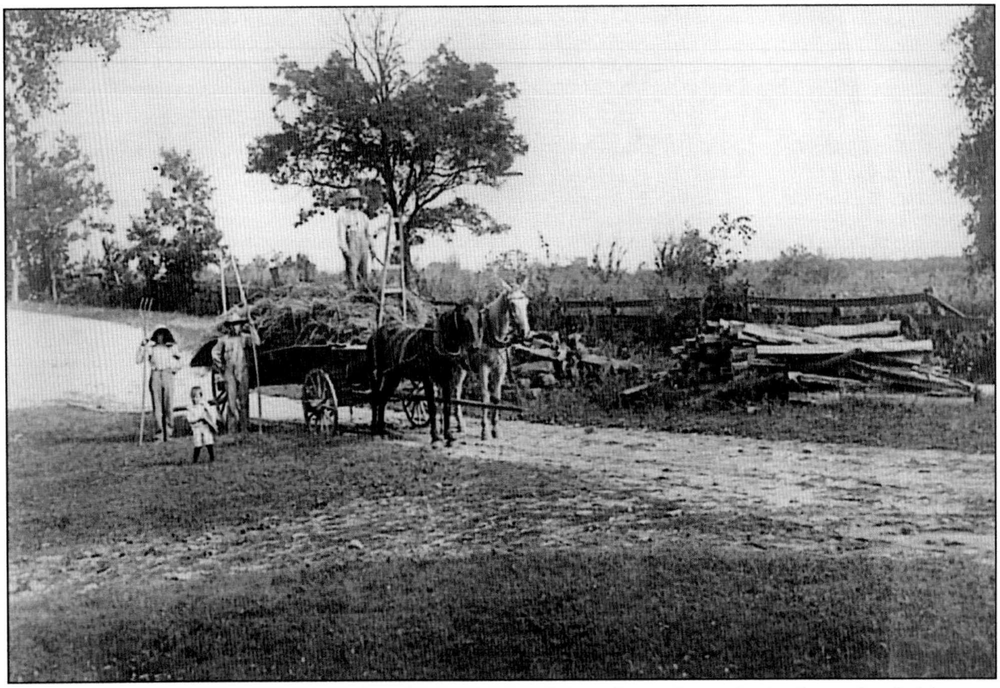

LOAD OF GRAIN. After the year's last load of grain (above) was brought in from the fields, one of the biggest jobs started when the farmers took the oat, wheat, or barley seed off the stalk. This task was called threshing. A huge metal and wood machine powered by a big tractor (below) was needed, along with 15 to 25 men. Threshing machines were brought to the farm to do the custom work. The farmer's wife would spend days getting enough food ready to supply the hungry crew. Today the modern combine replaces all of these men and does the job much faster.

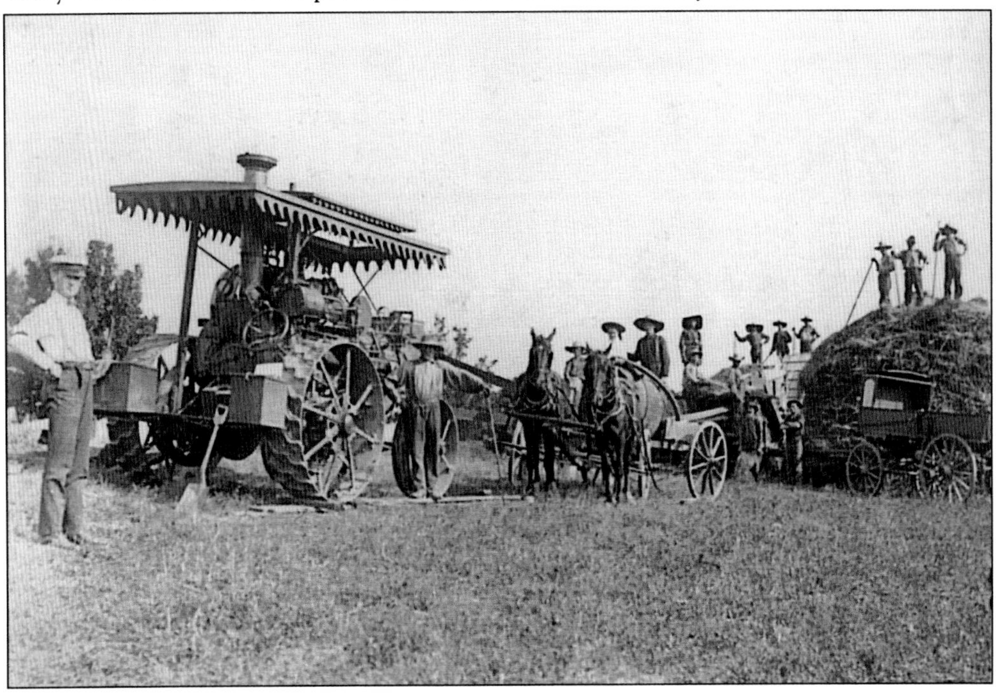

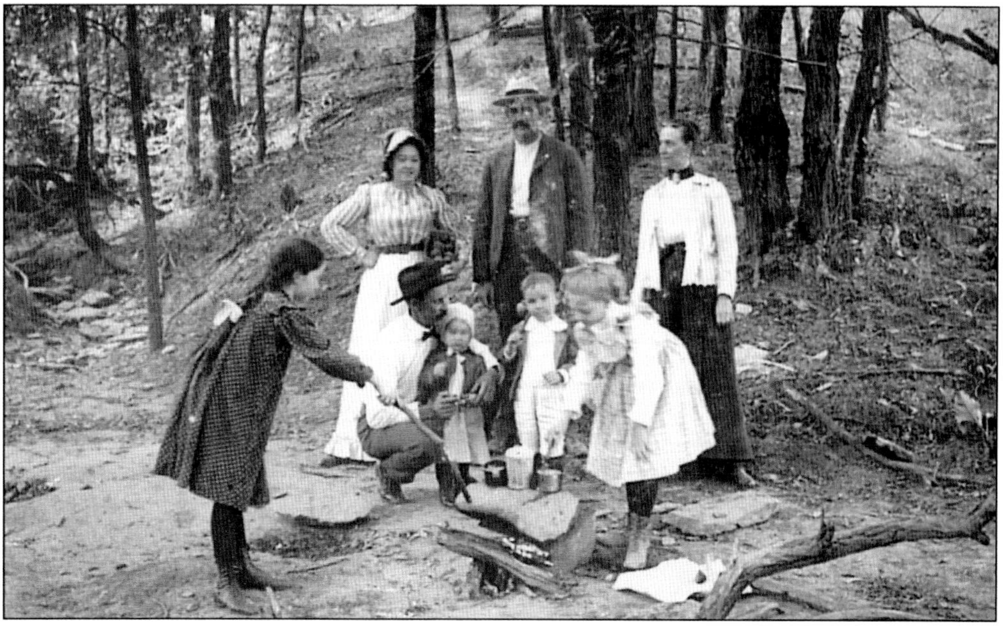

HAPPY HOLLOW PICNIC. A group picnics on East Alexandria Pike halfway down Youtsey's Hill at the current site of the Kerry Motors parking lot. Seen from left to right are: (foreground) Margaret Youtsey, Henry Meyers, Taylor Meyers, John Meyers, and Grace Koeninger; (background) Anna Weinel, William Albert Youtsey, and ? Koeninger.

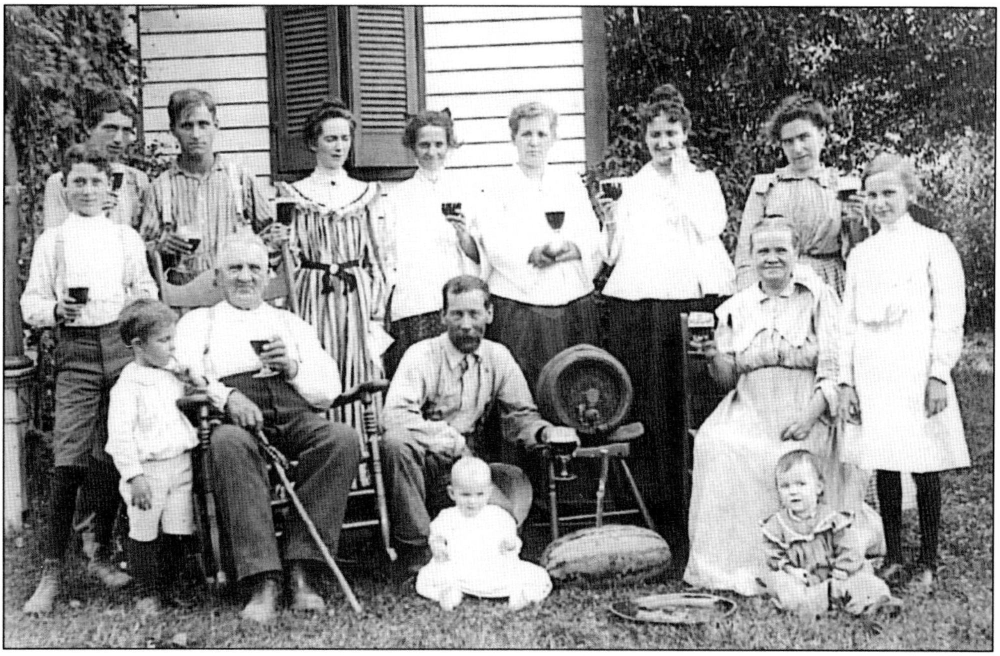

SUNDAY GATHERINGS. The normal thing to do on Sunday was to visit with relatives and neighbors, and catch up on the news of the week. Here neighbors gather at the Youtsey home. Seated from left to right are John Stewart Youtsey, Adam Leuger, and Eliza Jeanette Beggs Youtsey. The Youtsey family had seven children: Katherine, Mary C., George T., Jacob T., Margaret B., James J., and William A.

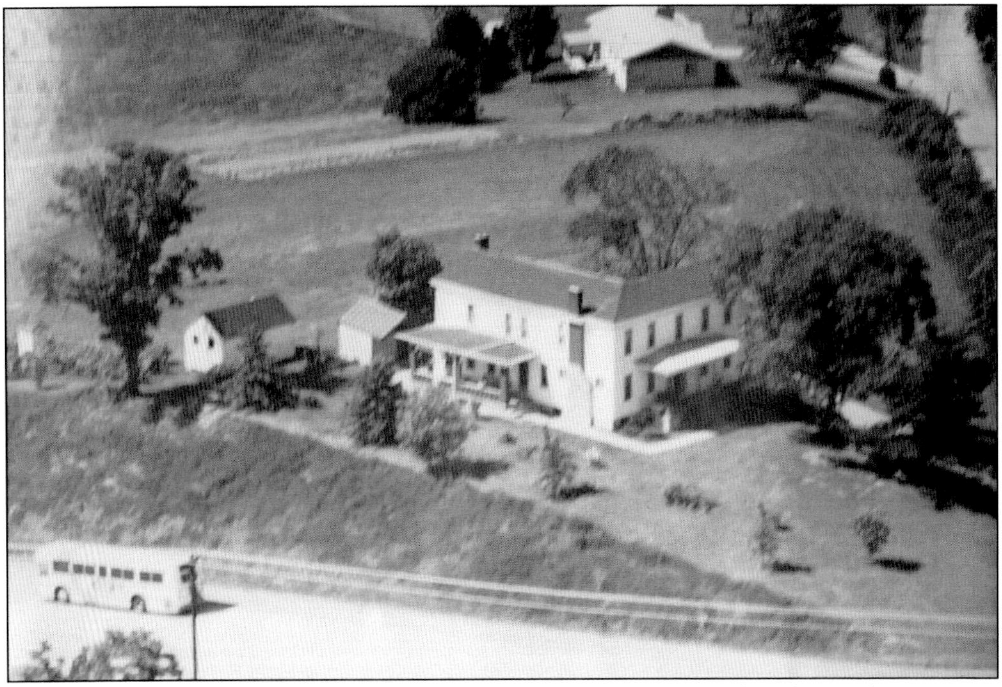

The Edward Schultz Home. Located at the top of Youtsey's Hill and on the northeast corner of Alexandria Pike's intersection with East Alexandria Pike, this house was moved several times due to road construction. When Alexandria Pike was widened to four lanes through town, it was destroyed and eventually replaced by fast-food restaurants.

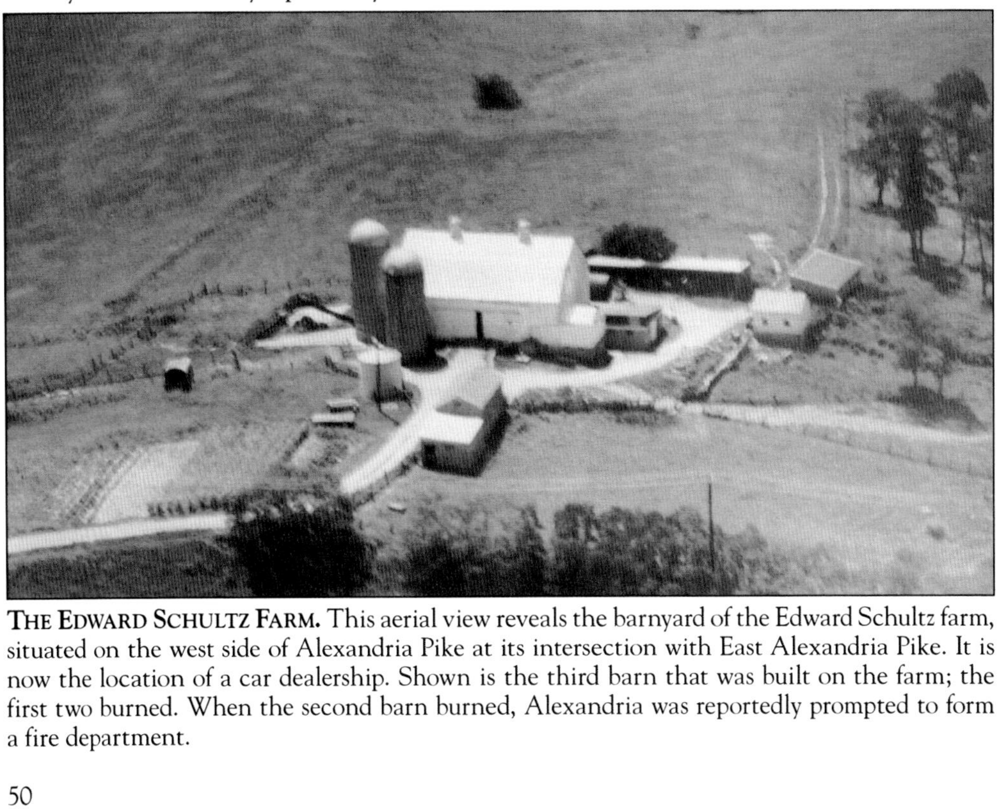

The Edward Schultz Farm. This aerial view reveals the barnyard of the Edward Schultz farm, situated on the west side of Alexandria Pike at its intersection with East Alexandria Pike. It is now the location of a car dealership. Shown is the third barn that was built on the farm; the first two burned. When the second barn burned, Alexandria was reportedly prompted to form a fire department.

Three

SCHOOLS AND CHURCHES

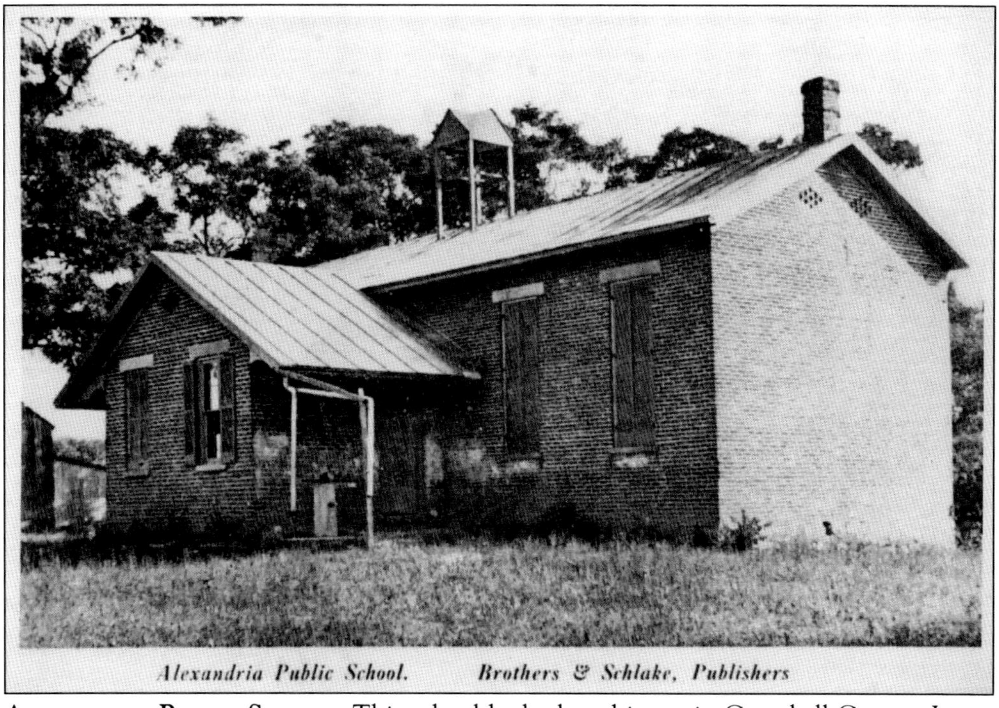

ALEXANDRIA PUBLIC SCHOOL. This school had a long history in Campbell County. It was first built before 1900 and was one of nearly 50 one- and two-room schools scattered across the county. Notice the chalk marks beneath the windows—the result of students clapping erasers against the building.

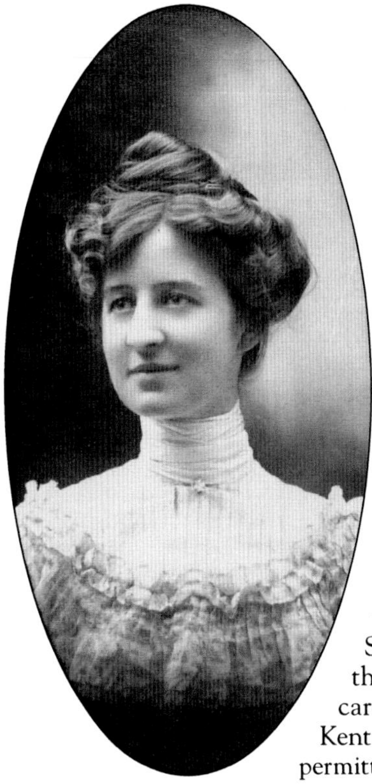

BLANCHE THATCHER. Blanche (left) was born on July 21, 1877, to Daniel Edward and Elizabeth Tarvin Thatcher. After attending the Teachers' Institute, she received her teaching certificate on May 25, 1909, allowing her to teach for the term of four calendar years. Along with her sisters Margaret Spilman Thatcher and Lou Thatcher, she taught throughout the Campbell County School System, finishing her teaching career at the Fifth District Elementary School in Covington, Kentucky. Below is her first Teacher's County Certificate, which permitted her to teach in Campbell County.

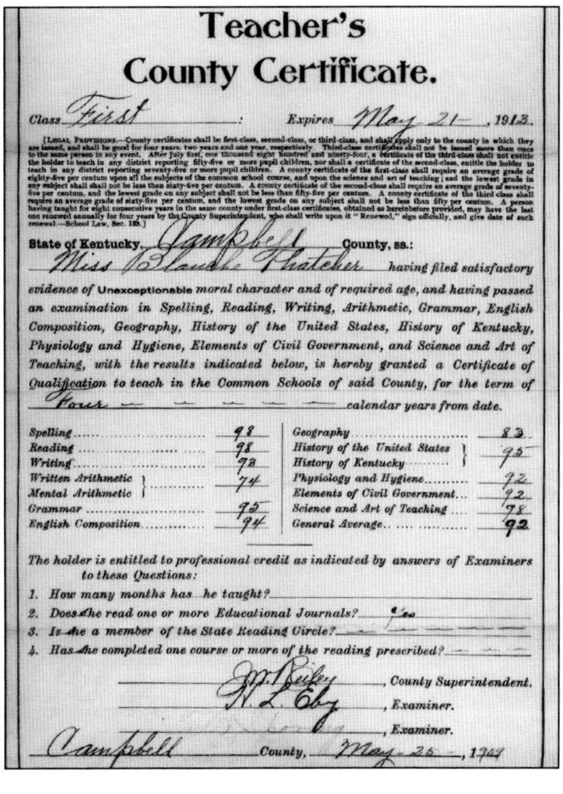

Teacher's County Certificate.

Class *First*: Expires *May 21*, 191*3*.

[LEGAL PROVISIONS.—County certificates shall be first-class, second-class, or third-class, and shall apply only to the county in which they are issued, and shall be good for four years, two years and one year, respectively. Third-class certificates shall not be issued more than once to the same person in any event. After July first, one thousand eight hundred and ninety-four, a certificate of the third-class shall not entitle the holder to teach in any district reporting fifty-five or more pupil children, nor shall a certificate of the second-class, entitle the holder to teach in any district reporting seventy-five or more pupil children. A county certificate of the first-class shall require an average grade of eighty-five per centum upon all the subjects of the common school course, and upon the science and art of teaching; and the lowest grade in any subject shall shall not be less than sixty-five per centum. A county certificate of the second-class shall require an average grade of seventy-five per centum, and the lowest grade on any subject shall not be less than fifty-five per centum. A county certificate of the third class shall require an average grade of sixty-five per centum, and the lowest grade on any subject shall not be less than fifty per centum. A person having taught for eight consecutive years in the same county under first-class certificates, obtained as hereinbefore provided, may have the last one renewed annually for four years by the County Superintendent, who shall write upon it "Renewed," sign officially, and give date of such renewal.—School Law, Sec. 133.]

State of Kentucky, *Campbell* County, ss.:

Miss Blanche Thatcher having filed satisfactory evidence of Unexceptionable moral character and of required age, and having passed an examination in Spelling, Reading, Writing, Arithmetic, Grammar, English Composition, Geography, History of the United States, History of Kentucky, Physiology and Hygiene, Elements of Civil Government, and Science and Art of Teaching, with the results indicated below, is hereby granted a Certificate of Qualification to teach in the Common Schools of said County, for the term of *Four* calendar years from date.

Spelling	98	Geography	83
Reading	98	History of the United States / History of Kentucky	95
Writing	93		
Written Arithmetic / Mental Arithmetic	74	Physiology and Hygiene	92
		Elements of Civil Government	92
Grammar	95	Science and Art of Teaching	78
English Composition	94	General Average	92

The holder is entitled to professional credit as indicated by answers of Examiners to these Questions:

1. How many months has he taught?
2. Does she read one or more Educational Journals? *Yes*
3. Is she a member of the State Reading Circle?
4. Has she completed one course or more of the reading prescribed?

J. M. Riley, County Superintendent.
W. L. Eby, Examiner.
, Examiner.

Campbell County, *May 25*, 190*9*

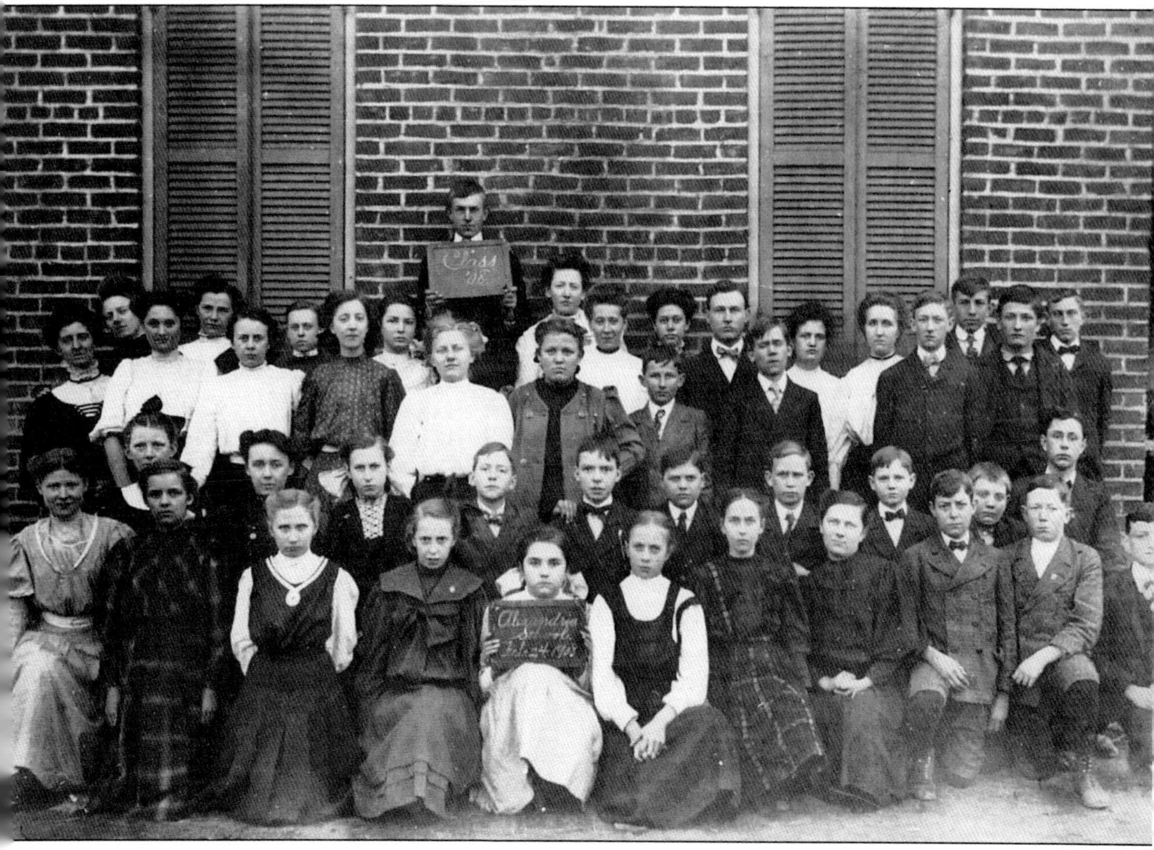

ALEXANDRIA PUBLIC SCHOOL CLASS OF 1908. Blanche Thatcher taught this class in 1908, perhaps as part of the student-teaching requirements in order to obtain her certificate. Pictured from left to right are: (first row) Cora Snyder, Marie White, Cornelia Matz Racke, Bessie Houston, Norma Rost, Anna Gosney Teschmer, Bessie Charles Gosney, Margaret Spilman, Albert Teschmer, Edwin Yelton, and Alois Schwalbach; (second row) Florence Reiley Peterson, Florence Brell Dunn, Lola Hart, Willis Shaw, Ralph White, August Nordwick, Clyde Gosney, George Racke, John Fields, and Ennis Shaw; (third row) Edith Fields Schlake, Augusta Funk, Ruth Thatcher, Mary Gilbert Hopper, Jack Thatcher, Atwood White, Bernard Boyers, Claude Fields, and Charlie Listerman; (fourth row) teacher Blanche Thatcher, Fan Thatcher, unidentified, Clifford Gosney, Eva Wright, Lida Robinson, Edith Parry Hodge, Hannah Lou Petty Smith, Lillian Racke, Ben Bowers, and two unidentified; (fifth row) Cooper Hart, with the sign.

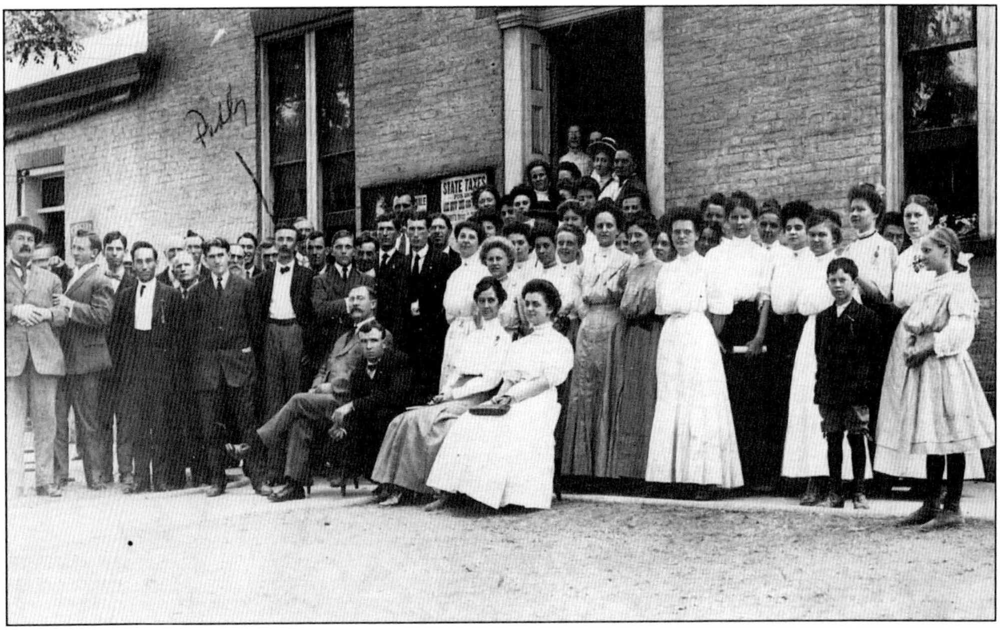

CAMPBELL COUNTY TEACHERS' INSTITUTE. The Teachers' Institute was the program through which permission was granted to teach school in Campbell County. Interested individuals attended classroom instruction, complete with examinations, in order to obtain their teaching certificate. They also attended classes to further their education, much like the teachers of today who participate in what is called "in-service days." On thoses days, teachers are free from class work and can use the time for additional education and planning. These photographs were taken in front of the Campbell County Courthouse in Alexandria.

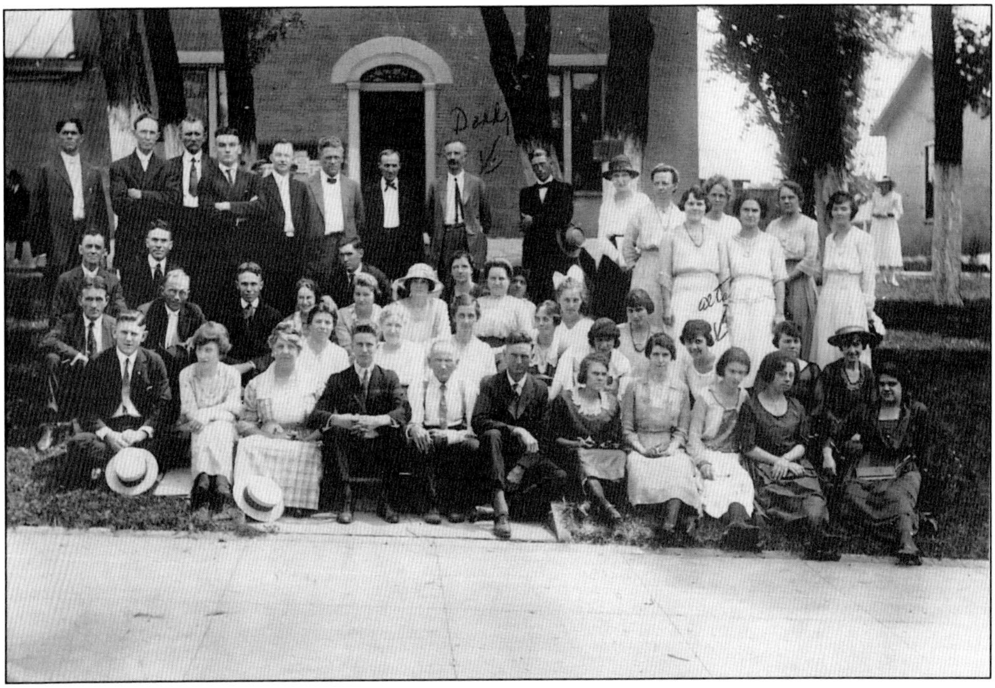

PROGRAM

Campbell County Teachers' Institute

To be held at the Court House
Alexandria, Ky.

August 29-30-31, September 1-2
1910

PROF. J. T. C. NOE, Instructor
J. W. REILEY, County Sup't.

TEACHERS' INSTITUTE PROGRAM, 1910. This program was given out to those attending the institute from August 29 to September 2, 1910. The first page states the objective of the institute, and subsequent pages detail the topics of discussions and lectures presented each day. Topics included the study of child life and how to proceed on the first day of school, complete with rules and discipline. Lessons in spelling, pronunciation, penmanship, grammar, language and composition, reading, arithmetic, geography, history, physiology, and civil government were also offered. Sessions were open to trustees of the institute as well. An overview of books purchased for the school libraries was provided. Throughout the week, attendees enjoyed a focus on music by participating in daily singing.

OBJECT OF THE INSTITUTE.

To give to Teachers practical ideas and enlarge the true teaching spirit, which will cause pupils to do more effective work and create better educational conditions in every community.

TEACHERS—The program is but an outline. Every subject before the Institute is open to you for discussion.

Make a note of those methods, devices, etc., which have helped you. Give them to others.

Make a note of those points upon which you need help. Seek a better way.

TRUSTEES—A Period on Thursday has been set apart for you. Come.

We cordially invite graduation pupils, parents and the public in general to all sessions of the Institute.

We extend our thanks to *The Church-Beinkamp Company, S. E. Cor. Fourth and Elm Sts., Cincinnati, O. Phone Main 754,* for the use of their piano during the Institute.

INSTITUTE FEE, $2.00.

COMMITTEE ON RESOLUTIONS.

Miss Vinnie North, Miss Avice White, Mrs. Hattie Speed Orr, Miss Edna Jolly, F. K. Springer, Edward Baker, Malcom Eads, M. B. Boyers.

COMMITTEE ON NECROLOGY.

Mrs. Elizabeth Maddox, Miss Ethel Baker, Miss Mary Hausler, G. W. T. Prickett, T. A. Daniel, Robert Wheeler.

MUSICAL DIRECTOR.

Solon E. Fletcher.

USHERS.

Charles Springer, M. F. Sporing.

MONDAY.

10:30 A. M.

Singing.
Invocation ....Rev. J. R. Nelson
Singing.
Organization, Enrollment, Distribution of Blanks, Etc.
Introductory Address Prof. J. T. C. Noe
Adjournment, 12:00 M.

1:30 P. M.

Singing.
Roll Call.
Organization of the County Teachers' Association.
Practical Suggestions for Our Week's Work. Instructor
The Study of Child Life—How. Why. Miss Ethel Baker
Defects in Children. How discover. How Manage. Miss Alpharetta Ebert
The First Day of School—Pupils are Strangers. How to Proceed. ....Edward Baker
Rules for the School—Seating of Pupils, Etc., T. A. Daniel
Recess, 2:40 P. M.

2:55 P. M.

The Teacher
Scholarship ....G. W. L. Prickett
As a Student ....Miss Cynthia E. Reiley
The Teacher's Library ....F. K. Springer
Professional Training ....H. W. Barr
Concluded by Instructor.
Adjournment, 4:00 P. M.

TUESDAY.

8:30 A. M.

Singing.
Invocation ....Rev. Charles Brown
Singing.
Roll Call.
Reading—
The Teacher's Aim ....Sr. Antoinette Kalk
Teaching Beginners—My Method. Miss Bernice Fulner, Miss Grace Ellis
Study of the Lesson by the Teacher. . Miss Edna Jolly
The Recitation—
Reading in Rotation: Criticism, When, How.
Oral and Silent Reading .....Ralph Rachford, Miss Mary Korn

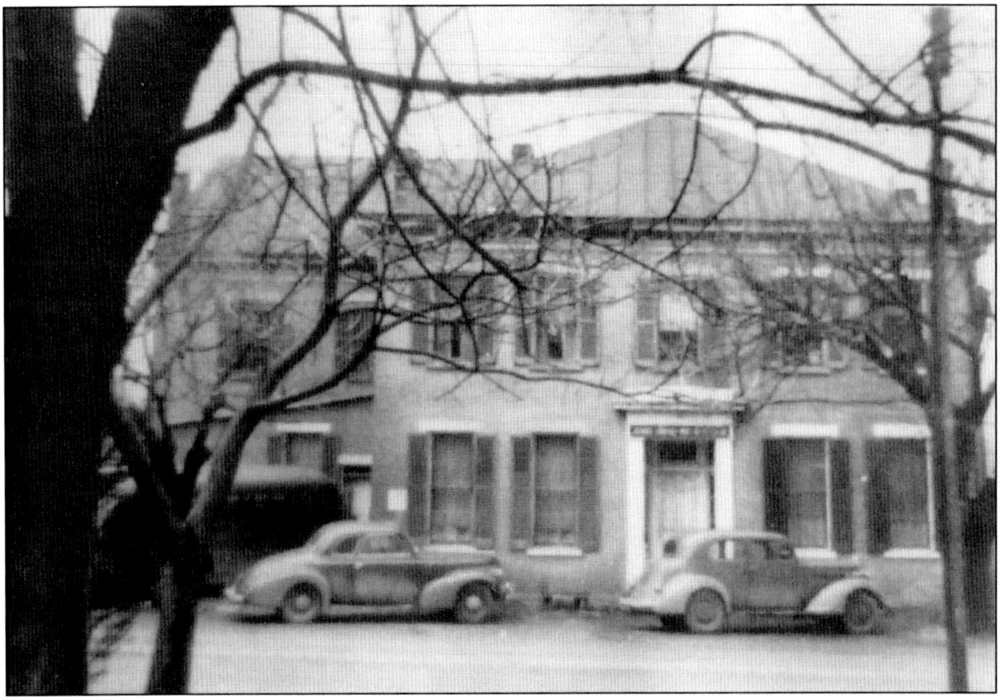

ORIGINAL CAMPBELL COUNTY HIGH SCHOOL. In 1908, the State of Kentucky passed legislation decreeing that each county establish a high school. The Campbell County Board of Education found an old brick building on Washington Street in Alexandria known as the Meister Brewery (above). The Campbell County High School was established in two rooms of this building in October 1909 and remained there until 1922. Shown below, the same building remains standing today.

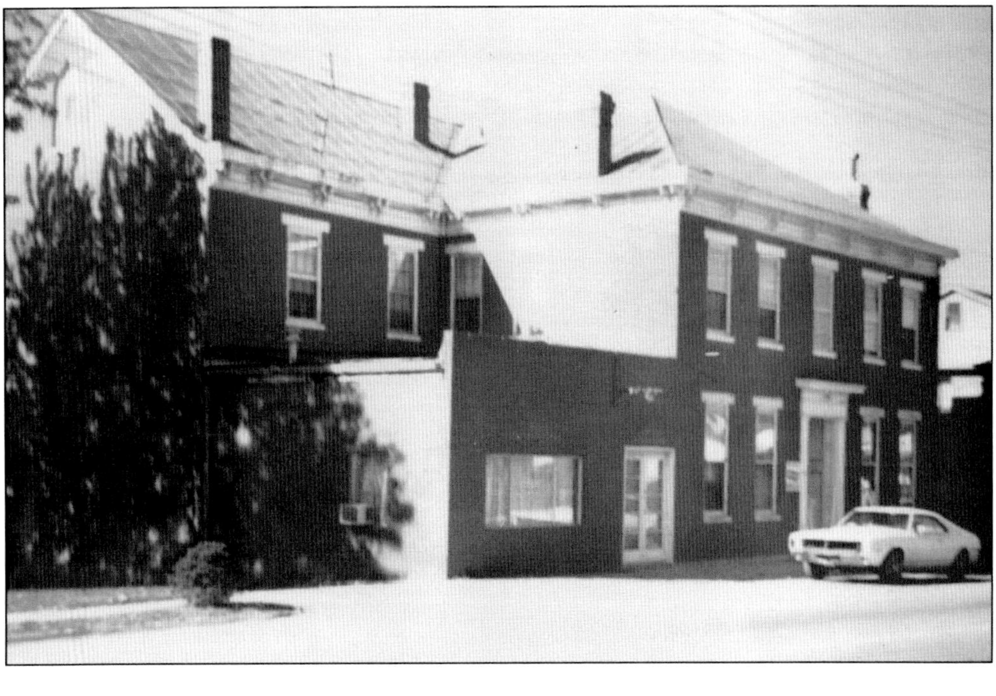

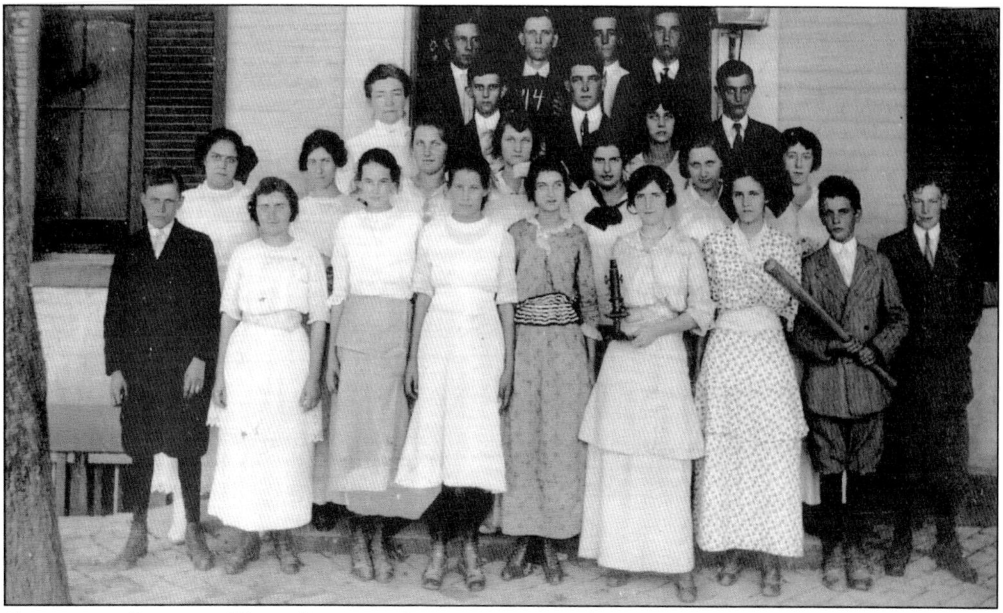

Campbell County High School Class of 1914. Shown from left to right are: (first row) Robert Gosney, Mary Phillips, Irene Stubbs, Geneva Stubbs, Welemina Walker, Elizabeth Grizzel, Mary Schlake, George Kuhl, and Henry Kees; (second row) Geneva Kinsler, ? Judd, Margaret Vogel, Florence Fields, Knelia Matz (Racke), Francis Houston, and unidentified; (third row) teacher Betty Reiley, John Kuhl, William Grizzel, Edna ?, and Clarence Reinhard; (fourth row) C. Martin, Verner Jones, Gordon Mattox, and Sherman Risch.

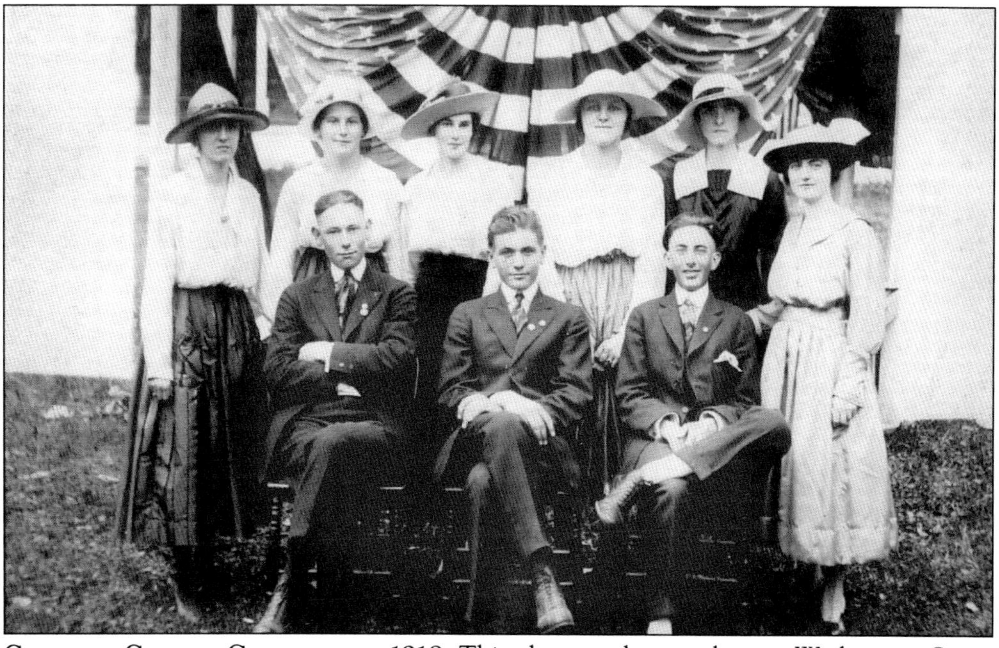

Campbell County Graduation, 1918. This photograph was taken on Washington Street in front of the Meister Brewery, which served as the students' high school. Pictured from left to right are: (first row) Henry Kees, George Kuhl, and Charlie Funk; (second row) Mary Schlake, Geneva Stubbs, Irene Stubbs, Margaret Vogel, Elsie Pelle, and May Phillips.

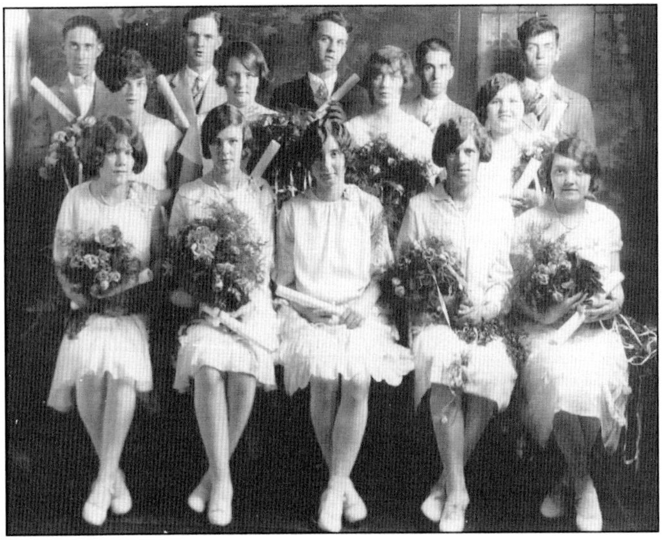

Campbell County High School Class of 1928. Posing after receiving their diplomas at the 17th annual commencement exercise are, from left to right: (first row) Sarah White, Louise Risch, Emma Enzweiler, Clara Weinel, and Elizabeth Shrewsberry; (second row) Victoria Goetz, Almira Wheeler, Florence Alford, and Frances Steffen; (third row) Herbert Smith, Stephen McVean, William Reiley, Harold Shaw, and Jack Huppert.

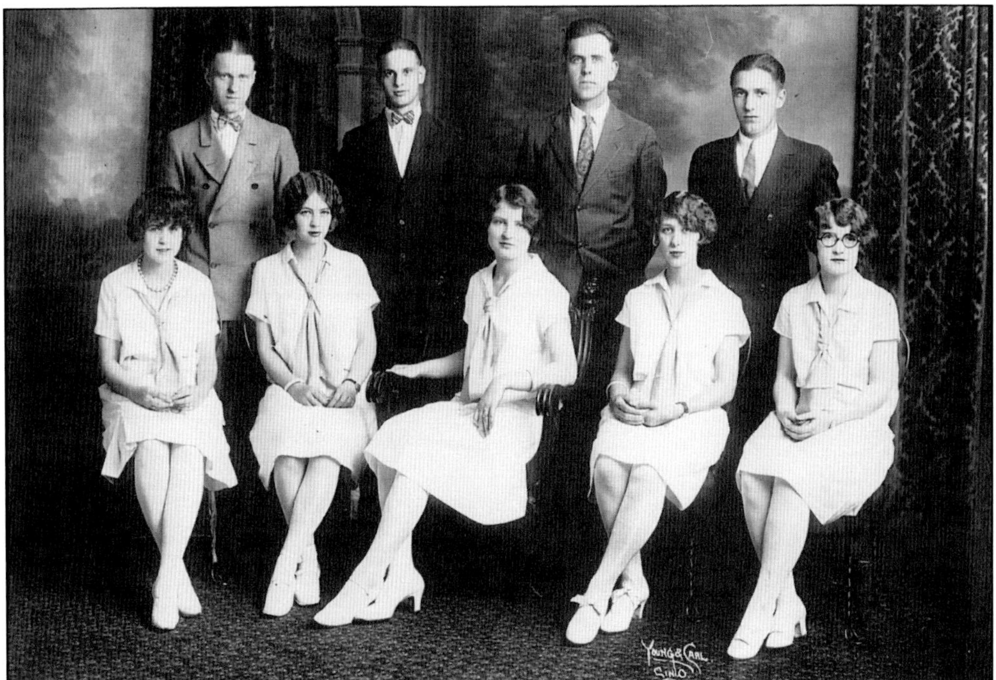

Campbell County Graduation, c. 1925. These graduating students are, from left to right, (first row) Mildred Miller, Mira Flora Wheeler, Edna Harris, Edith Lickert, and Marie Rardin; (second row) George Racke, Wesley Rapp, ? Bridwell, and Myron Hess.

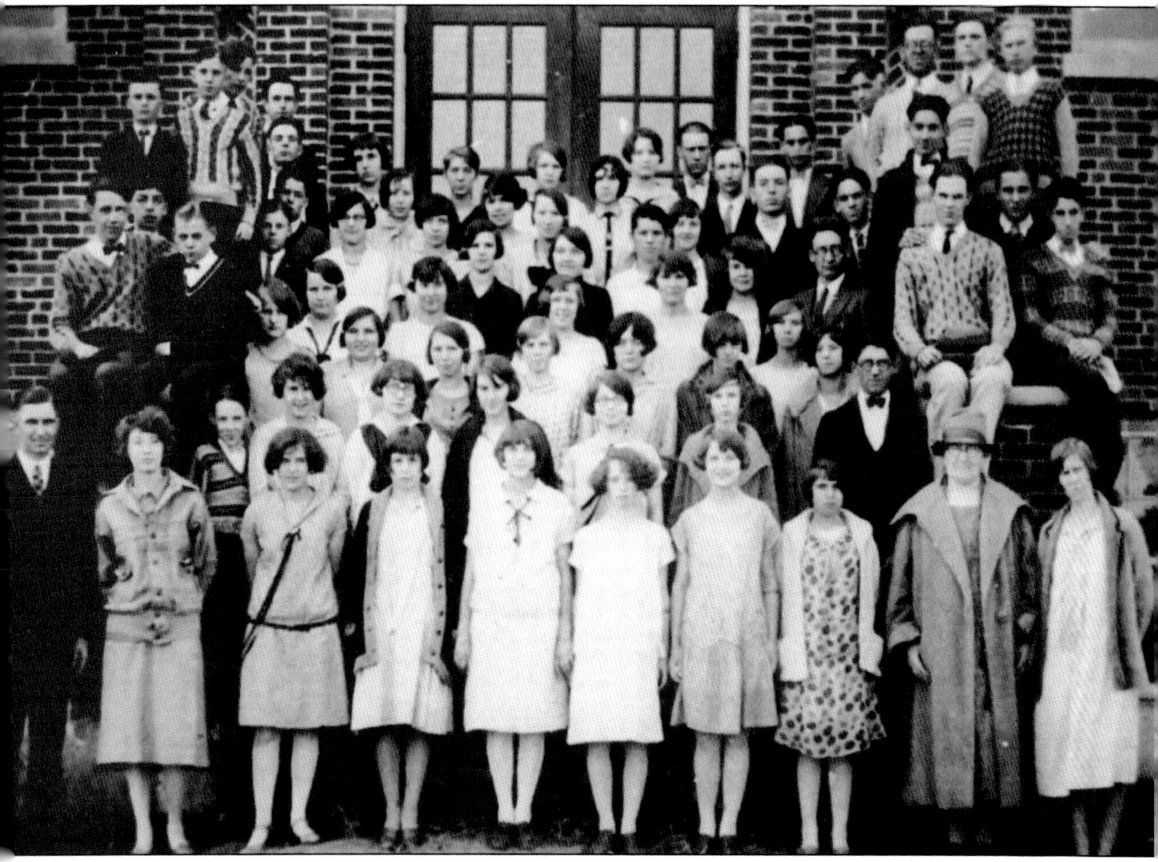

CAMPBELL COUNTY HIGH SCHOOL, 1920S. The entire student body gathers for a photograph. Among those shown are: ? Bailey, Ada Tarvin, Vic Goetz, Hazel Lees, Geneva Parr, Dot Baker, Ruth Harris, Margaret Steffen, teacher Betty Reiley, ? Bailey, Walter Neal, Mildred Miller, Marie Rardin, Marie Robinson, Neva Harris, Lelua Webster, Paul Brickles, Carrie Brauley, Frances Steffen, Carrie Trapp, Clara Eneman, Wilamena Smith, Leola Johnson, Helen Thornton, Alma Webester, Bill Reiley, Dudy Aiegler, Jack Hupper, Howard Risch, Roy Shaw, Bill Stubbs, Jack Robinson, Reginald Schalk, Almera Wheller, Erma Enzweiler, Margaret Baker, Erma Hale, Mildred Miller, George Graden, Henry Clay Rardin, Katherine Wagner, Florence Alford, Louise Risch, Eliza Shrewsberry, Clara Weinel, Violet Rardin, Charlie Ball, Herschel Hess, Chester White, Mary Reiley, Mildred Baker, Edith Lickert, Sara White, Mira Flora Wheeler, Catherine Goetz, Edna Harris, George Racke, Leonel Chalk, Wesley Rupp, Stephen McVean, Harold Shaw, Myron Hess, Herbert Smith, Bill Pape, Newell Baedwell, Franklin Shaw, and Robert Bach.

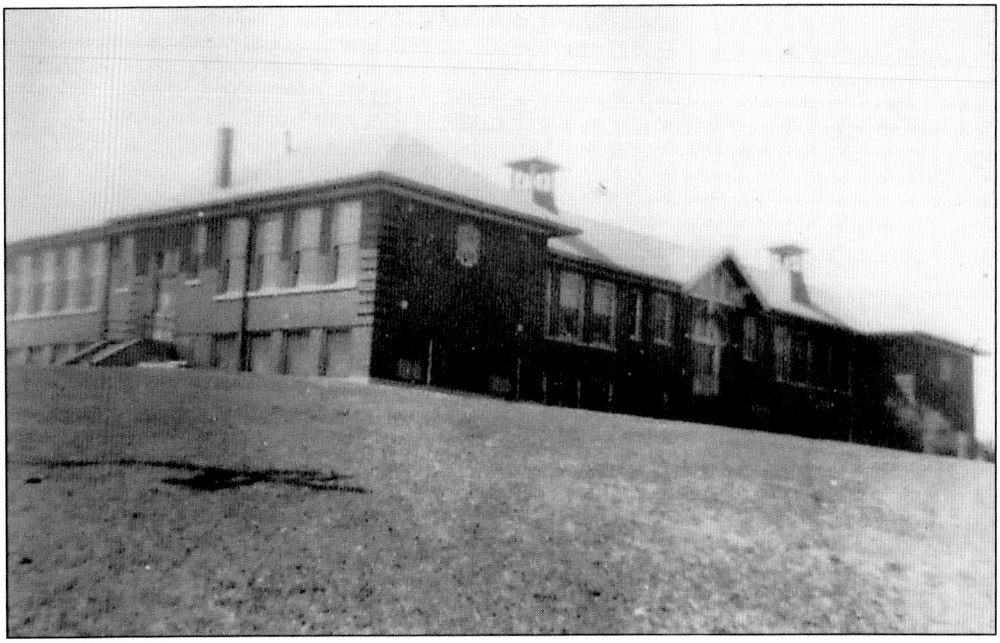

SECOND CAMPBELL COUNTY HIGH SCHOOL, 1922. In 1911, the board of education bought land behind the original building with the intention of constructing a new school on Jefferson and Grove Streets. It opened for the 1922–1923 year as both an elementary and high school. St. Mary's Parish later purchased the property and started a Catholic high school there. Ultimately, the Catholic Diocese of Covington made it into a district high school known as Bishop Brossart.

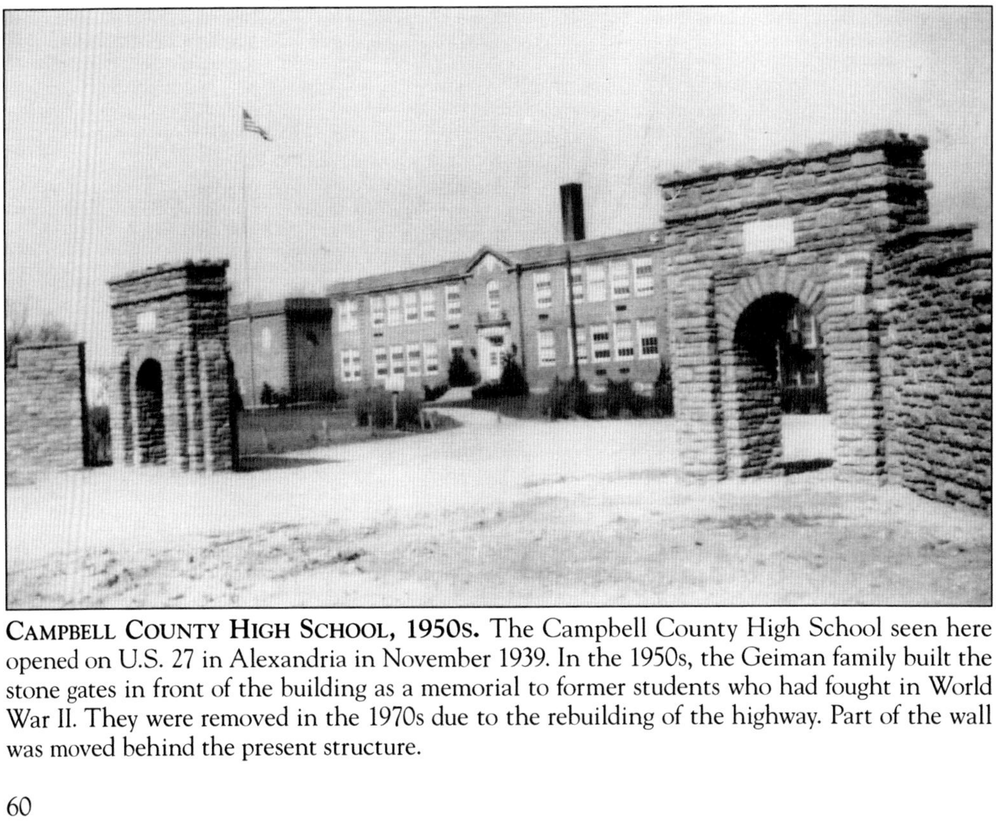

CAMPBELL COUNTY HIGH SCHOOL, 1950S. The Campbell County High School seen here opened on U.S. 27 in Alexandria in November 1939. In the 1950s, the Geiman family built the stone gates in front of the building as a memorial to former students who had fought in World War II. They were removed in the 1970s due to the rebuilding of the highway. Part of the wall was moved behind the present structure.

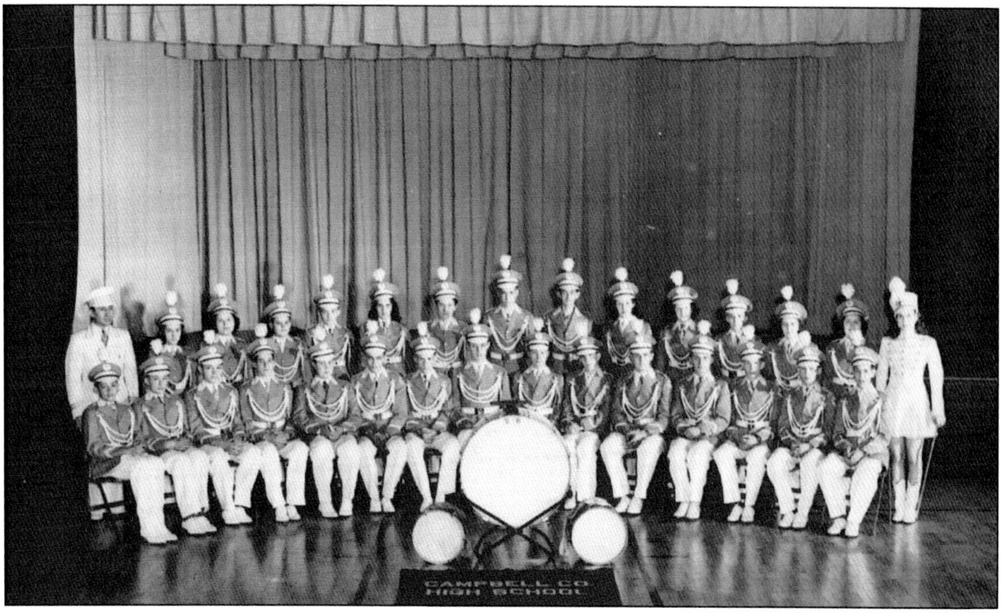

CAMPBELL COUNTY BAND, 1942. In 1939, a group of 12 students began music lessons at the Alexandria Methodist Church on Jefferson Street and formed the high school band the next year. Through fund-raising efforts, they earned enough money to purchase purple, gold, and white uniforms for 36 band members. W. W. Howard took on the duties of music director in 1939.

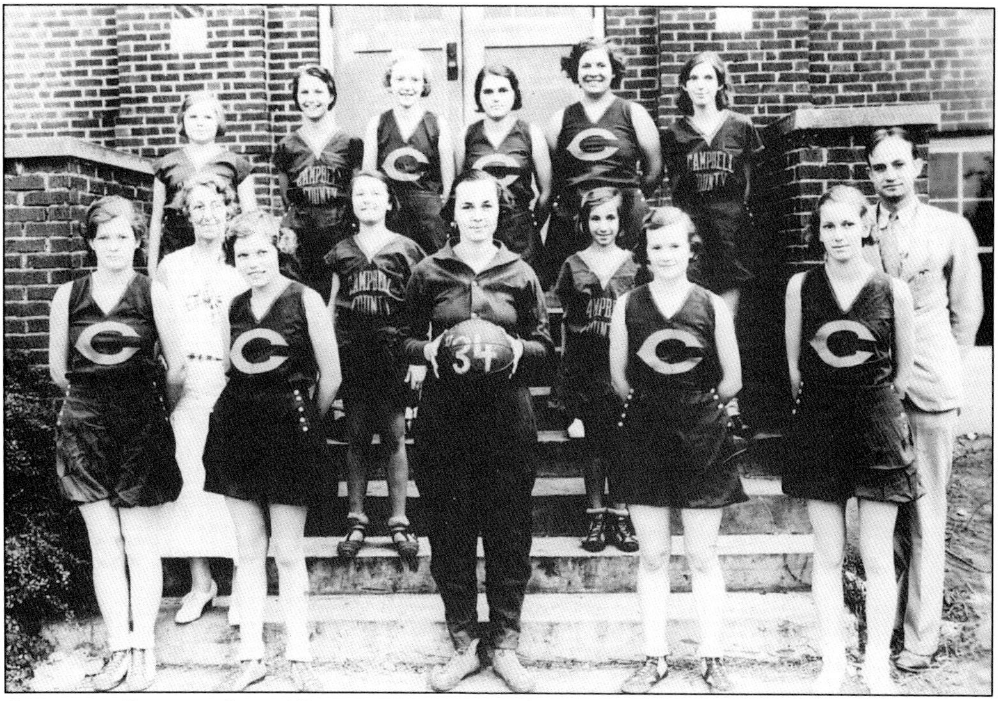

CAMPBELL COUNTY GIRLS' BASKETBALL, 1934. Shown from left to right are: (first row) Ida Lee Youtsey, Ferrol Parker, Louise McVean, Irene Rardin, and Wilma Hess; (second row) Ada McKee, Wilma Englert, Goldie Warner, and Letcher Woolum; (third row) Delores Ireton, unidentified, Rose Maddox, Kitty Lamb, Emma V. Stevens, and Kathryn Lytle.

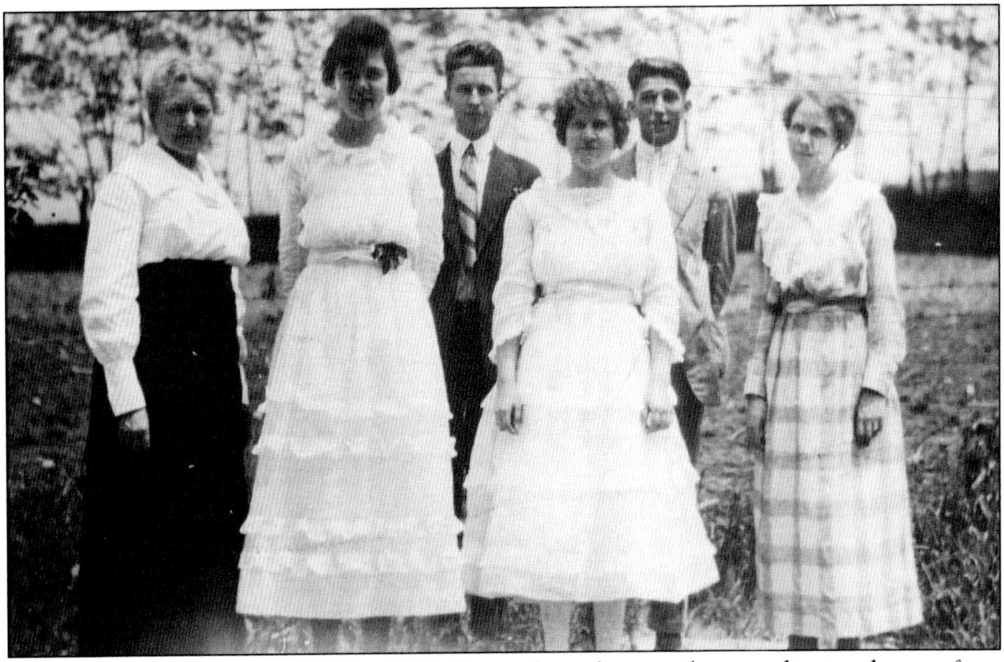

CAMPBELL COUNTY GRADUATION, 1920. Posing for a photograph on graduation day are, from left to right, (first row) Cynthia Elizabeth Reiley (known as "Miss Betty"), Alta Reiley, F. Racke, and Avice White; (second row) Howard Benedict and Raymond Lickert.

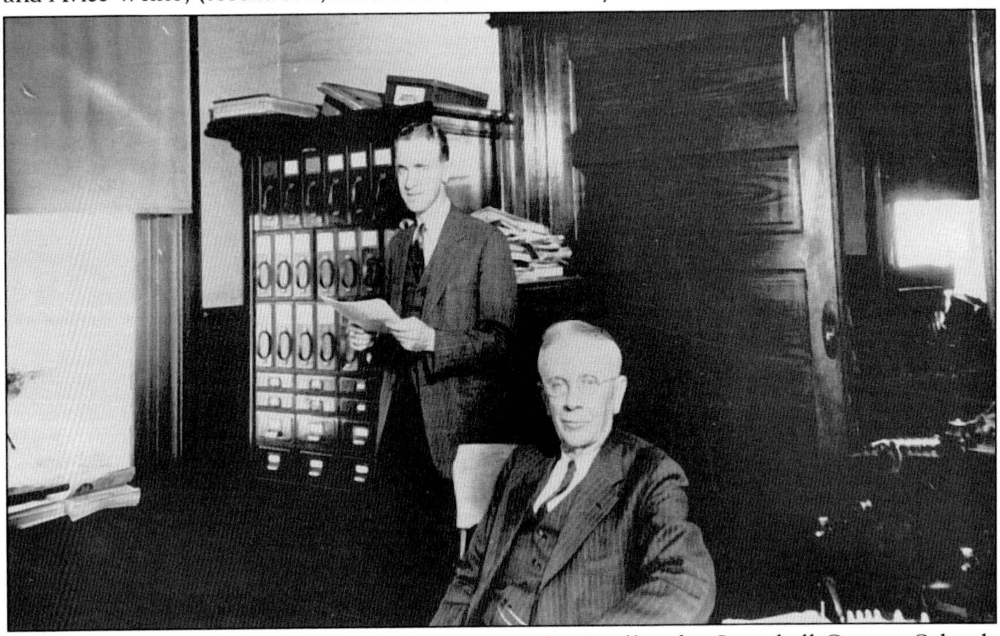

SUPERINTENDENT'S OFFICE. The first superintendent's office for Campbell County Schools was located in the back of a Washington Street insurance business. At the time of this image, William Chester "Check" Jolly was working as the attendance officer and John W. Reiley (seated) as superintendent. John Reiley lived on Reiley Road (named for his family). He was the longest-serving superintendent in Campbell County and possibly the state of Kentucky, holding the position for 40 years.

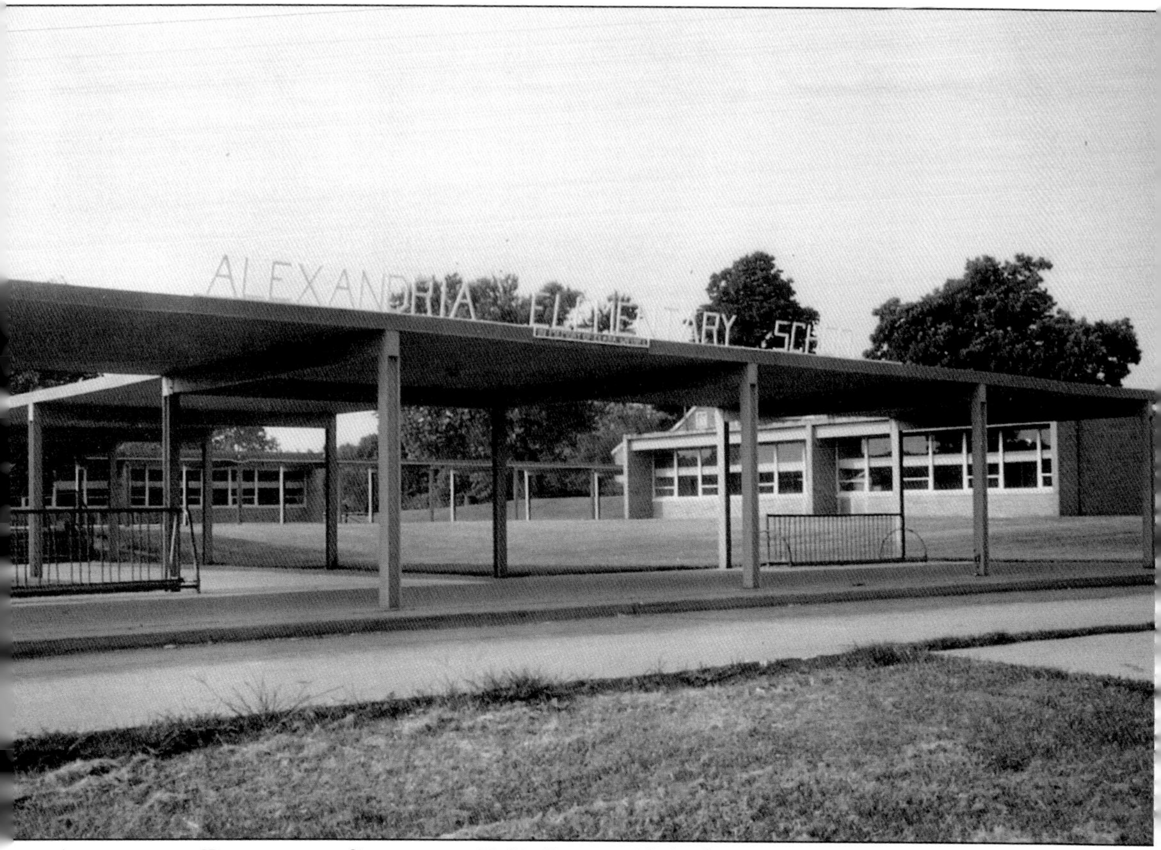

ALEXANDRIA ELEMENTARY SCHOOL, C. 1960. First established as a one-room school at Jefferson and Grove Streets, the Alexandria Elementary School sat attached to a new combined elementary and high school from 1922 until 1939. A modern high school had previously been built on U.S. 27, and another new Alexandria Elementary School was built adjacent to that structure. A two-story brick building with a full basement, this facility served the community's children until 1960–1961. That year, as part of a new concept, six separate buildings were completed as a final Alexandria Elementary School. All six were connected by covered walkways as shown above. Finally, in 2007, these six rooms were closed, and the elementary school was located on the AA Highway, thus ending the over-100-year history of the Alexandria Elementary School.

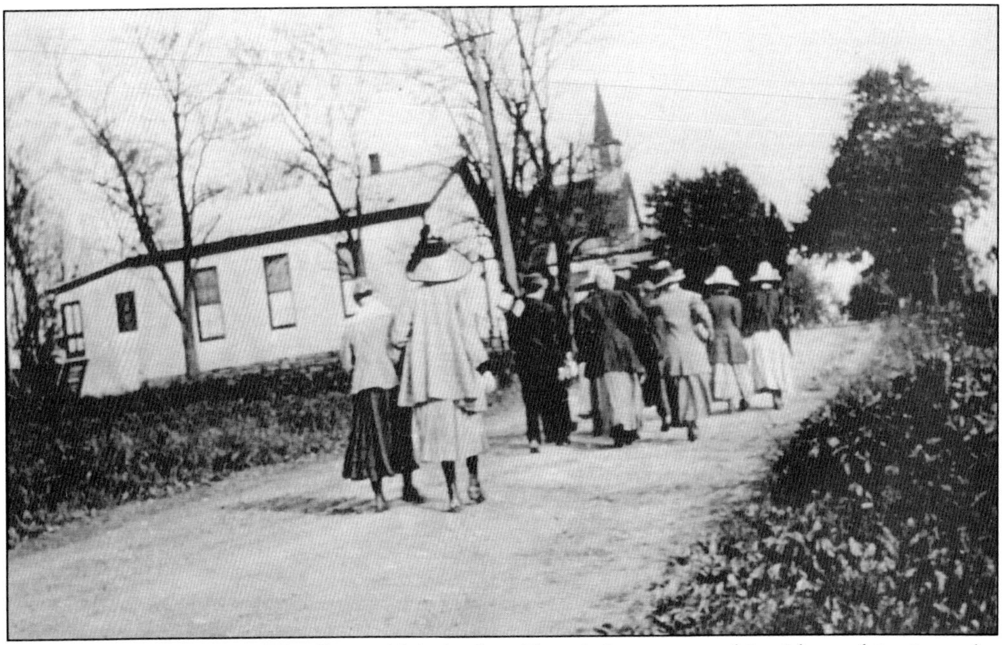

WALKING TO CHURCH. The Second Methodist Church has operated in Alexandria since the 1820s. Members first met in a log cabin on what is now Reiley Road. The church, which is the white-frame building located on the left, is on Washington Street. The building would later be used as a town hall before it was torn down. The women in the photograph are actually walking to the First Baptist Church next to the building.

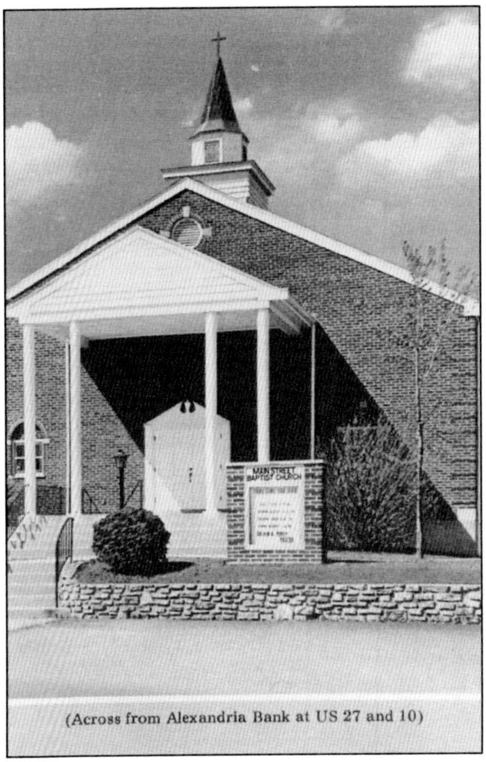

MAIN STREET BAPTIST CHURCH. Organized around 1957, this church was built on Main Street a few hundred feet west of U.S. 27. Rev. Calvin Perry led the church for 35 years. As more space was needed, the congregation moved south on U.S. 27 to Sun Valley, about four miles from the old building. In 2007, a new church opened on 18 acres. The building shown here was sold to the City of Alexandria.

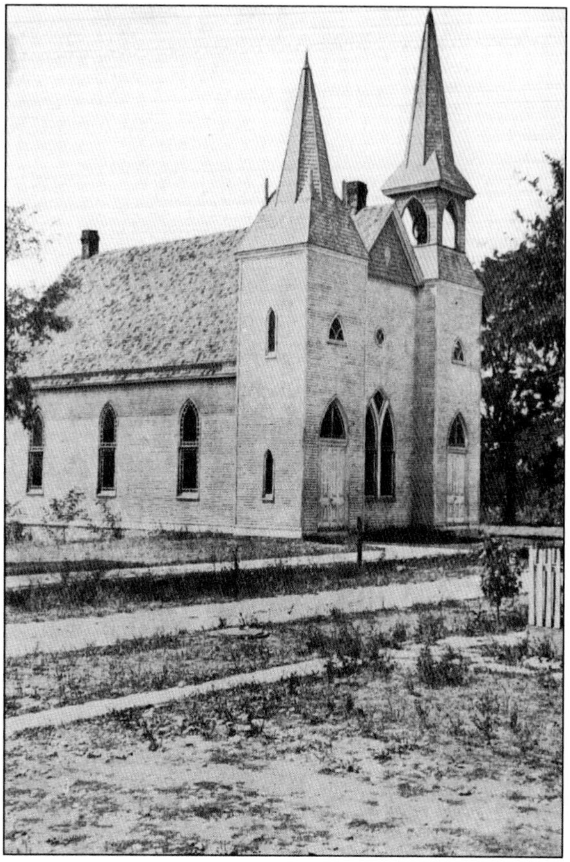

Second Methodist Church Building. Located on Jefferson and Greenup Streets, this frame structure (pictured right) was built in 1867. When the congregation experienced a surge in numbers, a fourth building (below) was erected in 1966 on land donated by the Zinn family. In the 1980s, a sanctuary was added. For more than 187 years, the Methodist church has been a part of the fabric of Alexandria.

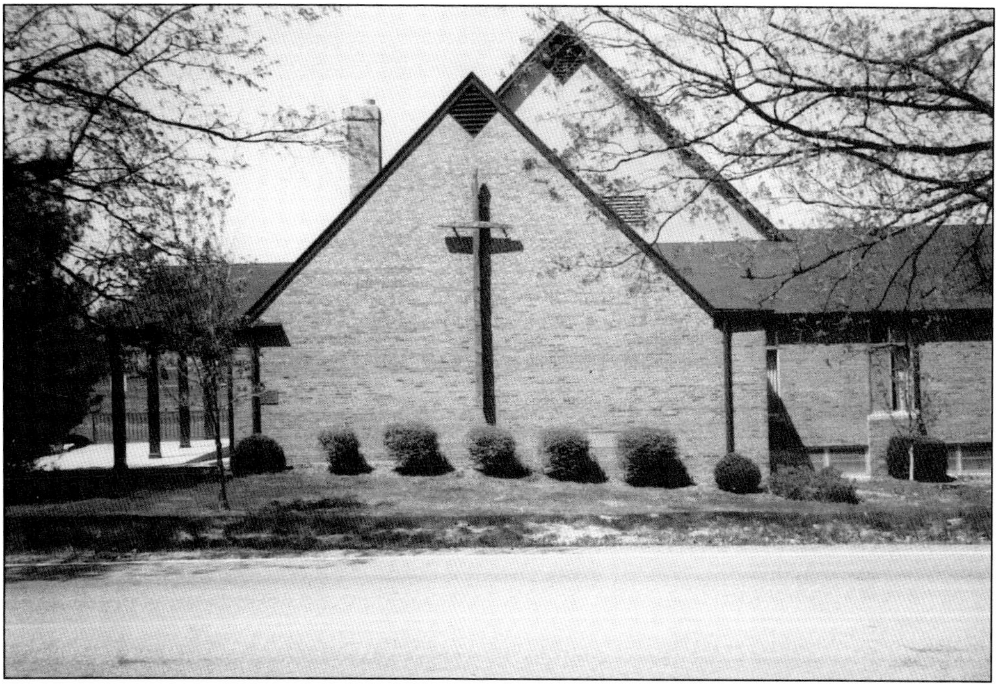

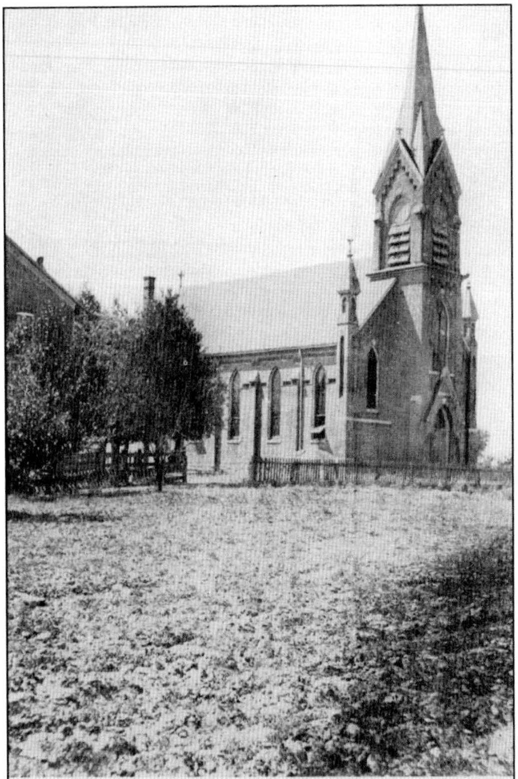

St. Mary's Church. Brothers & Schlake Publishers

ST. MARY CATHOLIC CHURCH. The St. Mary Catholic Church, as it appears at left, was first located on Jefferson Street on four acres of land purchased by 30 families in 1860 at a cost of $300. By 1889, having outgrown that structure, the congregation began to build a new church at a cost of $11,600. Opening in 1904, it was 102 feet long by 47 feet wide with a bell tower that stood 118 feet tall. By 1982, the parish had started plans for St. Mary Cemetery. That same year, with over 900 families, the parish decided to build a new street and church behind its elementary school. The dedication took place on December 11, 1983, and the former church was razed. Fr. Francis De Jaco, shown below (on the far right) along with St. Mary students, became pastor in 1932 and remained for 35 years, leaving in 1967.

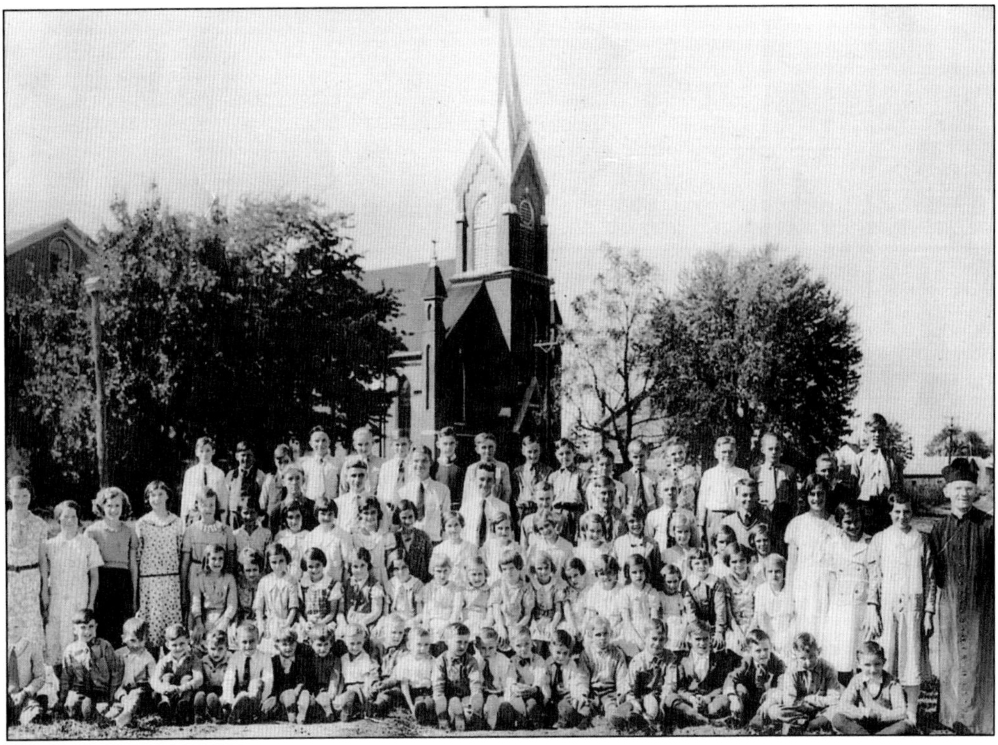

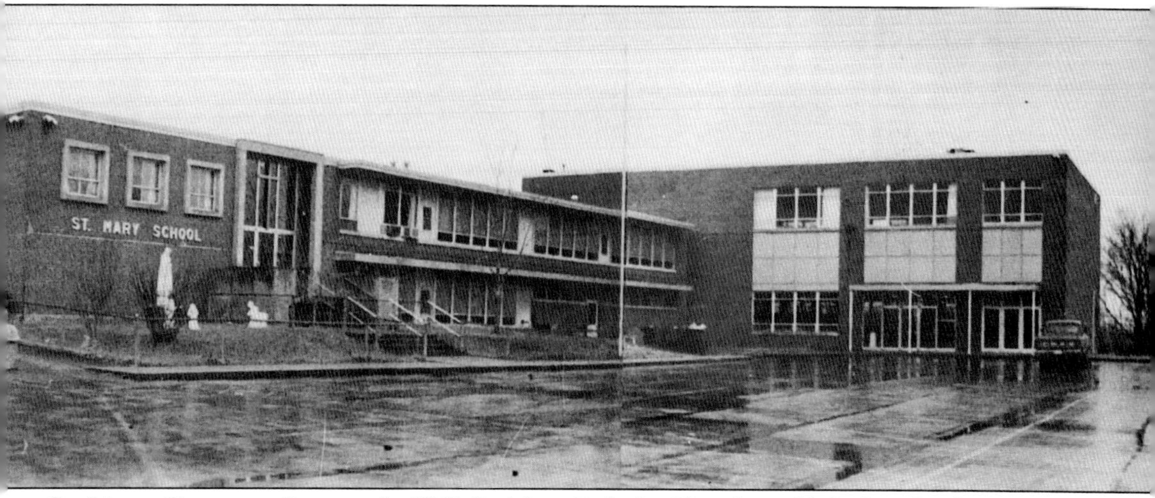

ST. MARY CATHOLIC SCHOOL. In 1867, St. Mary Catholic Church established a school serving 70 pupils in an adjacent room of the church. On October 1, 1876, the Sisters of Notre Dame assumed teaching duties. As the parish grew, space became a problem. In December 1949, the parish purchased the old brick building on Jefferson and Grove Streets that had been both the county high school and the elementary school. From 1950 to 1964, that property was St. Mary School, offering education for the 1st through 12th grades. In 1964, the Diocese of Covington acquired the building for use as a district high school known as Bishop Brossart. When this occurred, St. Mary built this new elementary school past the church and cemetery. The congregation added to the building in 1989.

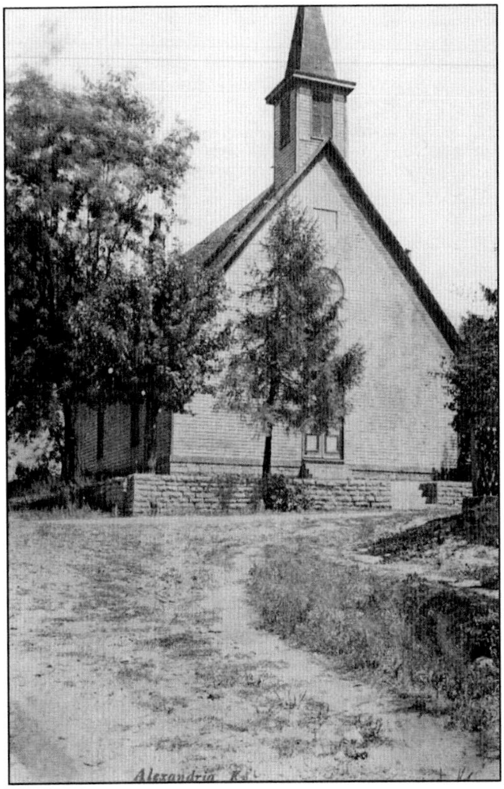

FIRST BAPTIST CHURCH, c. 1870. The First Baptist Church of Alexandria dates back to April 17, 1820. Members met in homes until the church was built as a wood structure on land donated by the Spilman family. A brick section was added to the front in 1944.

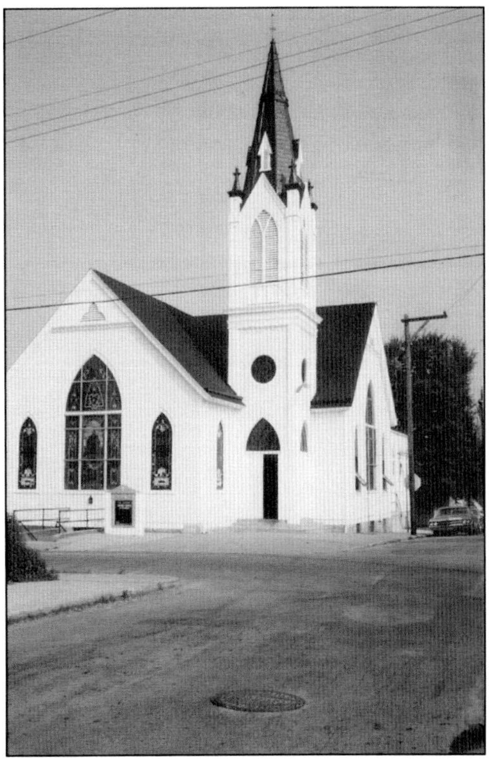

ST. PAUL'S UNITED CHURCH OF CHRIST. Organized by German immigrants, St. Paul's United Church of Christ began in 1850. The church property, located on the corner of Jefferson and Main Streets (where the Southern States Cooperative is today), also housed a parsonage and a school building. Though not initially affiliated with any particular denomination, the parish chose to become part of the Reform Church in 1934. In 2000, the congregation celebrated it 150th anniversary.

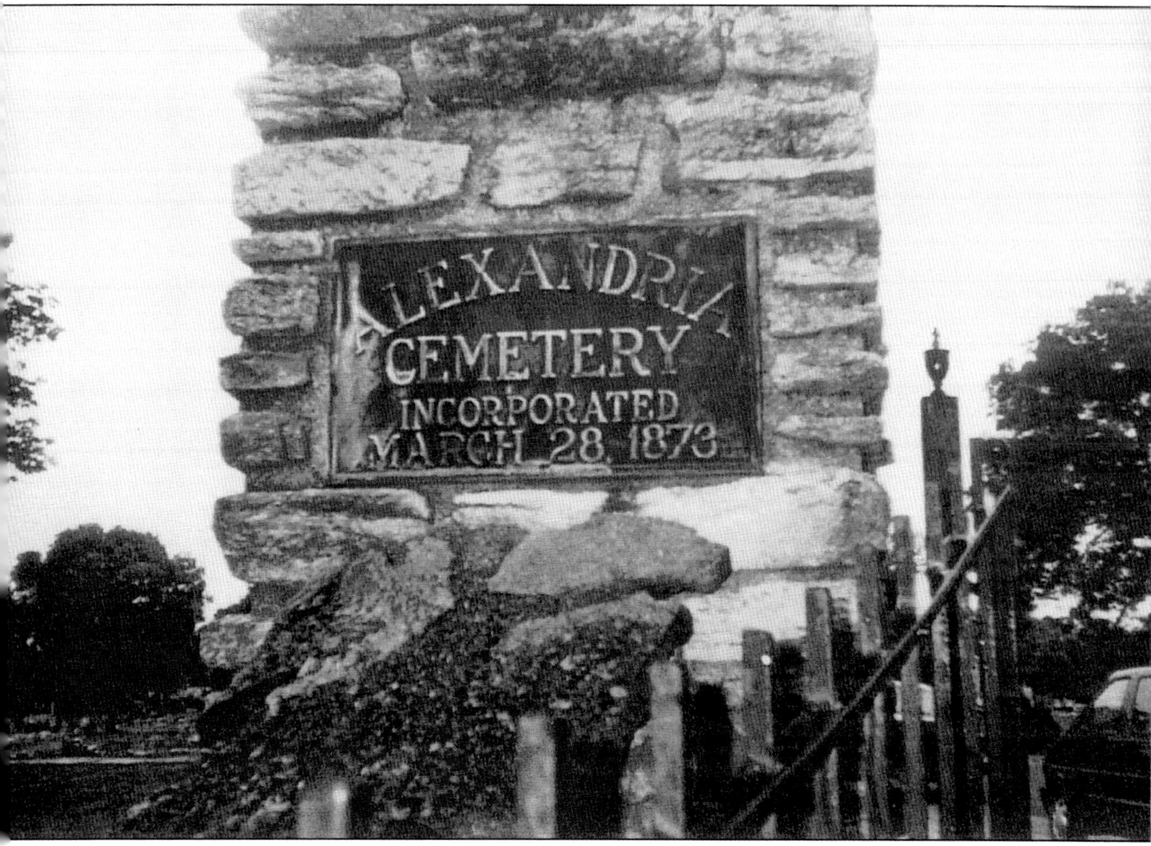

ALEXANDRIA CEMETERY. This cemetery was established on the Spilman farm on March 28, 1873. The first board of trustees included such family names as Reiley, Wright, Shaw, Hartman, and Beall. Today only half of the 35 acres are part of the cemetery property; the cemetery office is located in an old farmhouse on what was once the Petty farm. A mausoleum, which was built about 10 to 12 years ago, and an old vault house are also on the land. Probably the most prominent citizens buried here are former state senator Charlie Truesdale and county commissioner Mont Truesdale.

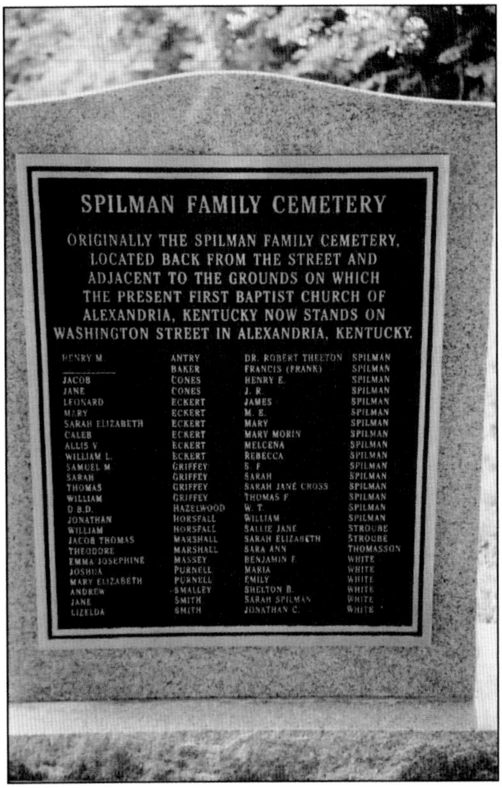

FAMILY CEMETERY MARKERS. The Spilman family cemetery originally lay back from the street and adjacent to the grounds on which the present First Baptist Church now stands on Washington Street in Alexandria. The Thatcher family cemetery was located behind the Thatcher Tavern, which is now Thatcher Court. As the cemeteries disappeared under development, these new markers were placed on the Thatcher lot in Alexandria Cemetery in September 2003.

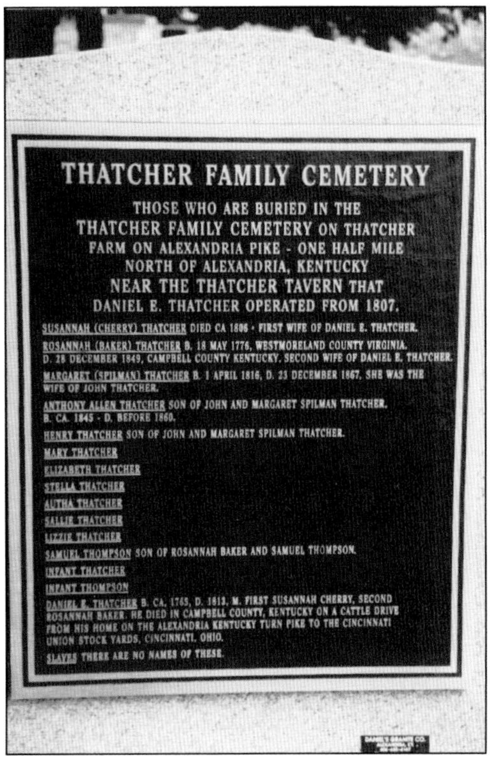

Four

INFRASTRUCTURE

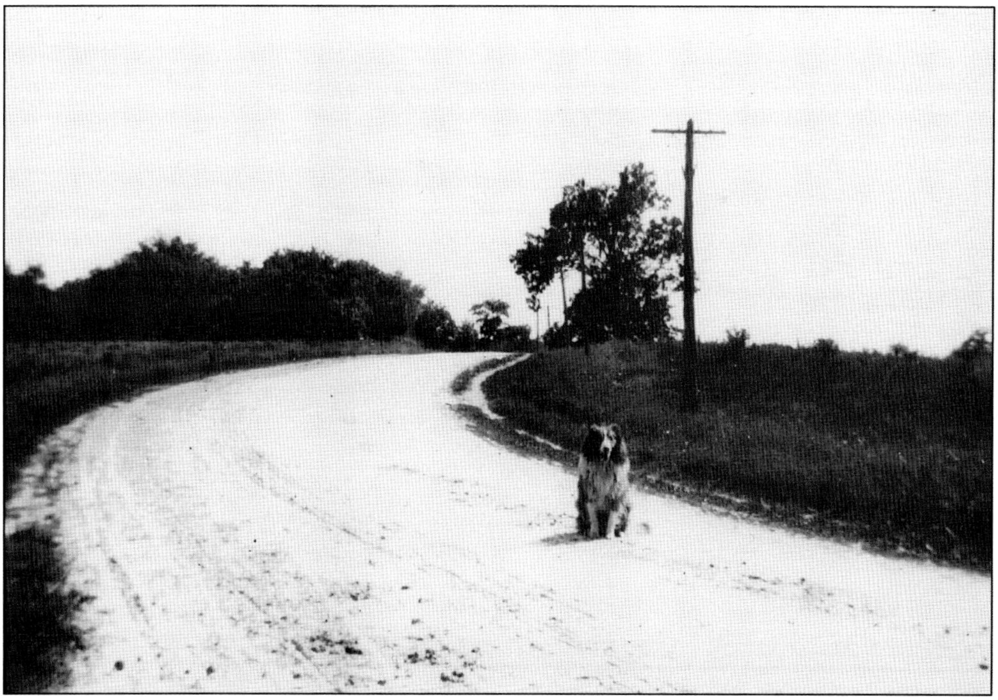

LONESOME HIGHWAY. Queenie takes a rest on the road to Newport. The location given is Alexandria Pike in the area of Sunset Drive heading north. Up ahead would be Poplar Ridge Road. This spot is now a thriving commercial center on a busy four-lane highway.

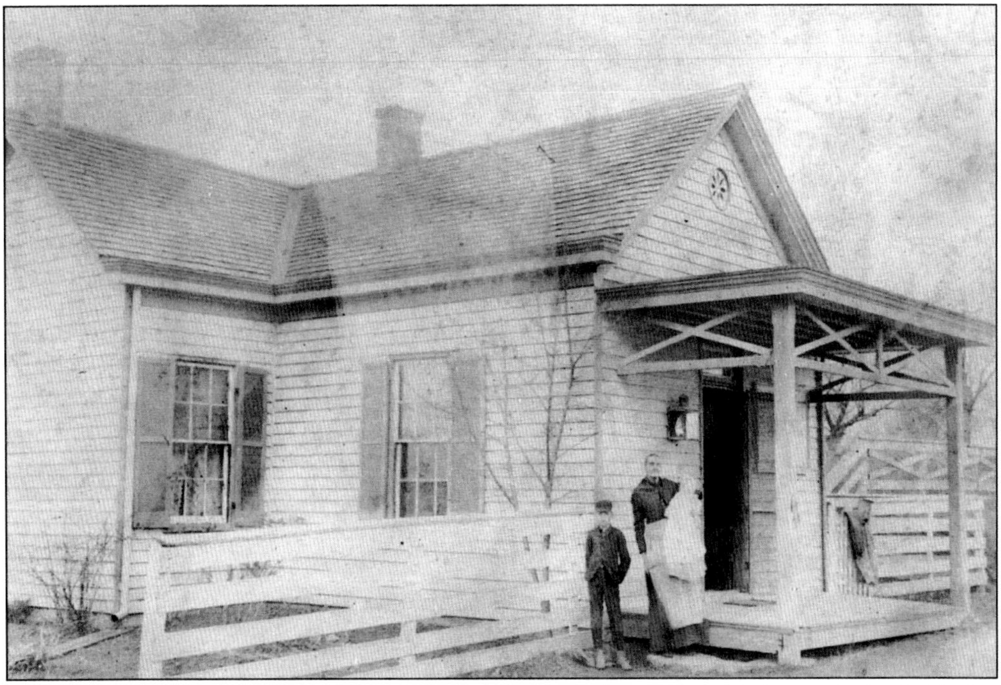

ALEXANDRIA TOLLGATE HOUSE. Pictured from left to right are Otto, Nellie, and Myrtle Neal at the tollgate house. At one time, almost all streets were toll roads on which individuals or families collected tolls to make their living. This tollhouse was located at the intersection of Washington Street and the old Alexandria Turnpike (later named U.S. 27). It was later moved directly across from Campbell County Middle School at Washington Street in the back of Thatcher Court. As a traveler came down the road, the tollgate attendant collected his money. The worker then raised the pole (pictured below), and the traveler went on his way. The attendant was provided with a residence next to the tollgate.

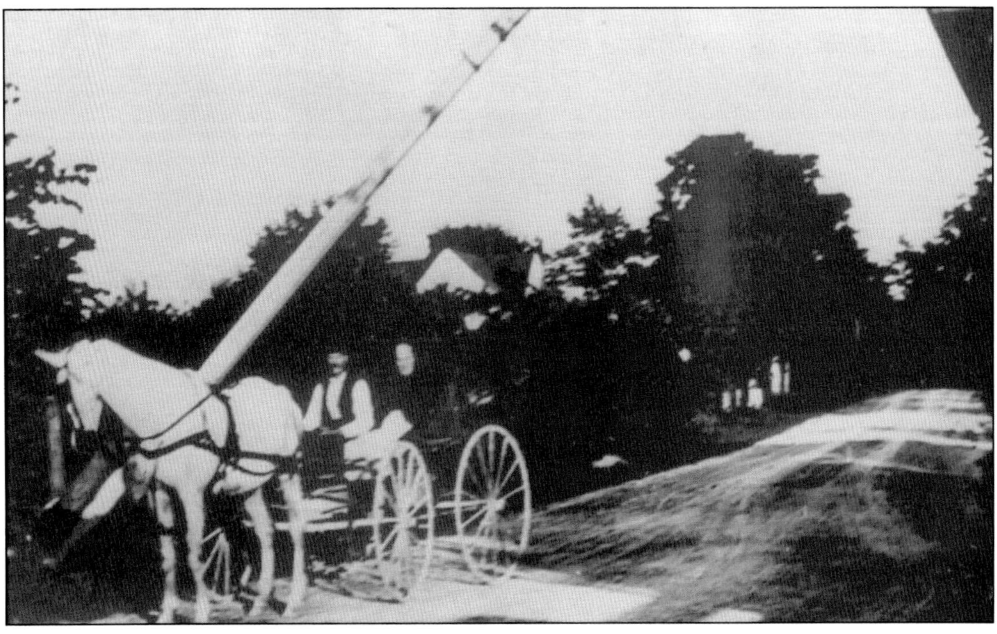

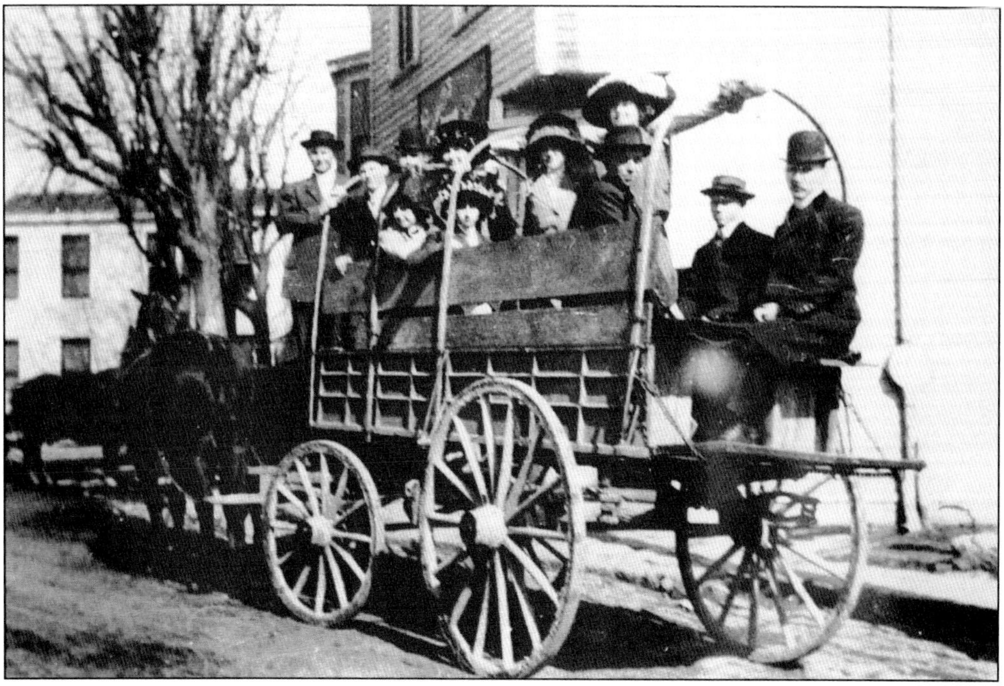

OMNIBUS. Said to be the first public transportation from Alexandria to Newport, this bus is shown at the corner of the Hess and Racke General Store. The old jail is visible in the background. Winfred Rardin (1874–1965) drove the bus. One can imagine how uncomfortable the long ride must have been.

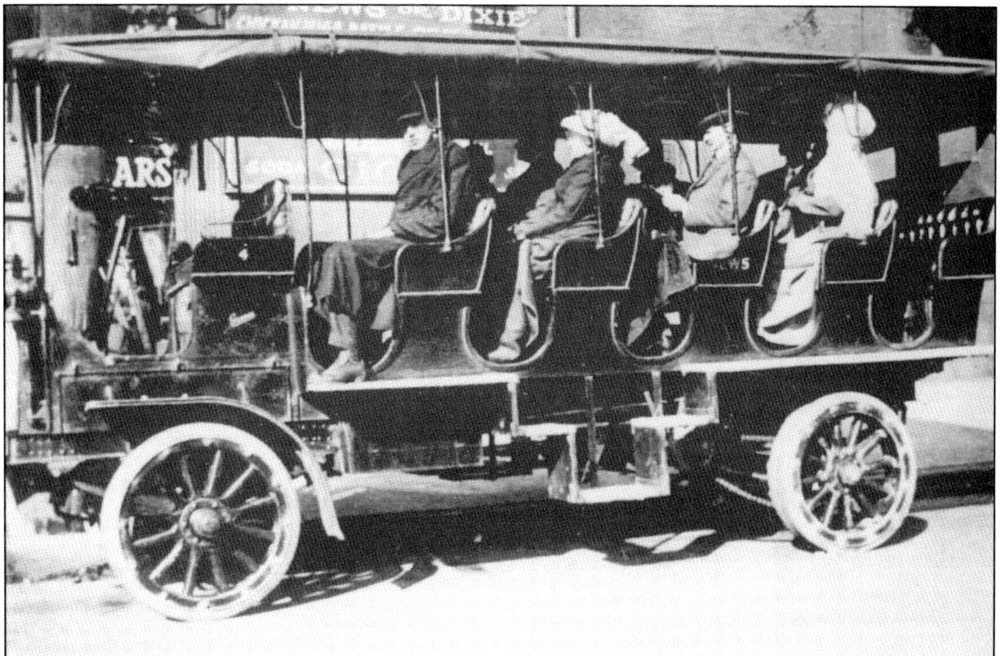

ALEXANDRIA'S FIRST MOTORIZED BUS. The chain-driven bus pictured here made two round-trips each day to Newport.

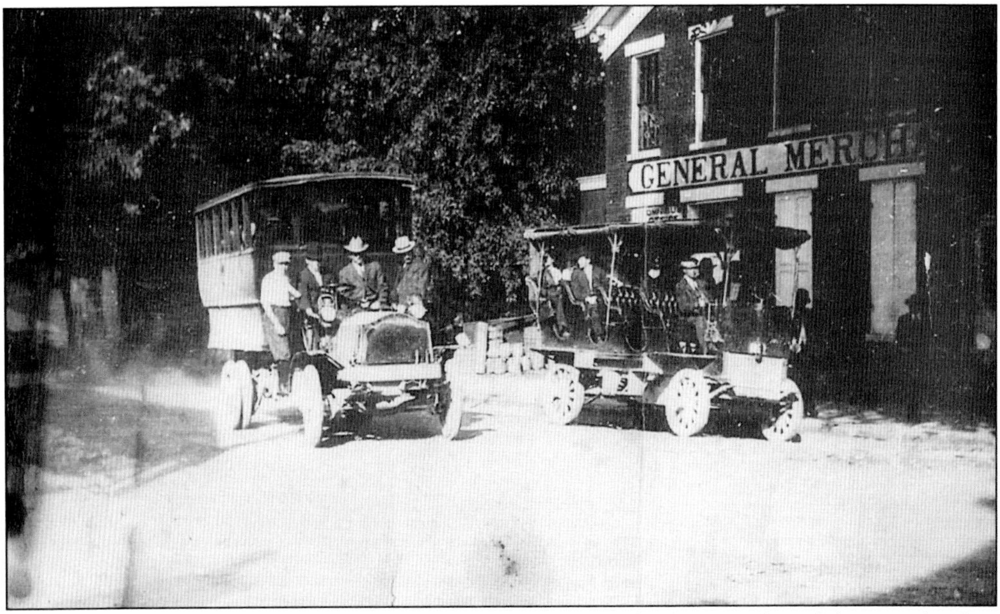

GOSNEY TRANSFER COMPANY. These chain-driven, two-cylinder tripod models were the first gas motorbuses to operate from Alexandria to Newport. The bus on the left also ran to Grants Lick. This view shows Gosney's Store at the intersection of Main and Washington Streets in Alexandria.

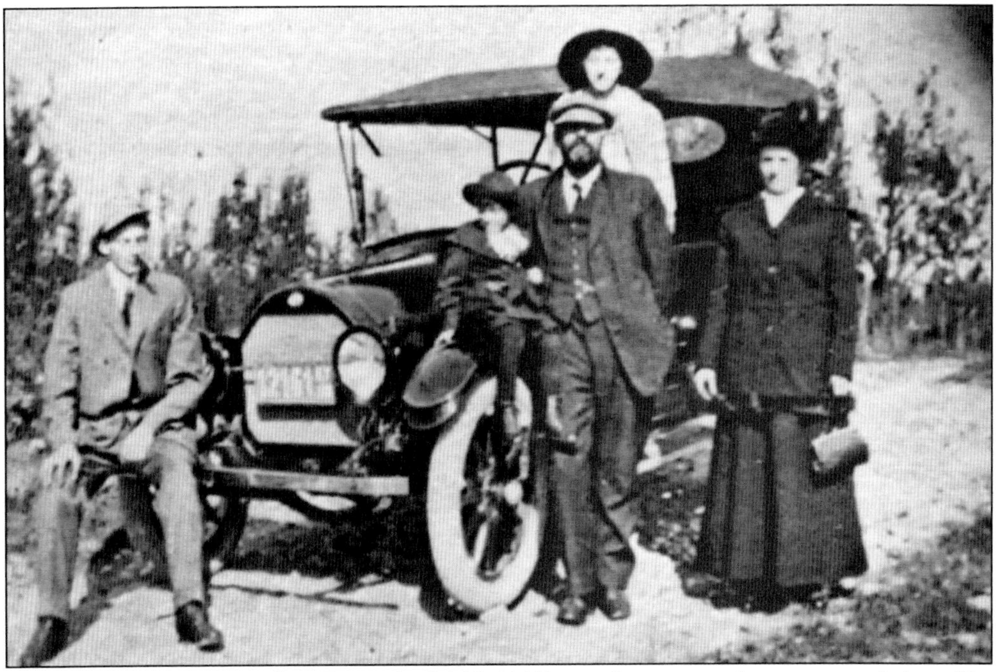

EARLY AUTOMOBILE. Matthew Enzweiler (1865–1928), standing next to his new car, is believed by some to have had the first automobile in Alexandria. The two ladies are his wife, Mary Margaret Steffen (1870–1960), pictured on the right, and her sister Susan Steffen (1872–1956). Susan was married to the gentleman sitting on the front bumper, Edward Bathalter (1864–1951). The child is unidentified, and the year of the photograph is unknown.

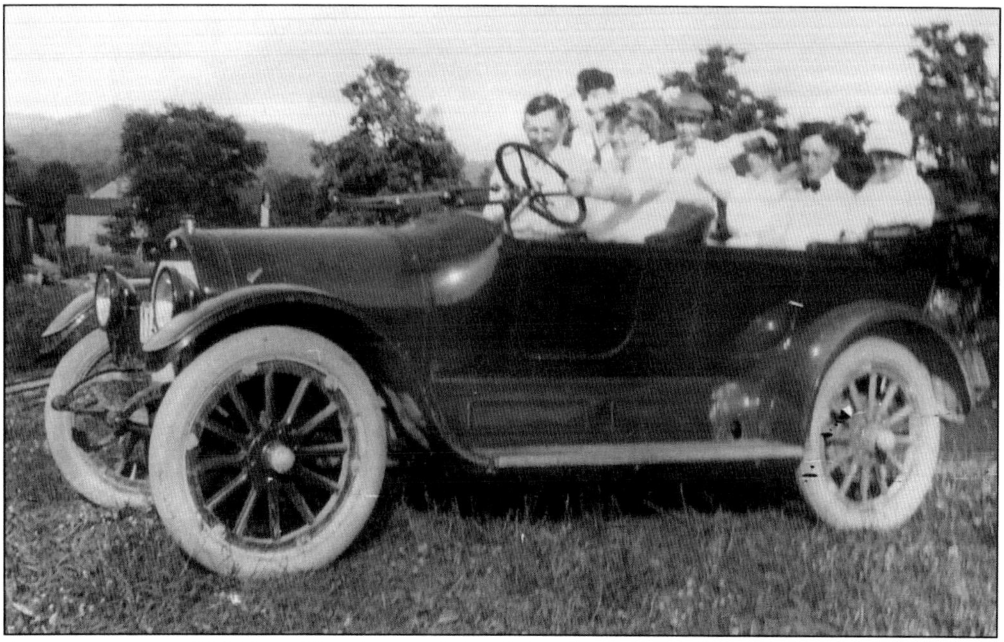

AUTOMOBILE, c. 1920. Ruth Thatcher sits behind the wheel alongside her husband, Wilbur Ehlen. Ruth was the youngest child of Frank and Mary Elizabeth Grant Thatcher. The couple traveled throughout the country with their primary residence in Bellefontaine, Ohio. Self-employed, Wilbur built machinery parts. This photograph was taken in the barnyard of High View Farm.

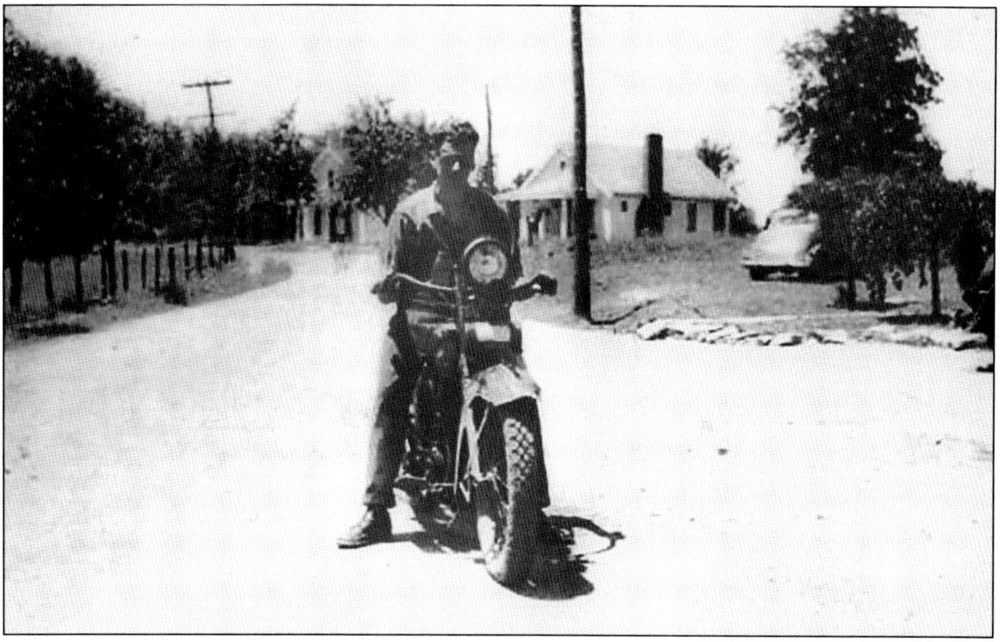

HERMAN R. "BUD" SEIBERT, c. 1938. Bud rides his motorcycle in front of Coleman's Garage on Main Street. This garage stood at the current site of the water tower. When U.S. 27 was rerouted to its current location, a deep cut was made into the hill between the garage and the houses in the background. Main Street is now 25 to 30 feet lower in this area. The houses remain on the west side of the intersection.

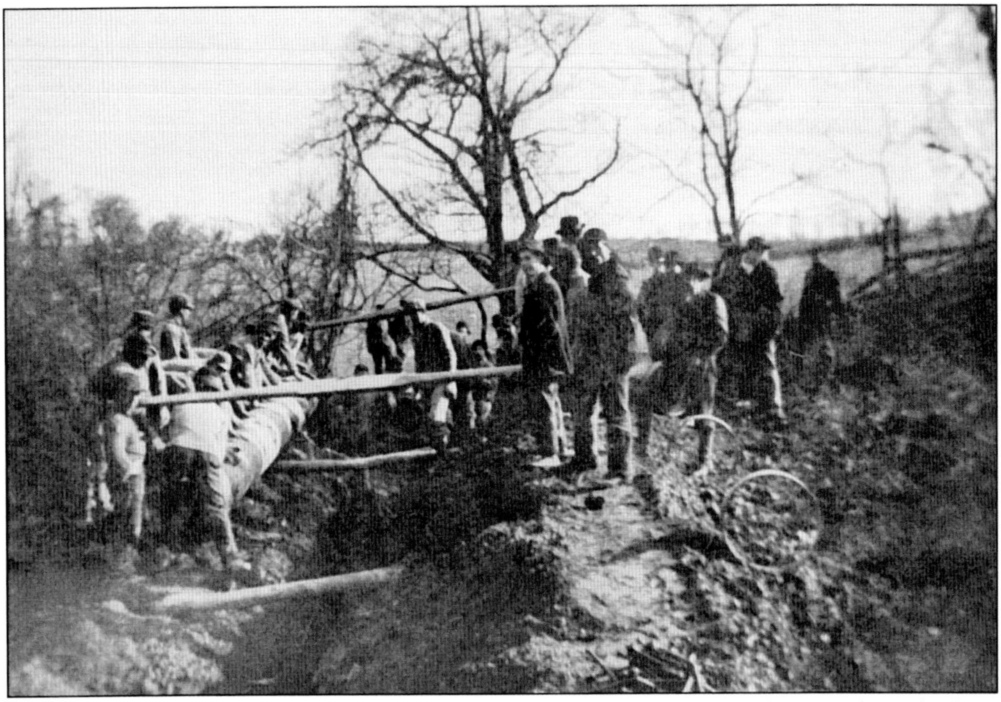

Arrival of Gas Lines. Progress came calling again when a major gas line was brought from West Virginia to Cincinnati, Ohio, about 1915. These photographs show the trench for the line, men laying pipe into the trench (pictured above), and the pup tents where the work crews lived during construction (pictured below). The photographs were taken in the pear orchard of the Thatcher farm just off Alexandria Turnpike.

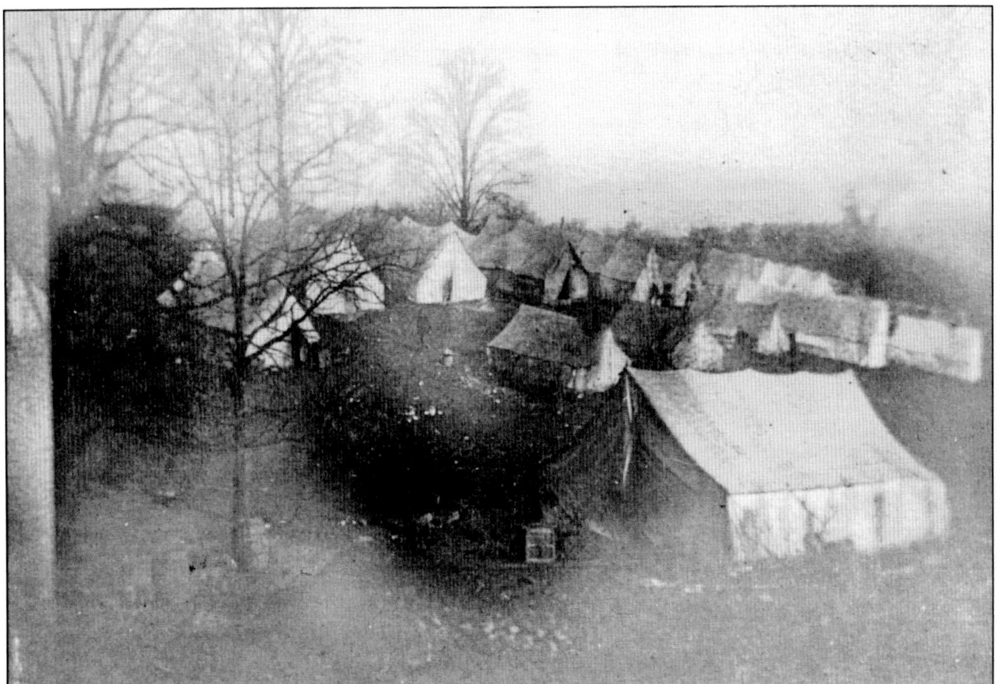

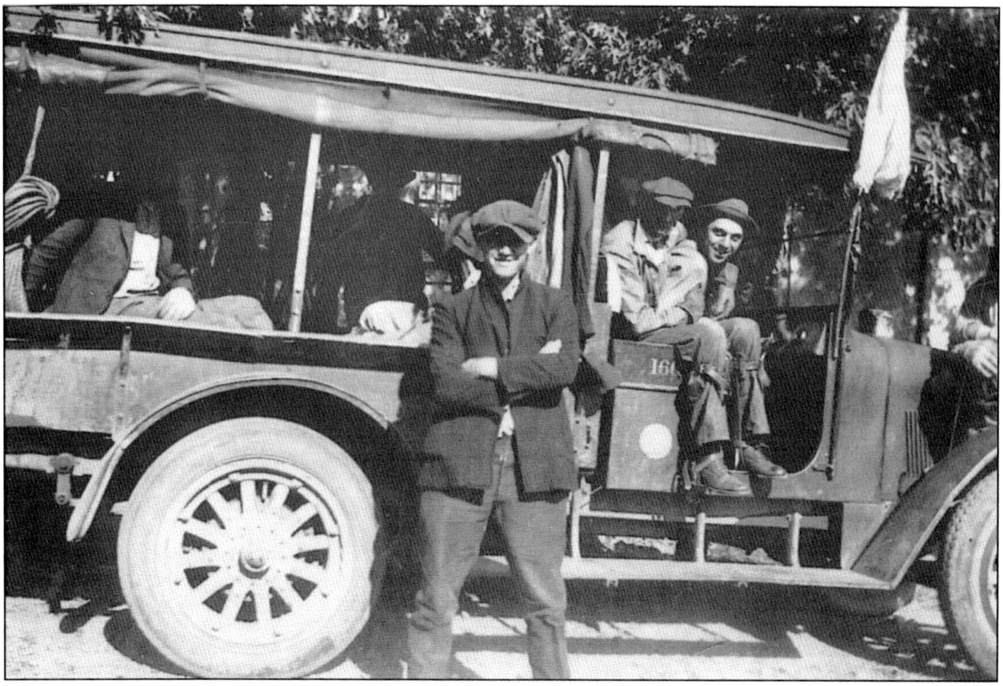

Telephone Crew and Truck, 1925. Few things have changed a rural community more than the arrival of electricity in 1916 and the telephone in the 1920s. These images highlight some of the linemen who installed the first telephone lines. Pictured above from left to right are unidentified, Joseph Schmidt, George Nordwich, and Joseph C. Neiser. Shown below from left to right are two unidentified, Joseph Schmidt, unidentified, George Nordwich, and Joseph C. Neiser. They are standing next to a trailer full of telephone wire spools. The telephone exchange was first located in Edgar Thatcher's home at the corner of Jefferson and Main Streets. A call placed to Alexandria was sent to the Thatcher Exchange and then routed to the person's home.

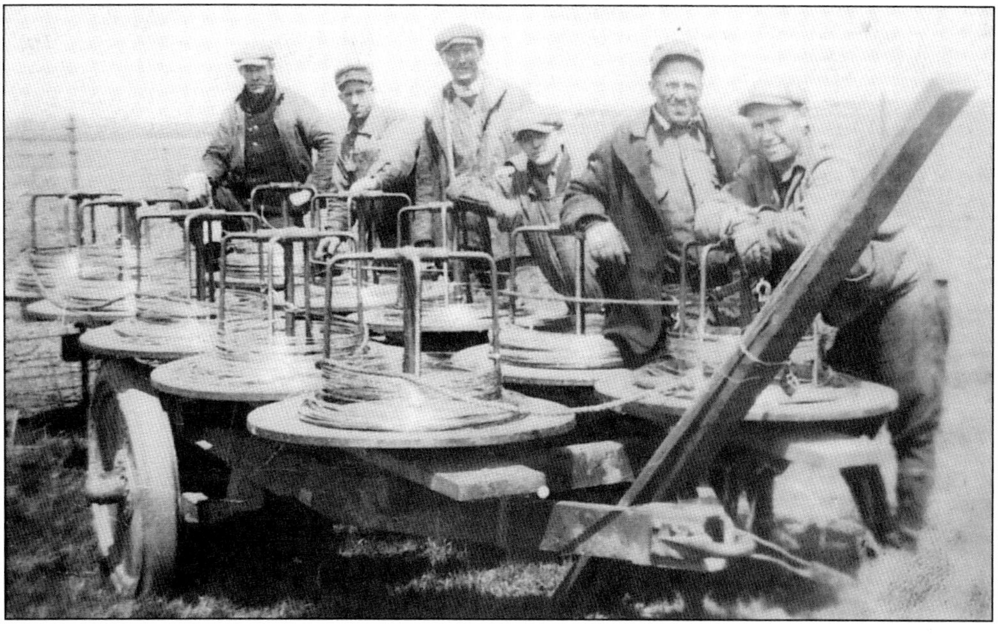

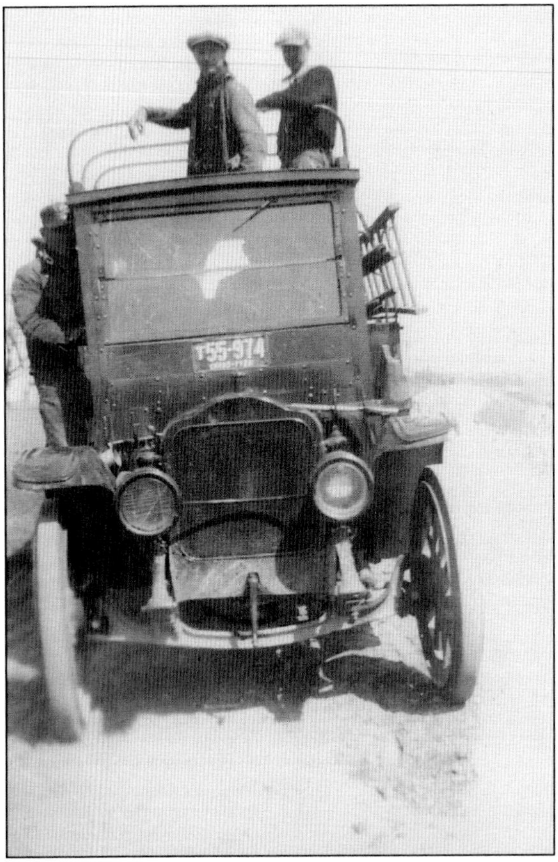

THATCHER EXCHANGE. In the left photograph, George Nordwick (center) and Joseph Schmidt (right) ride alongside an unidentified worker in the telephone equipment truck. These three men formed the first crew to install telephone lines to the Thatcher Exchange. The Thatcher Exchange operated out of a home (pictured below) formerly owned by Dr. John Orr. Edgar Allen Thatcher (1844–1916) purchased the residence around 1890. Edgar and his wife, Patience "Mollie" Gosney Thatcher (1849–1917), are seated on the front lawn. Beginning about 1930, the Citizens Telephone Company of Kentucky located its switchboard in the parlor of the home. The Thatchers' daughter Goldie was one of the first switchboard operators at the exchange. The Thatcher Exchange ran until the 1950s. At that time, a new building was erected at the end of Carmen Lane just east of the Alexandria Fairgrounds.

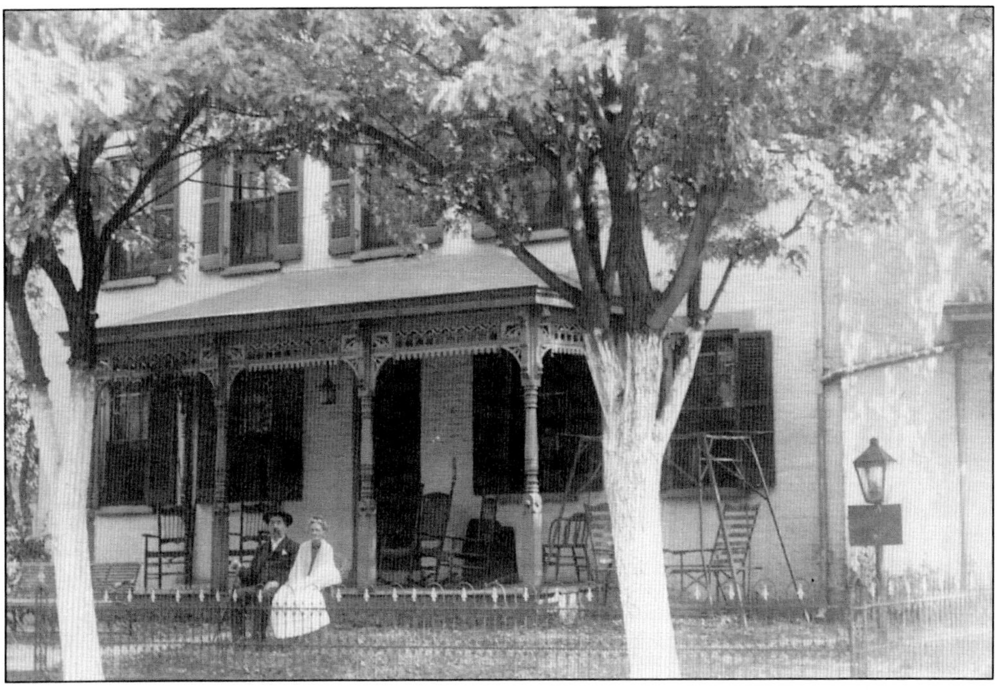

Five

BUSINESSES

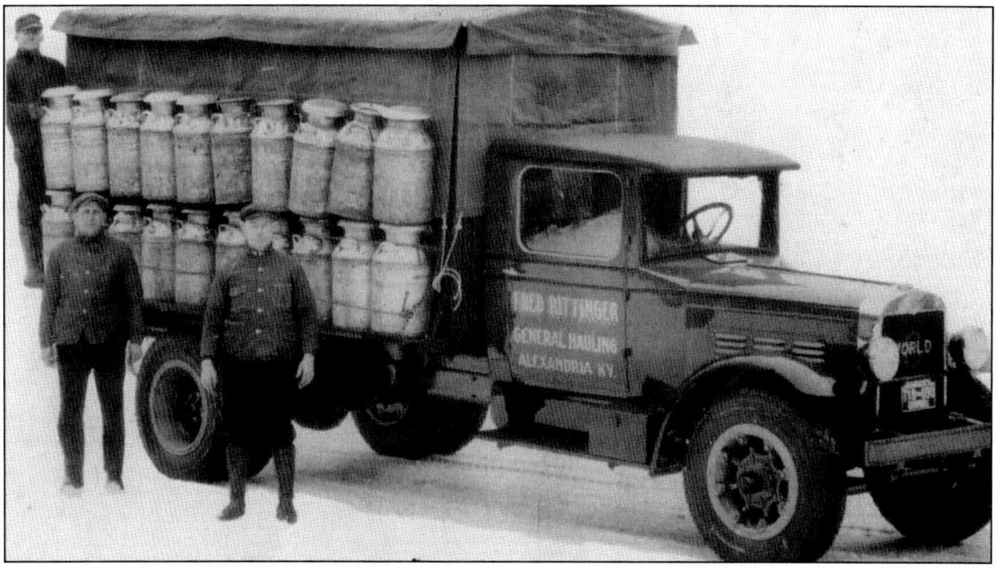

FRED RITTINGER GENERAL HAULING. Clifford Rittinger (left) and Fred Rittinger are pictured on a snow-covered road around 1930. The individual standing on the back of the truck is unidentified. On the outside of the truck is a load of milk cans. The logo on the radiator appears to read "World 8."

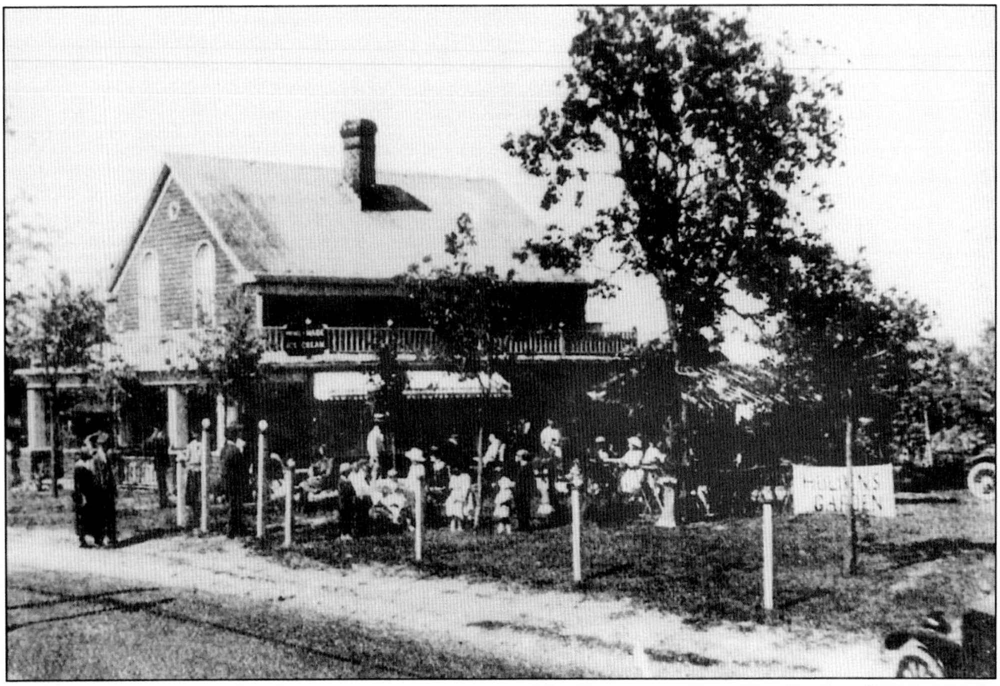

Holdens Garden. This home was once occupied by Benjamin Franklin Reiley (1813–1906), a farmer who served as a corporal in the 2nd Kentucky Infantry during the Spanish-American War. In 1837, Reiley married Susan Stroube in Alexandria. The residence later became Holdens Garden with a sign on the corner saying "Home Made Ice Cream."

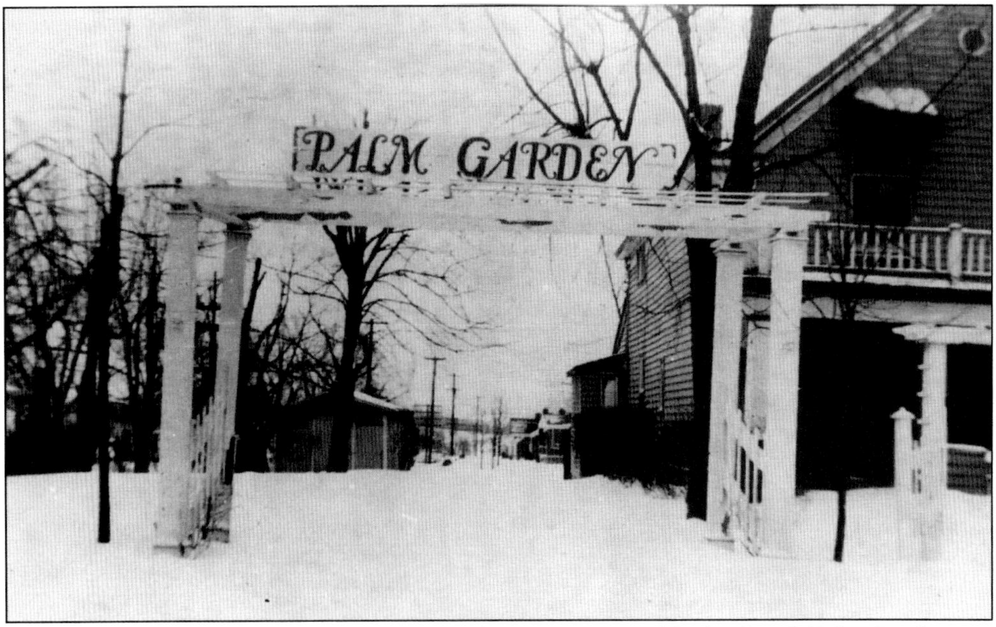

Palm Garden. Located at the intersection of Main Street and Reiley Road, Palm Garden was a landmark for many years. Guests could play tennis, volleyball, basketball, or indoor baseball at this recreational resort. In addition, Palm Garden offered chicken dinners, ice cream, and soft drinks. Holdens Garden was also a part of the complex. Apartments now occupy the property.

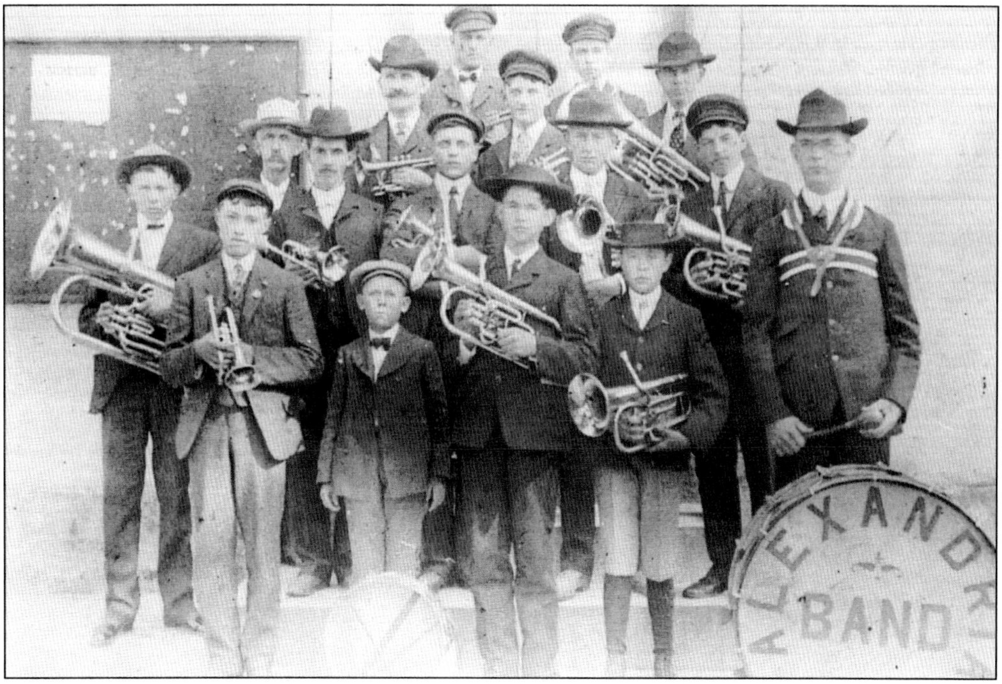

HOLDEN BAND. Though the drum says "Alexandria Band," the back of the photograph identifies this group as the Holden Band. A Mr. Holden stands on the left wearing a white hat. It appears that the band was composed simply of horns and drums.

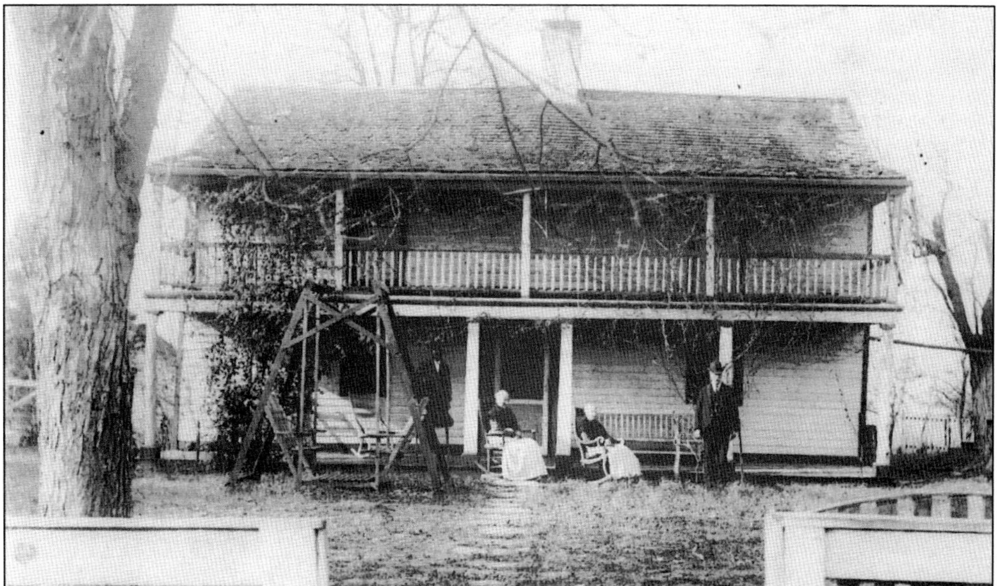

THATCHER TAVERN. In 1797, this tavern was built on what is now Thatcher Court near Alexandria Pike. Shown here from left to right are William Thatcher, Sara Thatcher, Rose Thatcher Robinson, and Clem Robinson. The family occupied the home until William's death in 1934. The Thatcher Cemetery was situated in back of the home. The Thatcher Tavern was the only accommodation that allowed turkey and cattle drovers to spend the night.

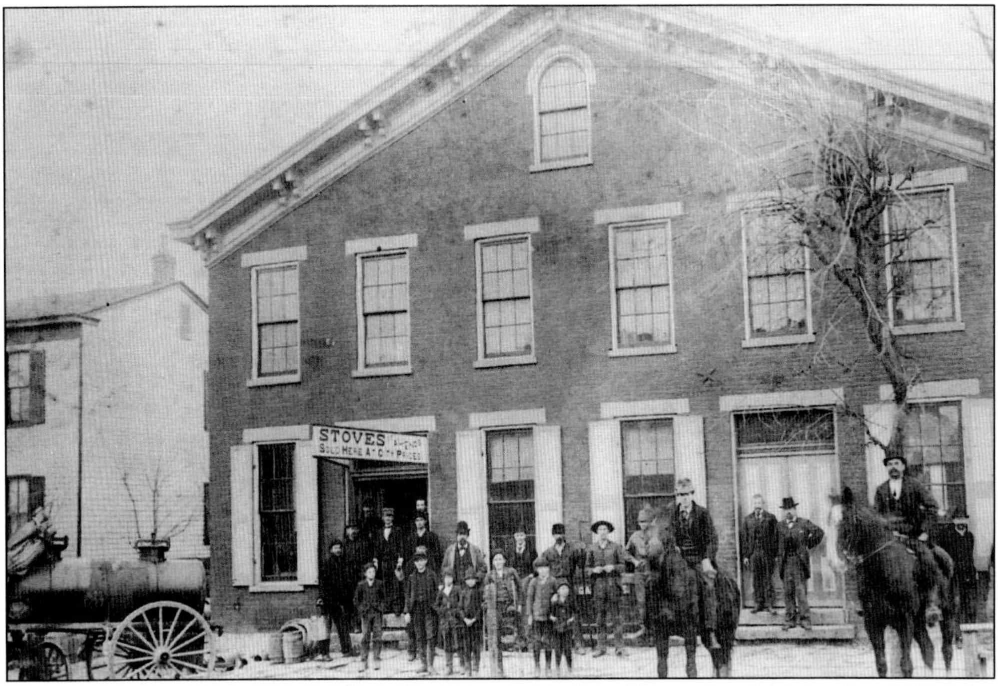

GENERAL STORE. This proud old building, constructed in the center of Alexandria before the Civil War, was home to many businesses over the years. Todd and Boesch, Youtsey Brothers, Gosney's, Carmacks, and Kentucky Motors all operated here. The structure also housed the post office for a period of time. In the center, Billy Thatcher stands with the aid of a crutch. Mounted on the horse to the right is William Grant.

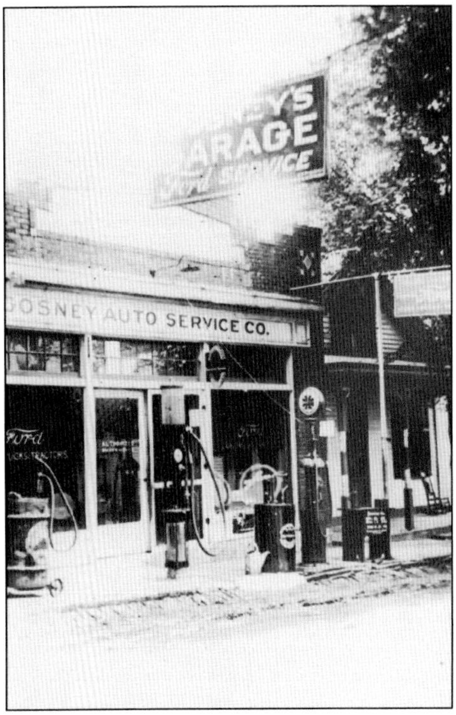

GOSNEY AUTO SERVICE. Clifford B. Gosney (1893–1971) sold Ford cars, trucks, and tractors, and offered gas and oil. In later years, he sold Dodge vehicles instead of Fords. Still later, Walter Schalk ran a Ford tractor business out of the same location. Today the front part of the building is gone, but the rear is still used for automobile repair by Seibert Auto Service.

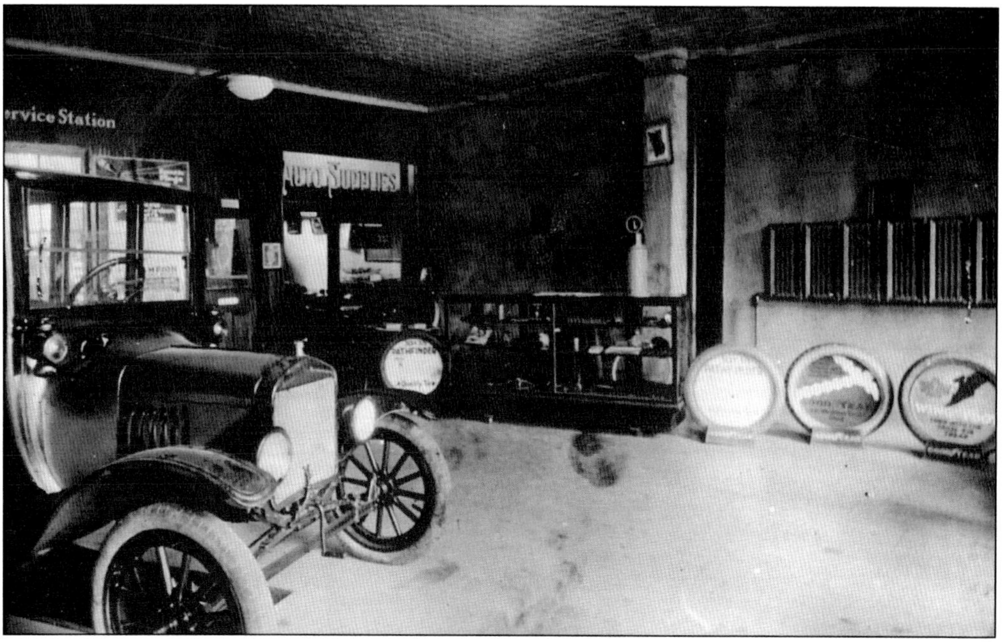

FORD MODEL T SHOWROOM. This interior view reveals Clifford B. Gosney's showroom, which was situated on Main Street between Washington and Jefferson Streets. On display is a 1921 or 1922 Model T. With dust on the fender, the car has probably been sitting for a while. The new tires have interesting names like Pathfinder and Wingfoot.

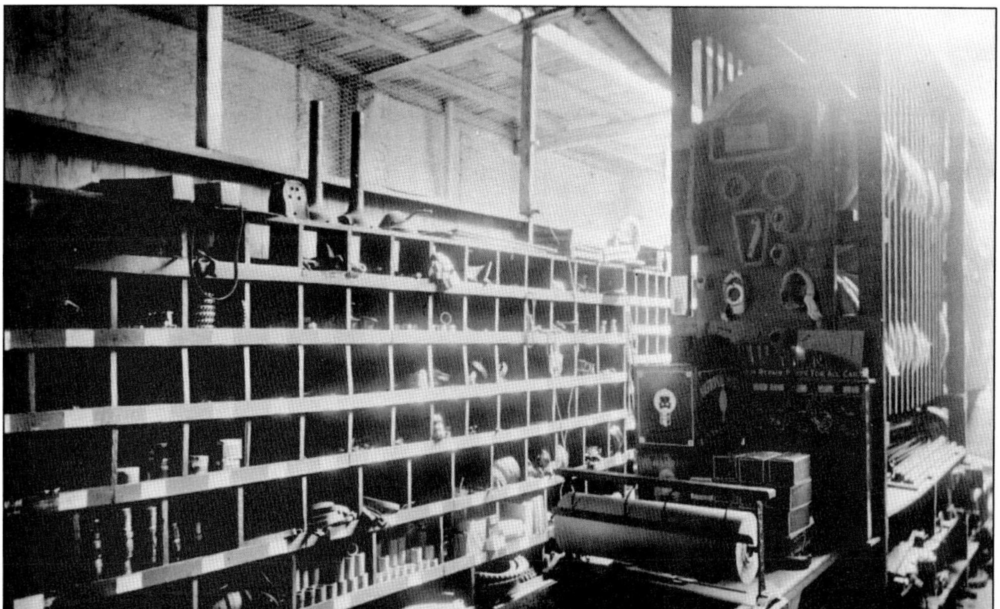

PARTS DEPARTMENT. Until the 1960s, no automotive parts stores operated in Alexandria. A service station or dealership had to stock a large variety of parts or make a long trip to Newport or Covington, Kentucky, or Cincinnati, Ohio. Bins of spare parts can be seen in this view of Gosney's Auto Service. Gaskets, fan belts, Champion spark plugs, and even rear axle housings can be identified.

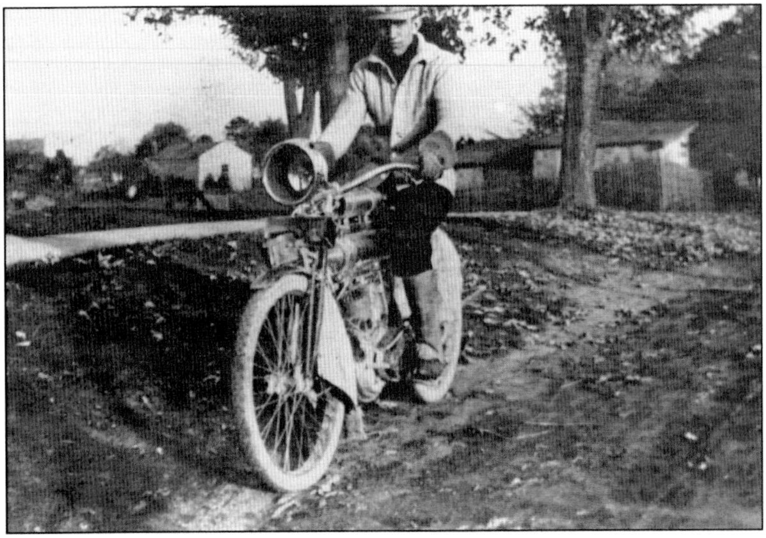

First Motorcycle. Here Clifford Gosney rides what is reported to be the first motorcycle in the town of Alexandria.

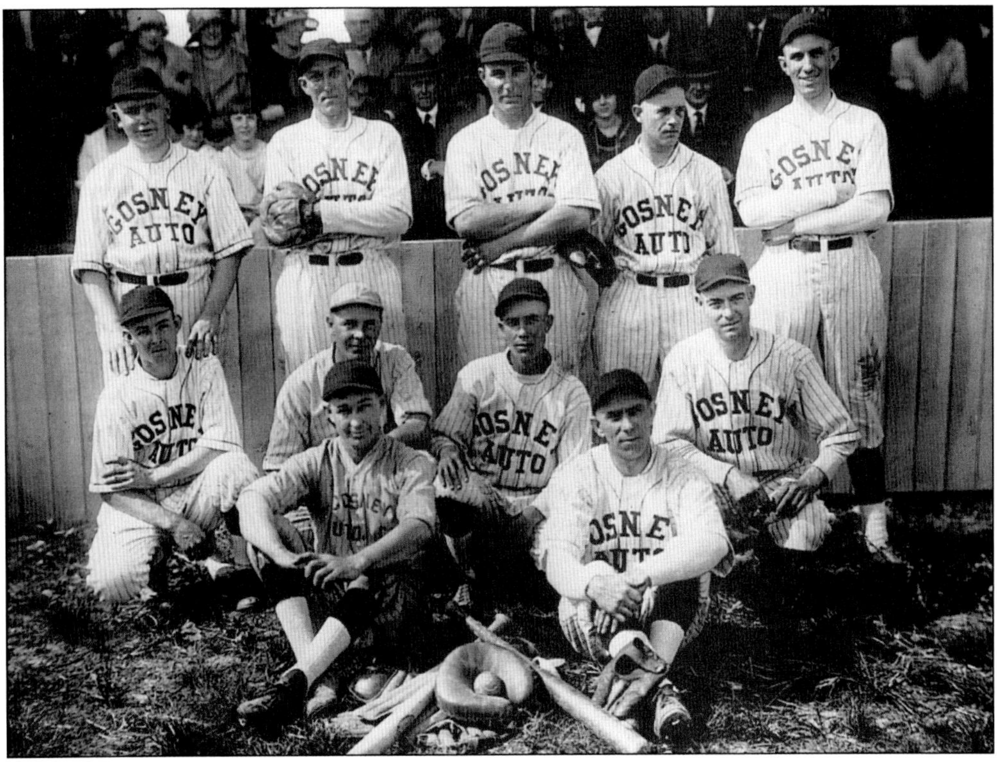

Gosney Auto Baseball Team. The Gosney team included the following players from left to right: (first row) Pomp Rardin, outfield; Charlie Schneider, third base; (second row) George Loss, pitcher; Bill Schort, shortstop; Phil Schaffer, pitcher; Albert Teschner, second base; (third row) Dr. A. E. Howe, manager; Fred Stormer, first base; Joe Schmidt; Clyde Gosney, catcher; and Clifford Gosney, center field. A nice crowd has gathered in the grandstand for this game.

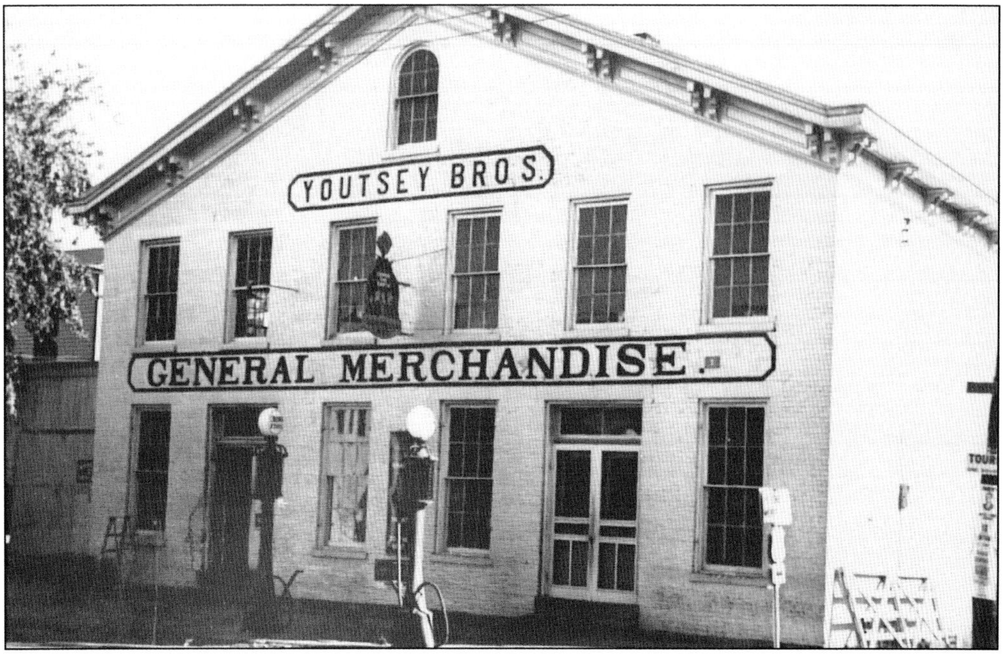

YOUTSEY BROTHERS GENERAL MERCHANDISE. A familiar Alexandria landmark, this building has served as a general store under several owners from its spot at the intersection of Main and Washington Streets. In 1886, it housed the first Alexandria Post Office, with John Todd holding the position of postmaster. In later years, it was home to Kentucky Motors. The globe on the gas pump to the left reads "Crown Ethyl."

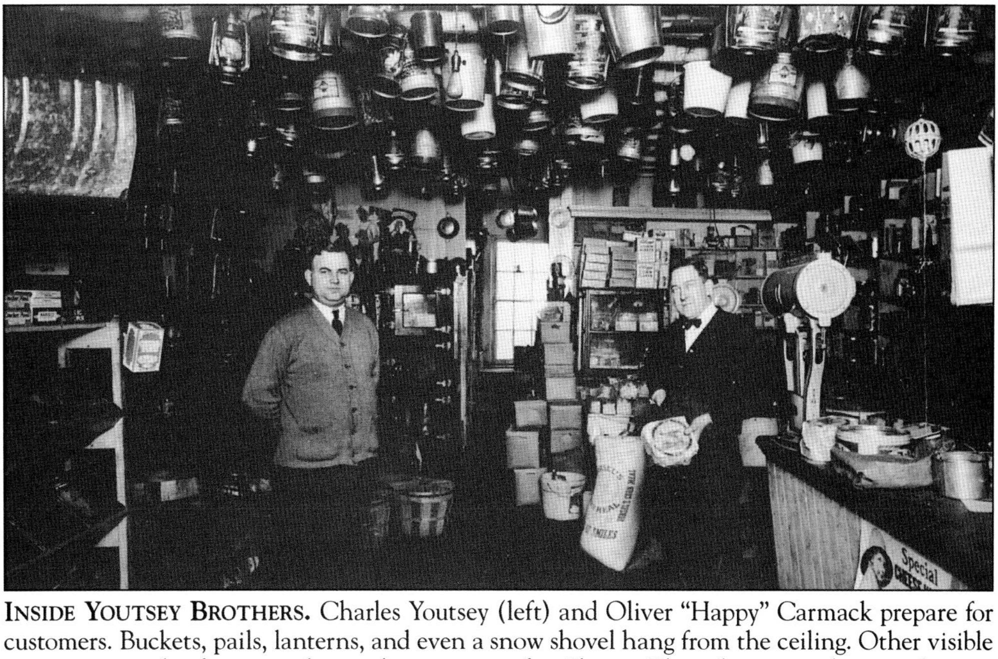

INSIDE YOUTSEY BROTHERS. Charles Youtsey (left) and Oliver "Happy" Carmack prepare for customers. Buckets, pails, lanterns, and even a snow shovel hang from the ceiling. Other visible items are a sack of cornmeal, an advertisement for Cheese Klips cheese crackers, and many canned goods. The store carried almost everything a patron could need and would take orders for many additional items.

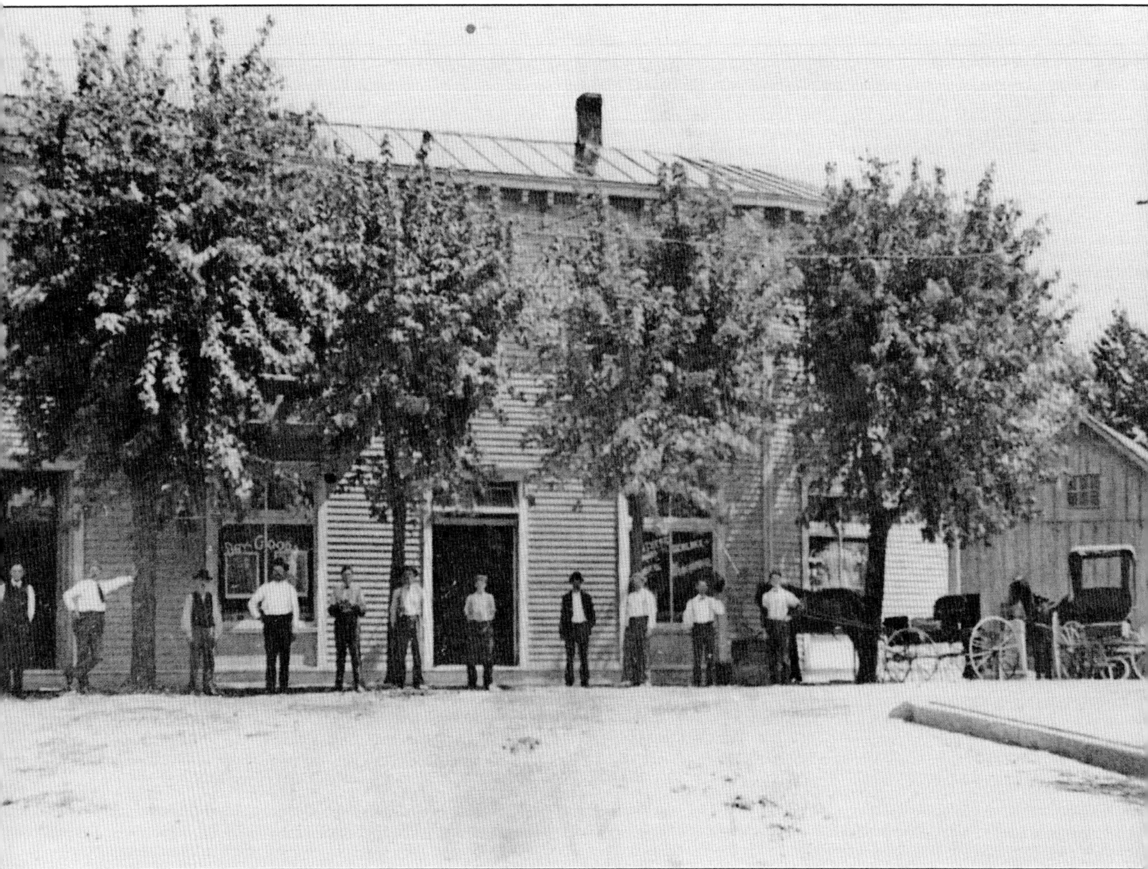

HESS AND RACKE GENERAL STORE, c. 1905. Operating for many years in Alexandria, this business was conveniently located just across from the courthouse on Main Street. The building contained the store, the omnibus office, and other offices, including Yelton and Racke Undertakers.

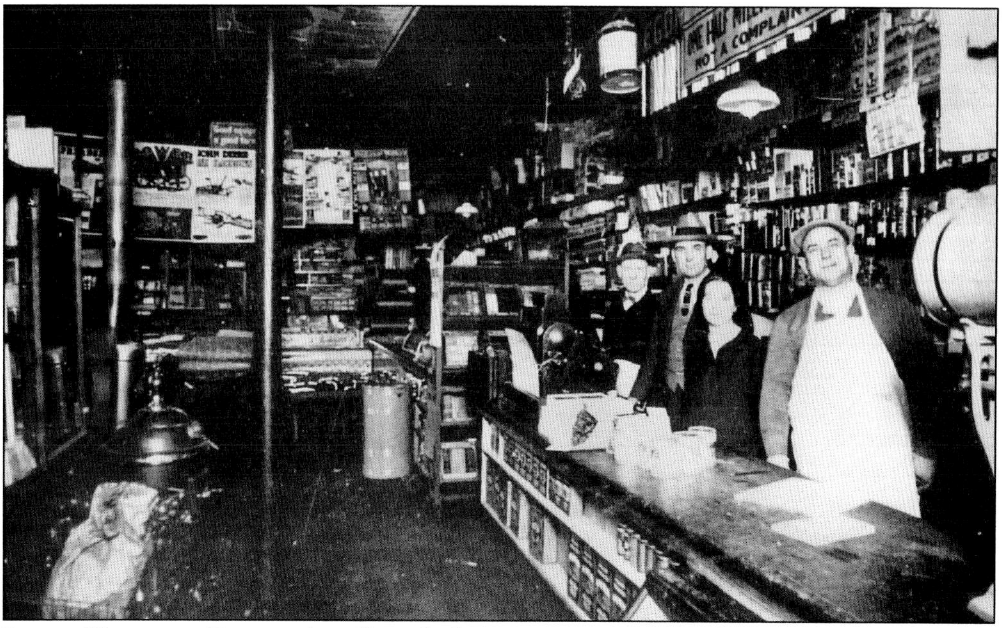

INSIDE HESS AND RACKE. A well-stocked country store, Hess and Racke sold many things. Shown in this image are grocery goods, a scale to weigh purchases, and a cash register. One of the advertisements in the background features farm equipment by John Deere. Pictured from left to right are unidentified, William Racke, Eula Harris Shaw, and Bill Hess.

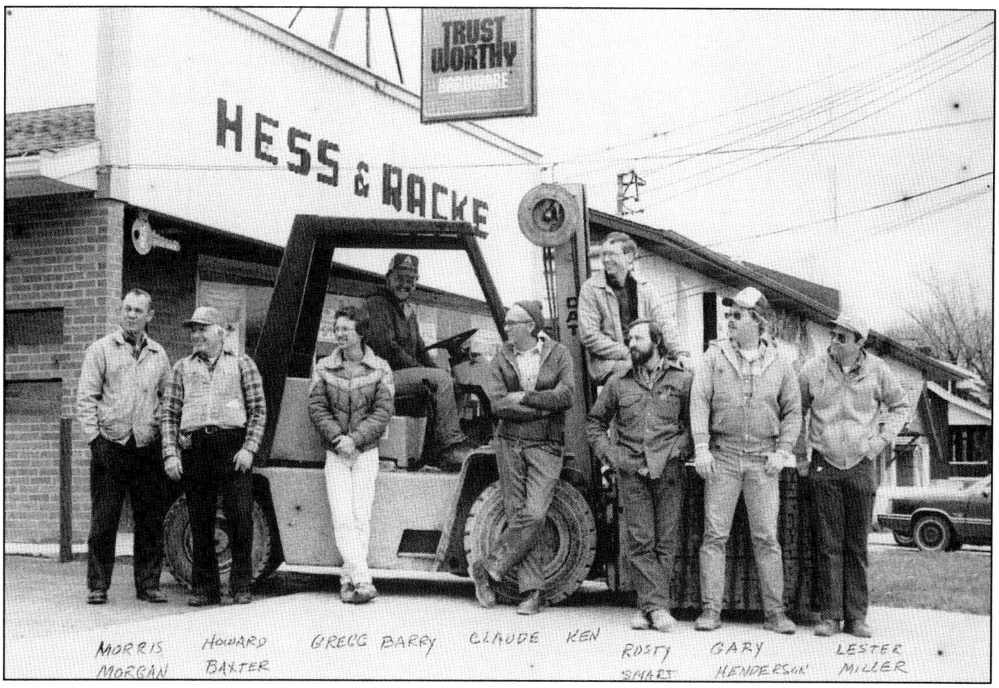

HESS AND RACKE HARDWARE, 1986. Family members and employees pose for a photograph. Seen from left to right are Morris Morgan, Howard Baxter, Gregg Racke, Barry Racke, Claude Blackburn, Ken Racke, Rusty Smart, Gary Henderson, and Lester Miller. The store, now located on Washington Street, offers hardware and home-building items.

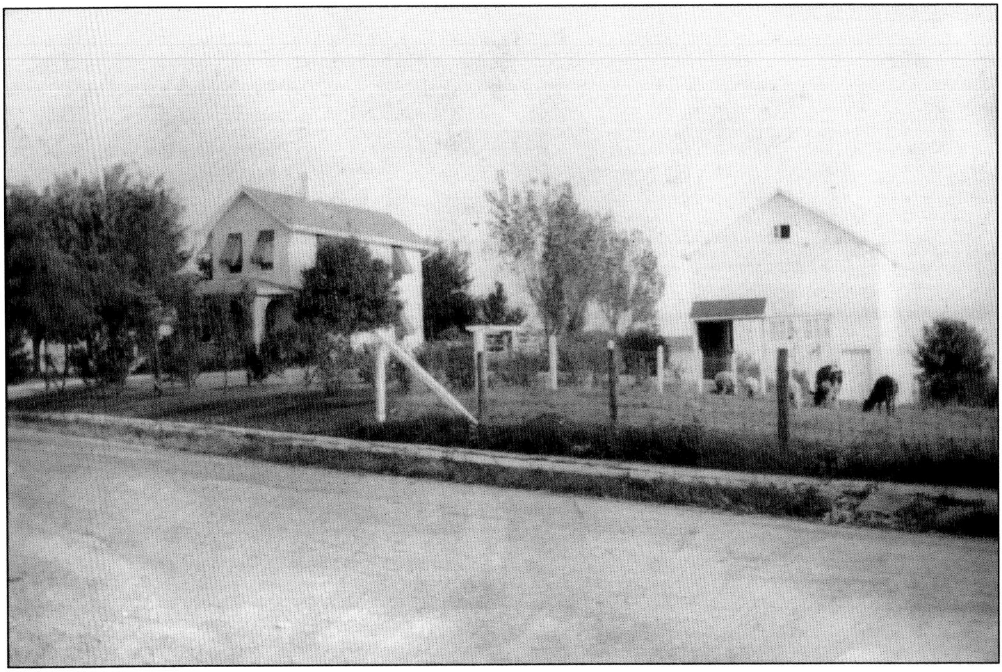

ANDREW THURNER FARM. Andrew M. Thurner, president of the Bank of Alexandria in the late 1930s, owned a fine home and farm on the south side of Main Street. Sheep and dairy cattle enjoyed a pasture and farm pond to the right of this view on the corner of Main Street and Alexandria Pike. Bank expansion resulted in the removal of these buildings and the pond.

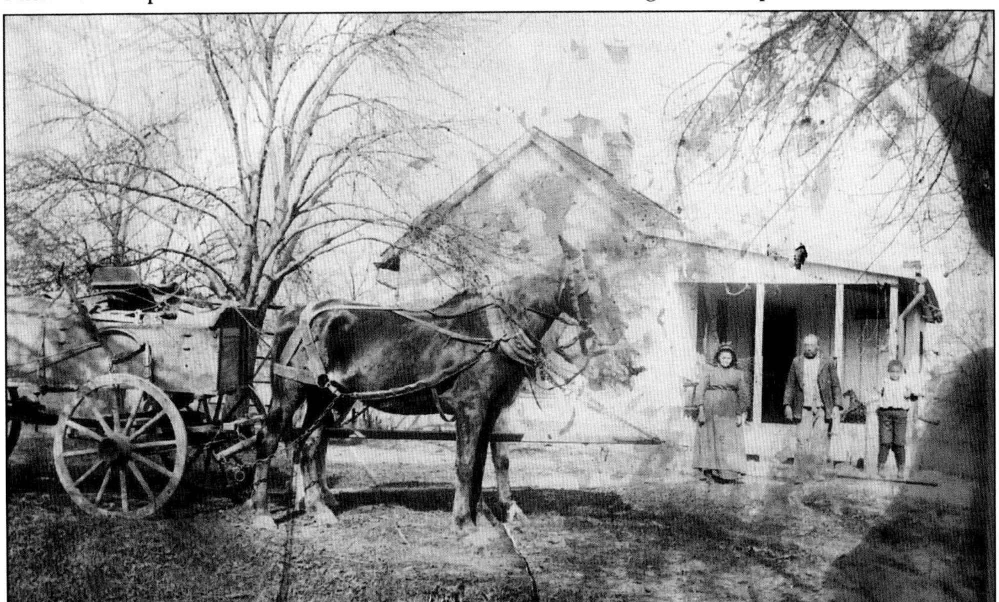

SAM FREEMAN. Worker Sam Freeman, his wife, Josephine, and their children resided in this small house on the High View Farm property. Freeman loaded his horse-drawn wagon and delivered bricks from the Spilman kiln to build the Bank of Alexandria. He was reportedly the first depositor of the bank when it opened. The Thatcher family buried him and some of his family members in Alexandria Cemetery.

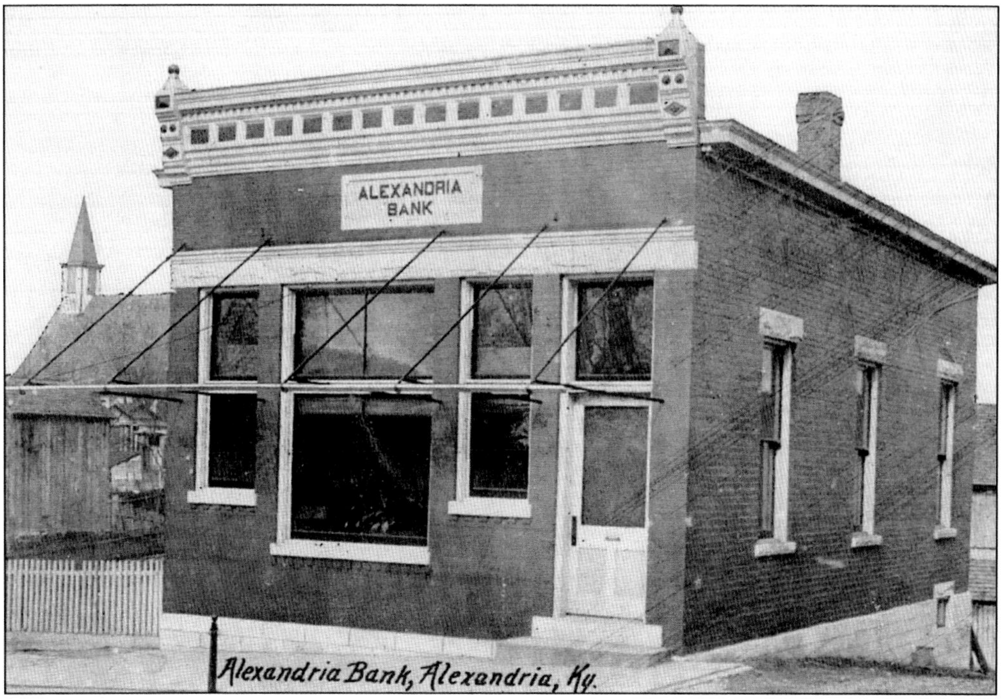

BANK OF ALEXANDRIA. In 1903, the Bank of Alexandria opened across from the courthouse on Main Street with Dr. Newton G. Zinn as president and Andrew Thurner as vice president. Quite successful, the bank is said to be one of the few in northern Kentucky that did not close during the Great Depression.

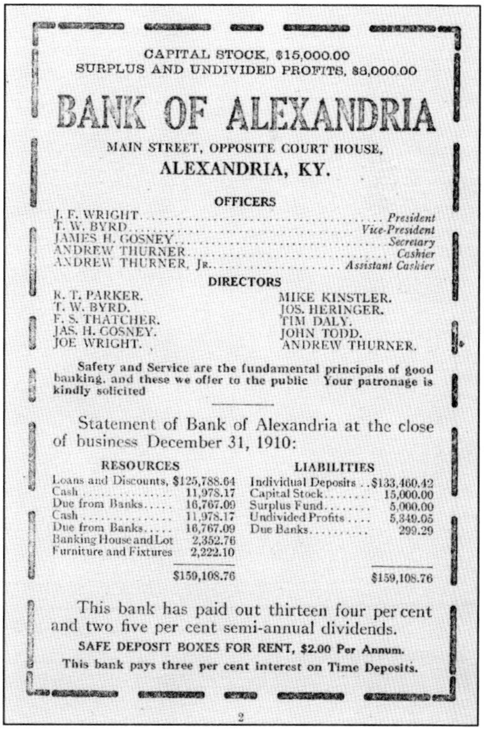

CAPITAL STOCK, $15,000.00
SURPLUS AND UNDIVIDED PROFITS, $8,000.00

BANK OF ALEXANDRIA

MAIN STREET, OPPOSITE COURT HOUSE,
ALEXANDRIA, KY.

OFFICERS

J. F. WRIGHT.......... President
T. W. BYRD.......... Vice-President
JAMES H. GOSNEY.......... Secretary
ANDREW THURNER.......... Cashier
ANDREW THURNER, Jr.......... Assistant Cashier

DIRECTORS

R. T. PARKER.	MIKE KINSTLER.
T. W. BYRD.	JOS. HERINGER.
F. S. THATCHER.	TIM DALY.
JAS. H. GOSNEY.	JOHN TODD.
JOE WRIGHT.	ANDREW THURNER.

Safety and Service are the fundamental principals of good banking, and these we offer to the public Your patronage is kindly solicited

Statement of Bank of Alexandria at the close of business December 31, 1910:

RESOURCES		LIABILITIES	
Loans and Discounts,	$125,788.64	Individual Deposits ..	$133,460.42
Cash	11,978.17	Capital Stock	15,000.00
Due from Banks.....	16,767.09	Surplus Fund..........	5,000.00
Cash	11,978.17	Undivided Profits	5,349.05
Due from Banks.....	16,767.09	Due Banks..........	299.29
Banking House and Lot	2,352.76		
Furniture and Fixtures	2,222.10		
	$159,108.76		$159,108.76

This bank has paid out thirteen four per cent and two five per cent semi-annual dividends.

SAFE DEPOSIT BOXES FOR RENT, $2.00 Per Annum.

This bank pays three per cent interest on Time Deposits.

2

STATEMENT OF THE BANK OF ALEXANDRIA, 1910. This document was published not only as a statement of the bank's holdings, but also as a public advertisement.

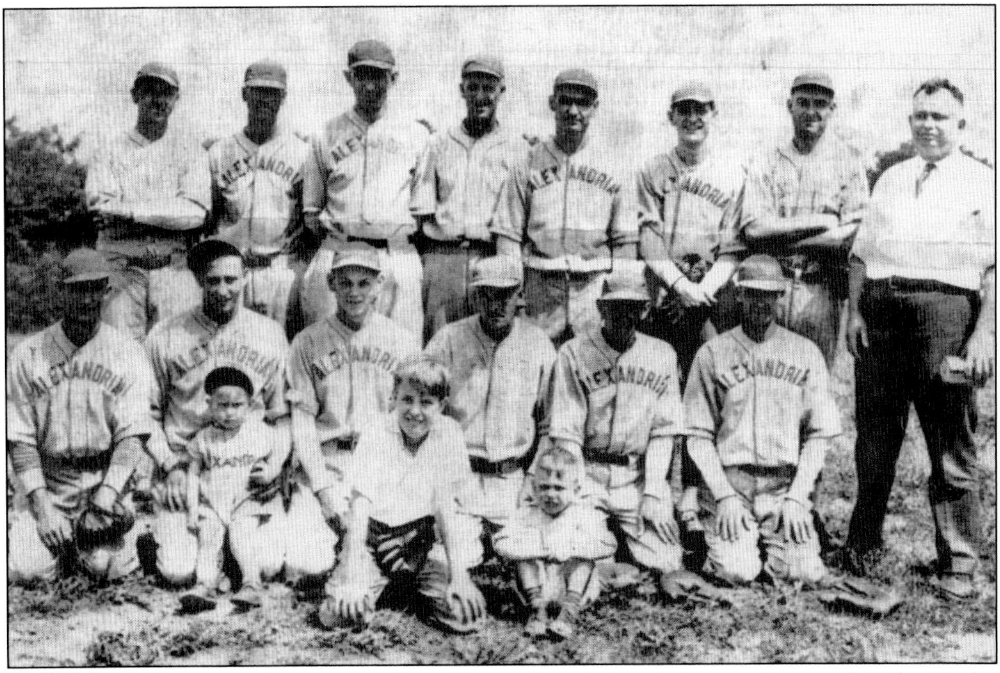

ALEXANDRIA BASEBALL TEAM, c. 1930s. Shown from left to right are: (first row) Eddie Ziegler Jr., Melvin Schaefer, and Nelson Howe; (second row) Bobby Cropenbaker, Carl Ziegler, Dude Ziegler, ? Stubbs, Ed. Ziegler, and Joe Kinny; (third row) Bill Short, Bill Watson, Cliff Gosney, Ed Schaffer Sr., Bill Crailer, unidentified, Butch Tischner, and manager Dr. A. E. Howe.

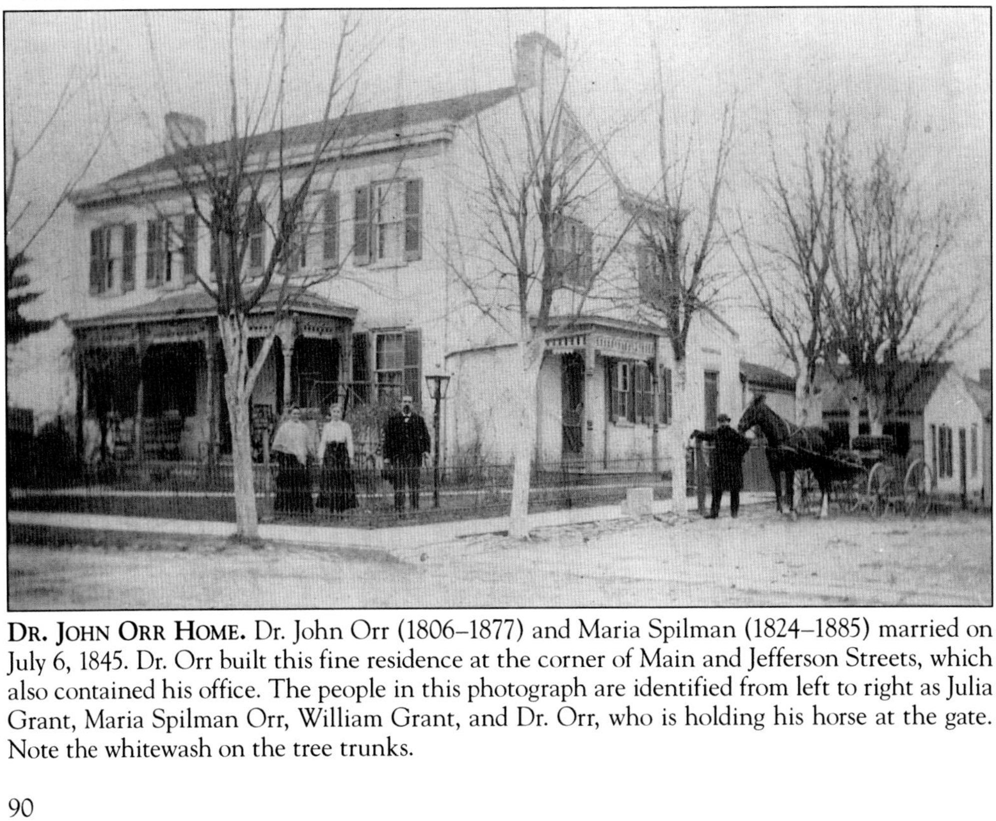

DR. JOHN ORR HOME. Dr. John Orr (1806–1877) and Maria Spilman (1824–1885) married on July 6, 1845. Dr. Orr built this fine residence at the corner of Main and Jefferson Streets, which also contained his office. The people in this photograph are identified from left to right as Julia Grant, Maria Spilman Orr, William Grant, and Dr. Orr, who is holding his horse at the gate. Note the whitewash on the tree trunks.

Dr. A. E. Howe Home. This Main Street building served as the home and office of Dr. A. E. Howe. Now only a parking lot remains on the location where many residents of the town went for aid and comfort. Patients would come away with some of Dr. Howe's famous purple salve and green liniment, a favorite cure.

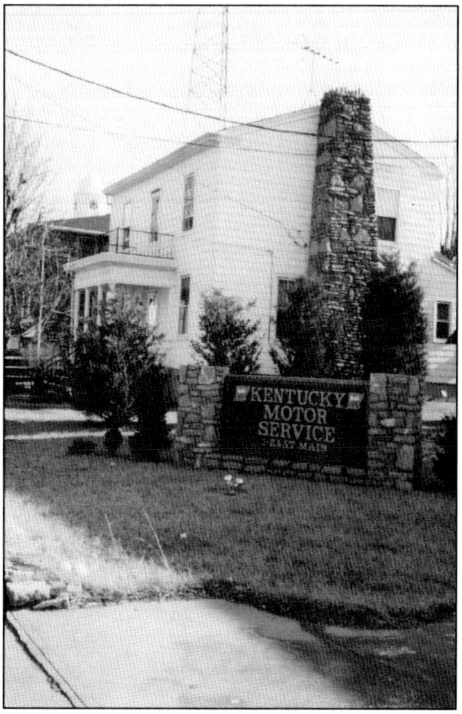

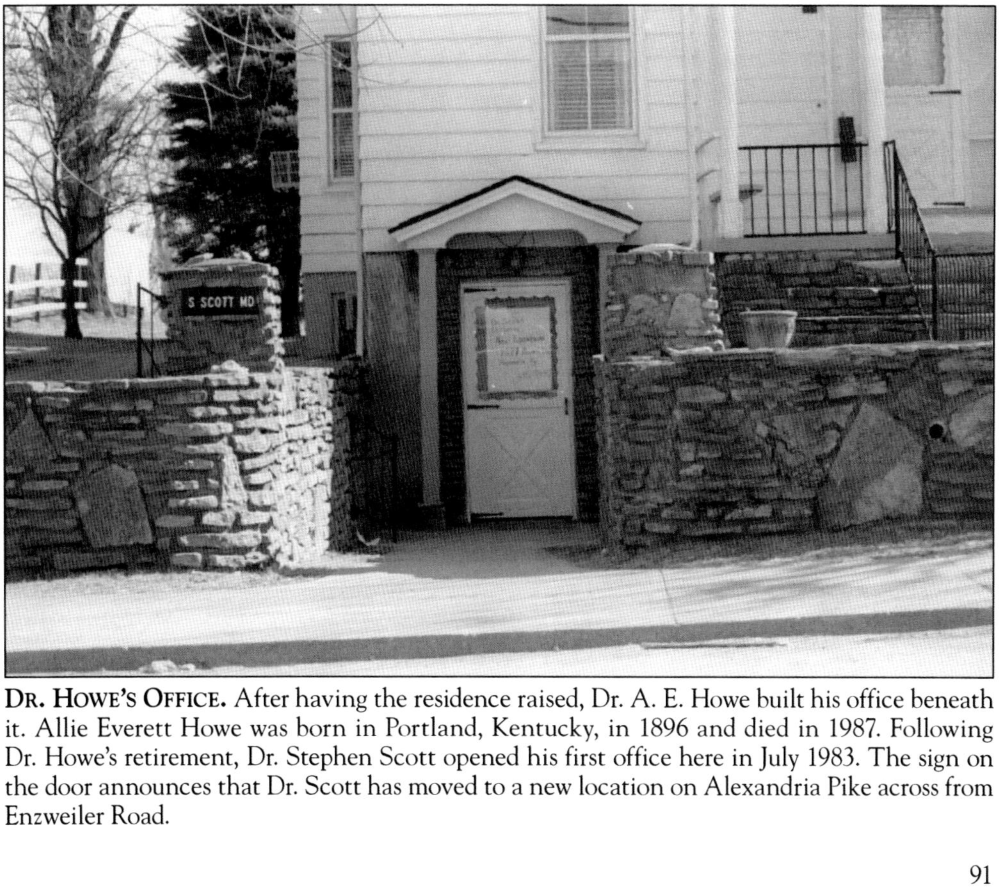

Dr. Howe's Office. After having the residence raised, Dr. A. E. Howe built his office beneath it. Allie Everett Howe was born in Portland, Kentucky, in 1896 and died in 1987. Following Dr. Howe's retirement, Dr. Stephen Scott opened his first office here in July 1983. The sign on the door announces that Dr. Scott has moved to a new location on Alexandria Pike across from Enzweiler Road.

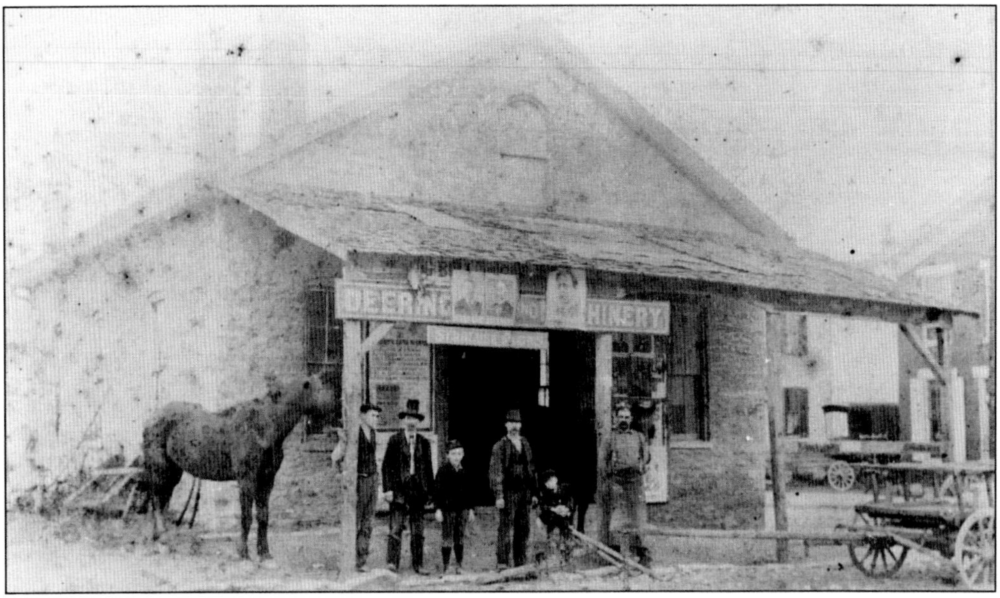

ALEXANDRIA BLACKSMITH SHOP. Few places were more important to an early town than the blacksmith shop, which fixed not only horseshoes, but also almost anything metal. Above, men stand on the corner of Washington and Main Streets beneath a Deering Machinery sign. Deering was one of the most popular brands of horse-drawn farm machinery. Visible are a wagon, a buggy, and the old general store at the far right on Main Street. Later a bank and drugstore would be built on this corner. Today the building serves as a computer shop. The home below, which belonged to local blacksmith Matt Smith, stood on Washington Street directly behind his shop, shown above. The First Baptist Church would later purchase this gingerbread house, tear it down, and build a gym on the site.

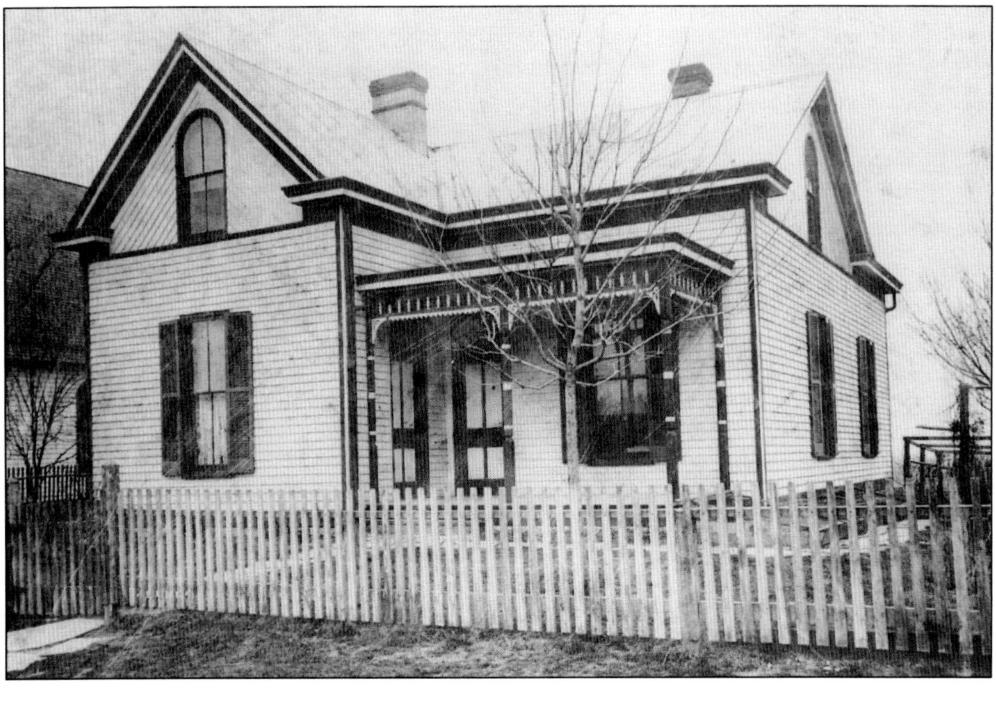

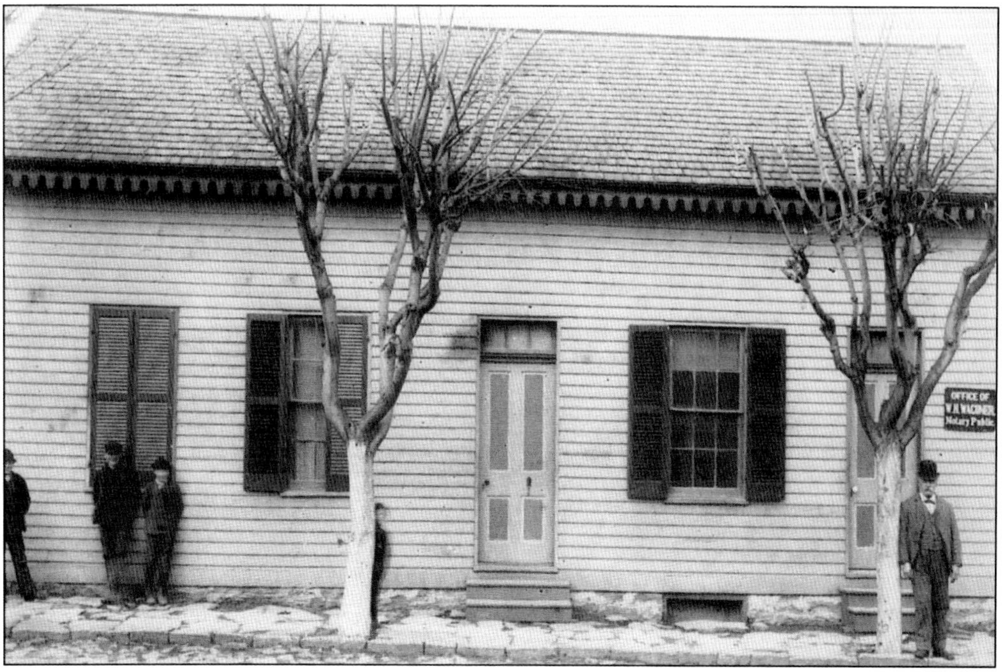

WILLIAM H WAGONER, c. 1890. This Main Street building first housed the office of notary public W. H. Wagoner and is the current location of Country Cousins Bakery. William H. Wagoner (1839–1908) is listed as a schoolteacher in the 1870 census. The 1880 census gives his occupation as a printer and the 1900 census as attorney-at-law. The children in this photograph are unidentified.

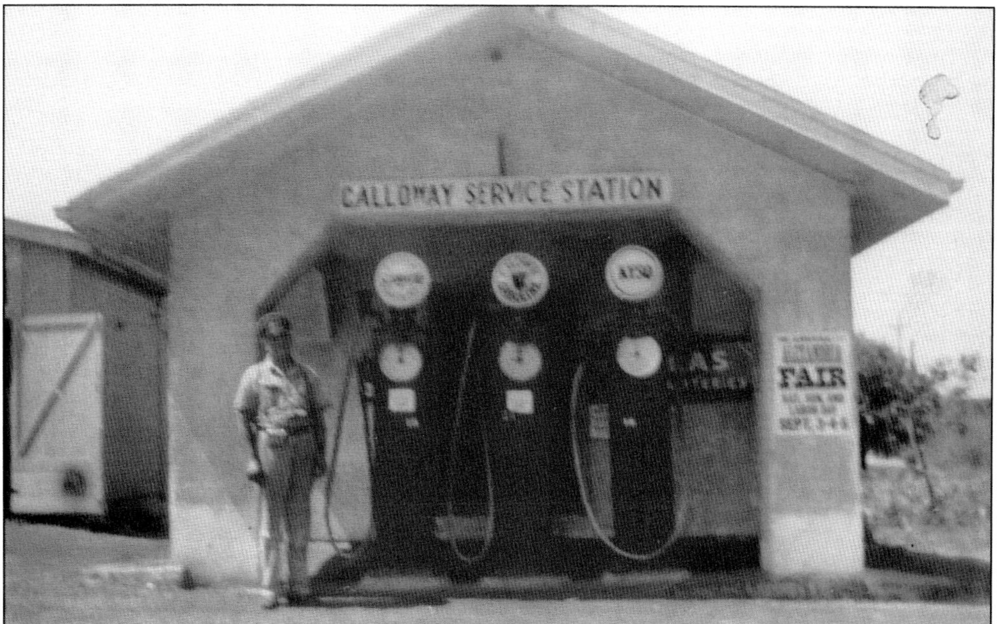

GALLOWAY SERVICE STATION, 1935. Edgar H. Galloway operated this service station, which sold Crown gasoline on Washington Street just south of Grove Street. Note the advertisement for the Alexandria Fair. The site now houses the Farm Bureau of Kentucky offices.

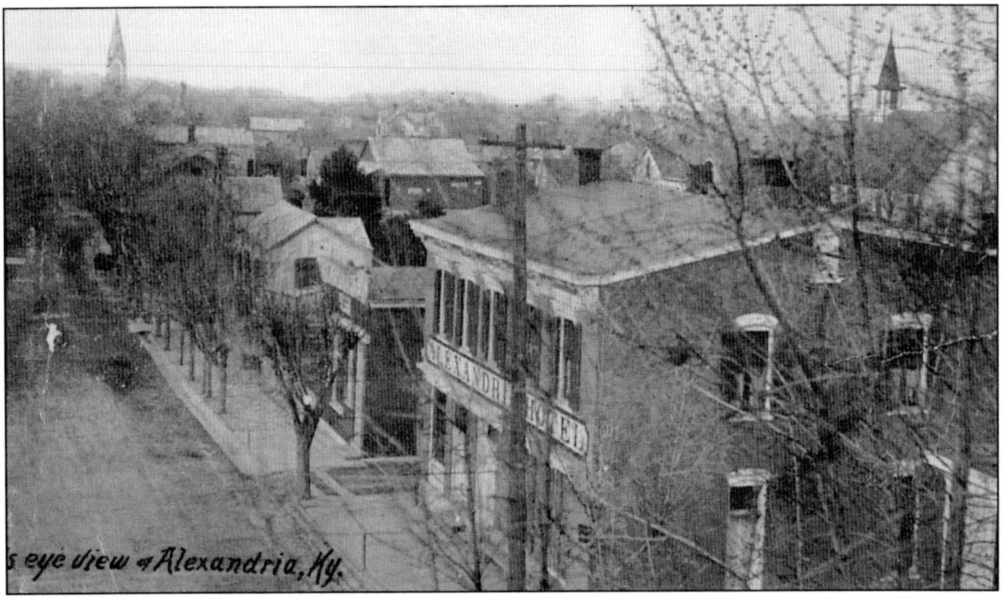

A Bird's-eye View of Main Street, c. 1920. Likely taken from the upper floor of Hess and Racke, this view looks west along the north side of Main Street. In the foreground on the right are the Alexandria Hotel and the adjacent Bank of Alexandria. In the distance are the steeples of St. Paul's Church (left) and the Baptist church on Washington Street.

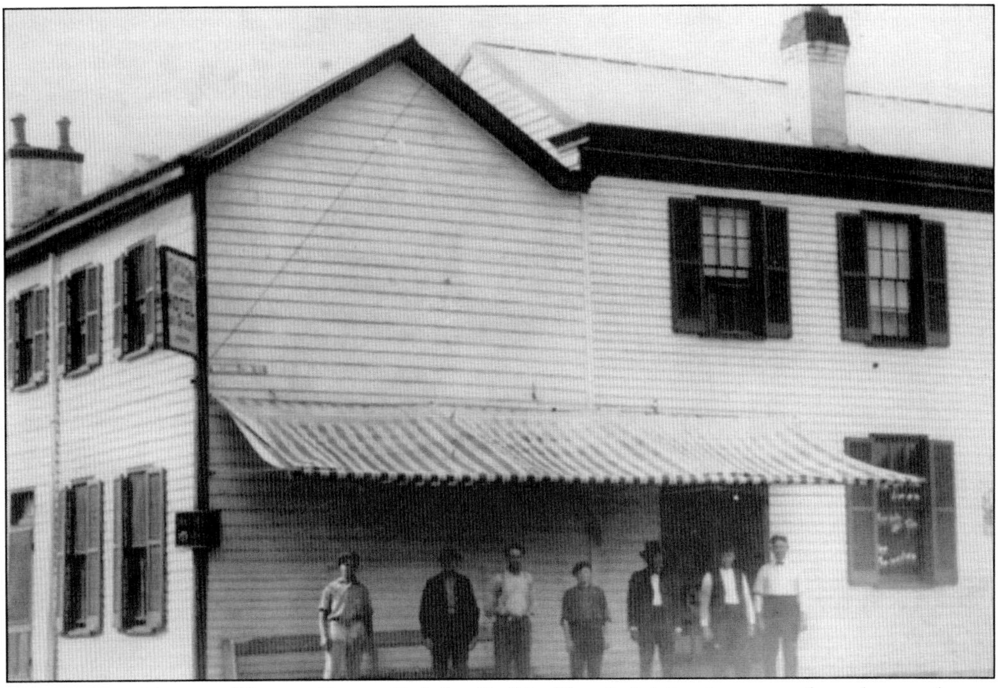

Miller and Engert Hotel. First called the Griffey Hotel, this business stood on the northwest corner of Washington and Main Streets. The large sign on the corner appears to read "Kentucky Home Hotel." Pictured from left to right are Len Schroat, William Patton, Matz Miller, ? Schwalbach, John Miller, ? Enzweiler, and George Nordwick. The Maple Lawn Restaurant later occupied this site in a new building.

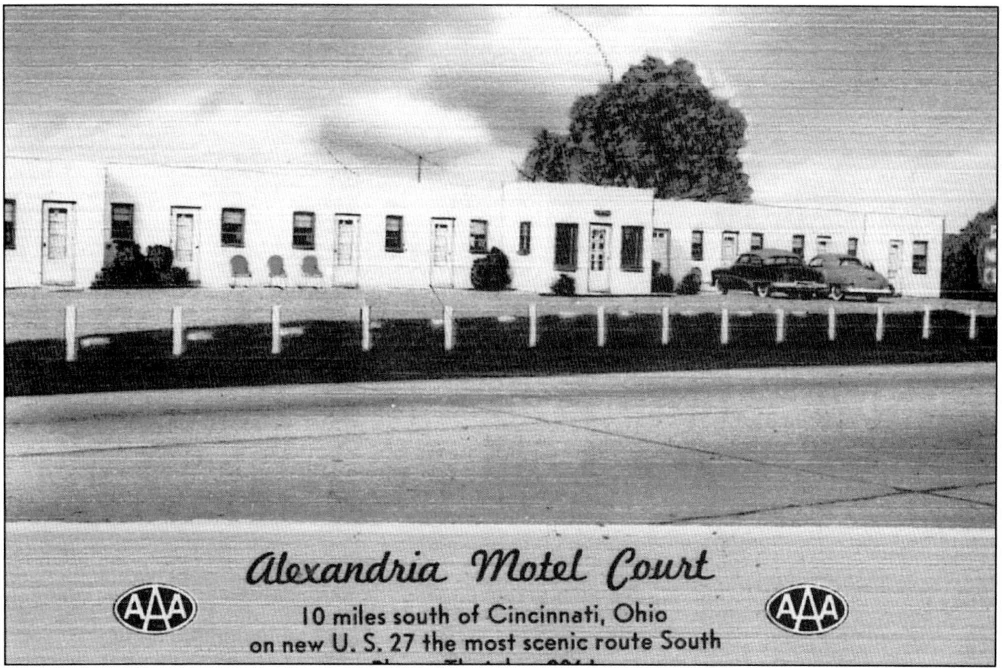

ALEXANDRIA MOTEL COURT. Built by a Mr. Blair sometime in the early 1950s, this accommodation was later known as the Guardian Angels Motel. It was a popular place for downstate visitors to stay while at the fair. A car wash now stands here. At one time, at least three motels were operating in Alexandria.

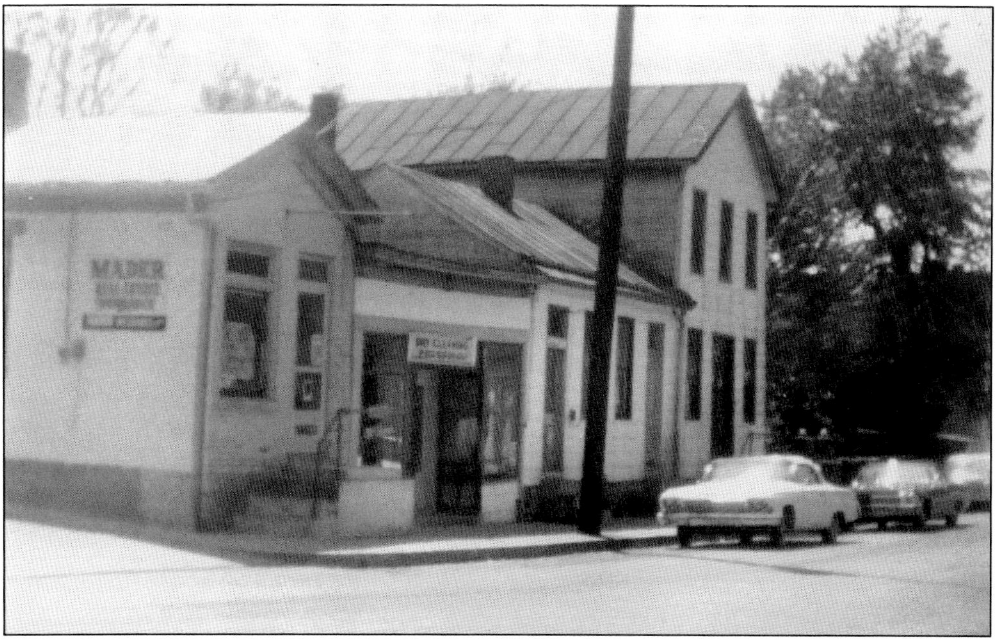

MAIN STREET. These four buildings are now gone. In their place is an apartment complex just to the right of the county courthouse. Seen from left to right are Dr. Rich's dentist office, later Mader Insurance; the second post office, later Art Woeste's Dry Cleaner; a law office and beauty shop; and Ershells Funeral Home and the third post office.

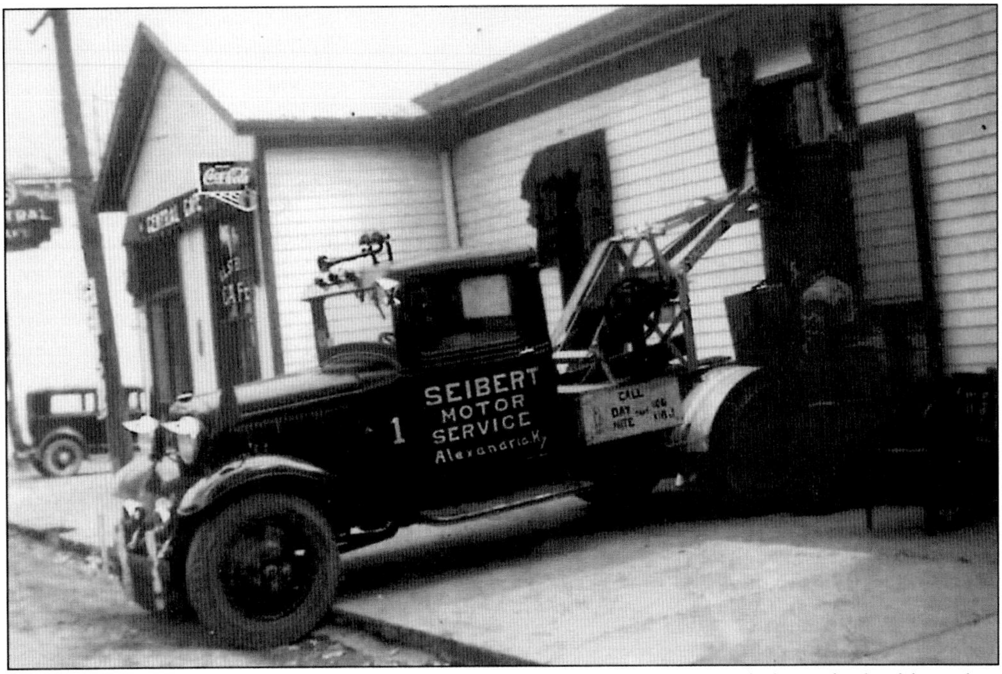

SEIBERT MOTOR SERVICE. A 1932 Ford Model BB tow truck moves a safe from the building that houses the Central Café on Main Street. This photograph was taken sometime prior to 1940. The Seibert family has operated an automotive service business in the Alexandria area since before 1917. Previously, the family had been in the wagon-building and blacksmithing business. The pictured tow truck is still owned by the Seibert family.

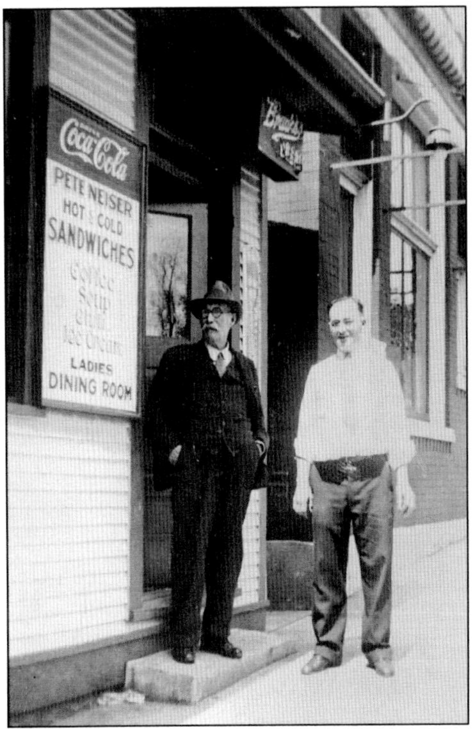

PETE NEISER'S CAFÉ. In 1923, Pete Neiser opened his business across from the county courthouse on Main Street, operating it well into the 1980s. Here Robert Gosney Sr. (left) and Pete stand in front of the café. Upon its closing, the bar was moved to VFW No. 3205 on U.S. 27. Today the Woeste Law Office occupies the building.

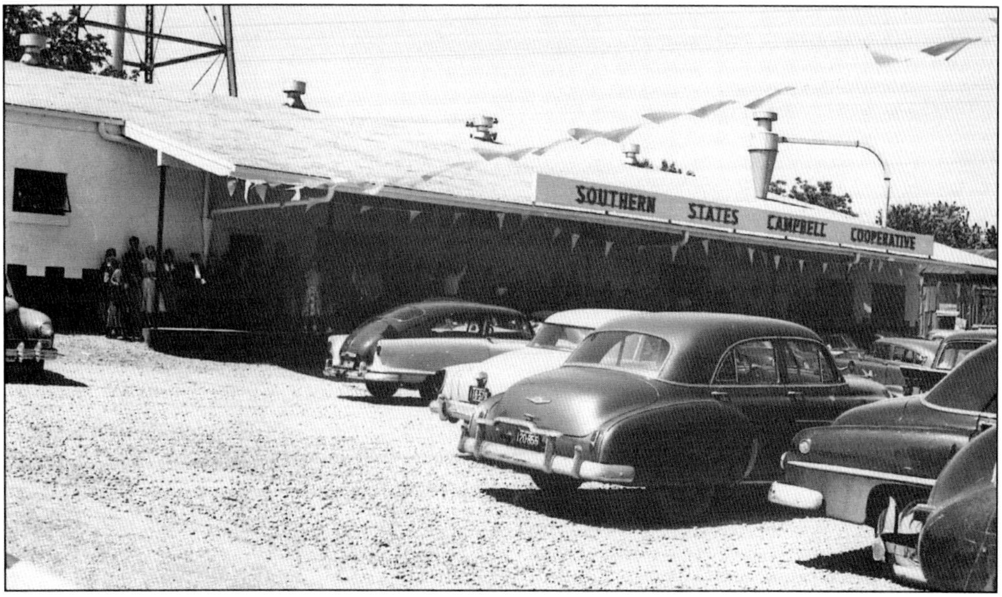

SOUTHERN STATES CAMPBELL COOPERATIVE. On May 23, 1953, a large crowd turned out for the opening of the Southern States Campbell Cooperative on Jefferson Street just south of Main Street and just behind the old water tower. The tower and the old Thatcher Telephone Exchange building were later removed to provide more room for the business and frontage on Main Street. The farmer-owned cooperative offers a wide range of services for the residents of Alexandria.

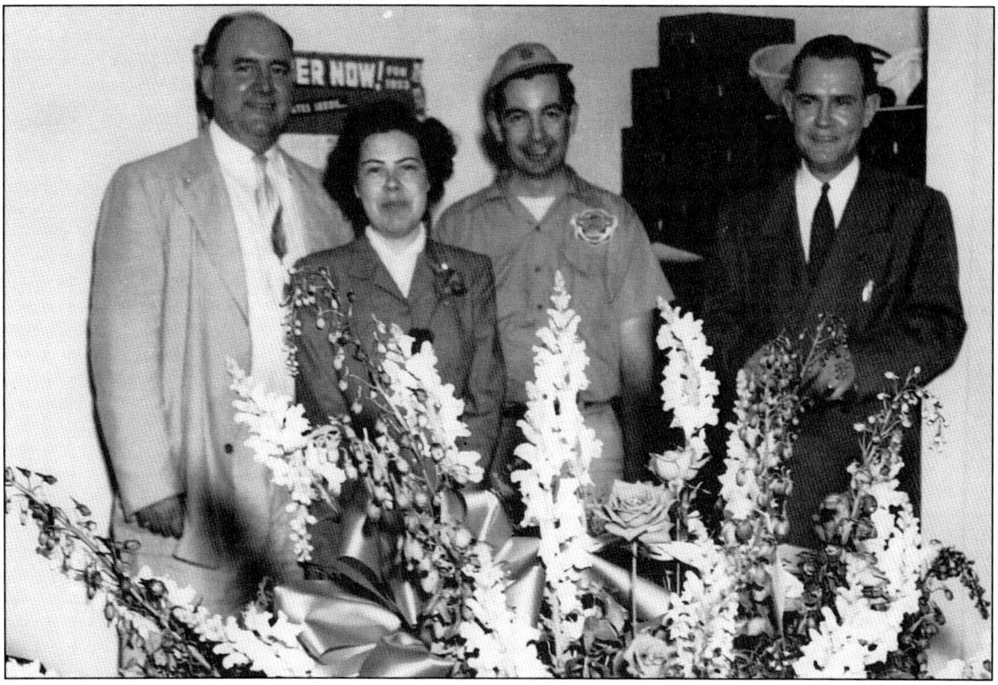

GRAND OPENING CREW. Southern States Campbell Cooperative workers present for the grand opening were, from left to right, Mike Powers, Elizabeth Thatcher Klem, Bruce Hutchinson Jr., and C. F. Lane. The festivities included drawings for door prizes, roses for the ladies, and bag openers for the men.

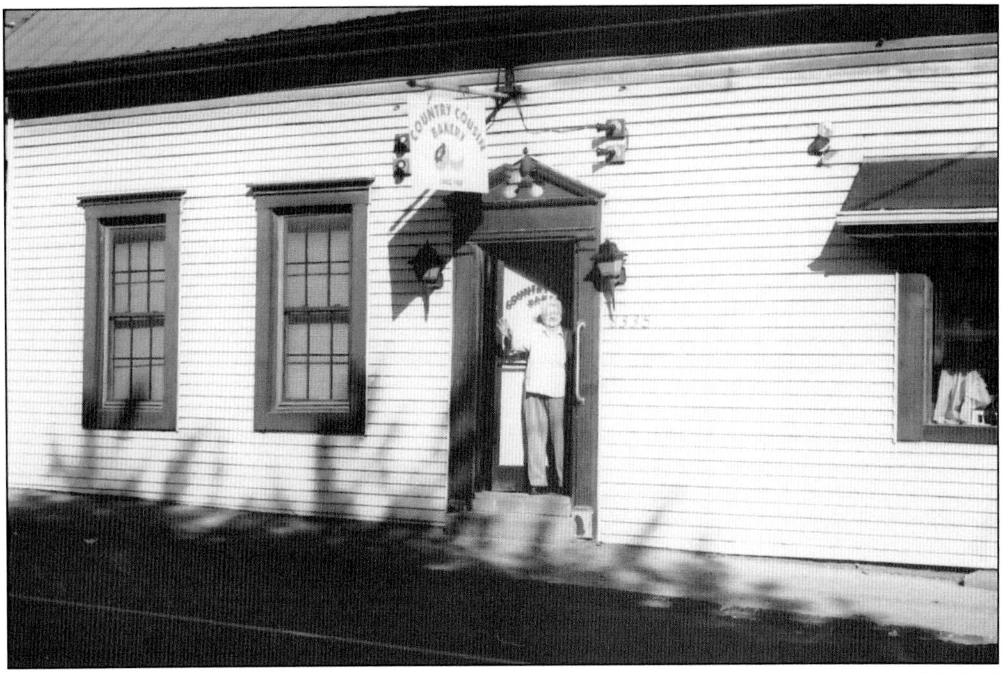

COUNTRY COUSINS BAKERY. Marion and Mary Reinhardt (above, in doorway) established Country Cousins across from the courthouse on Main Street in 1968. For years, it was the only place in the area to stop for that morning donut, peanut or coconut sweet roll, or Danish pastry. The bakery's favorite saying remains hanging on the wall inside: "We count our blessings, not our calories." Shown below from left to right are workers Alta Marksberry, Dottie Kremer, Terri Holtz, Mary Ellen Holtz, Marion Reinhardt, Mary Reinhardt, and Michael Reinhardt.

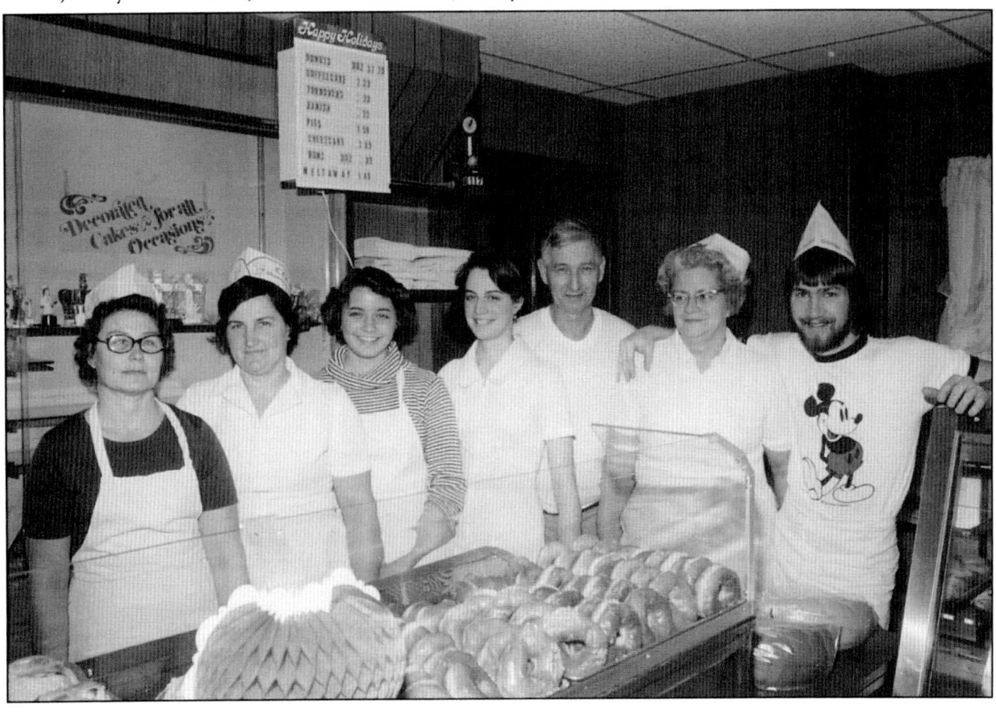

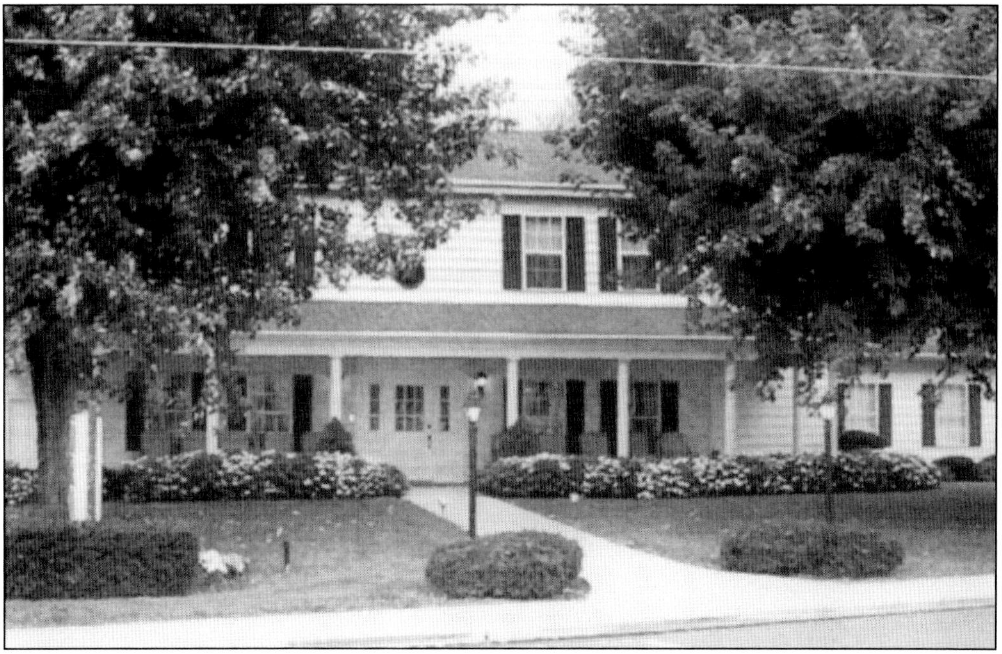

ALEXANDRIA FUNERAL HOME. This funeral home was established in 1961 in the original residence of the William Steffen family, which was built in the late 1800s. Operated by Marvin Bryon, it is located on Washington Street next to Cassons Realty. Beautiful flowers adorn the building throughout the summer months.

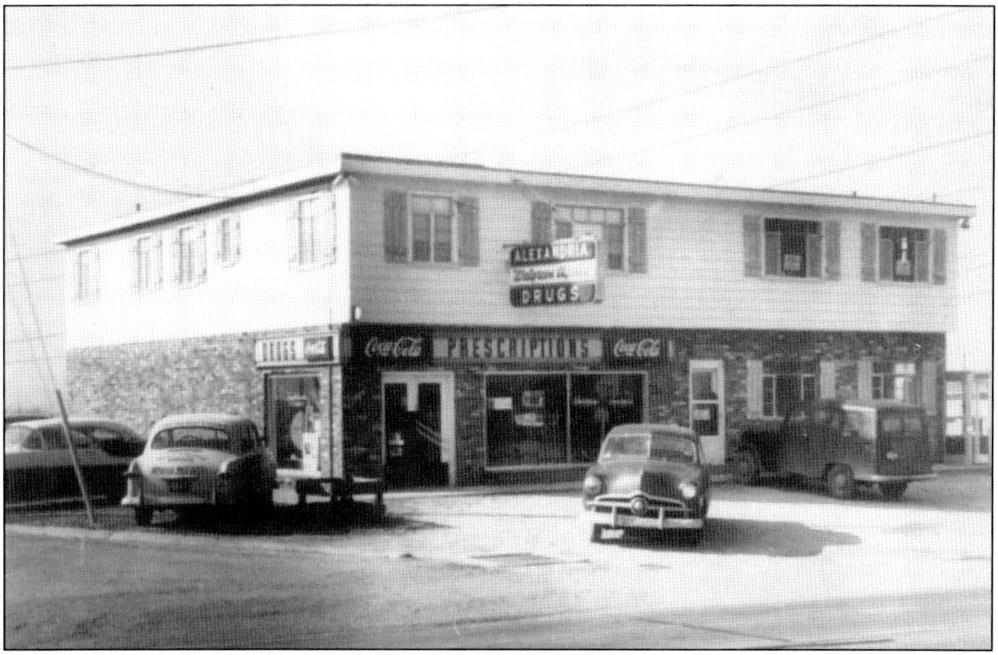

ALEXANDRIA DRUGS. In the mid-1950s, Peter Orzali opened this drugstore on Alexandria Pike at the corner of Sunset Drive. Prescriptions were delivered to patients' homes using the 1951 Ford seen second from the left. In addition to prescriptions, the store offered cosmetics, books, magazines, and gift items. Today Tom Rust owns and operates the store.

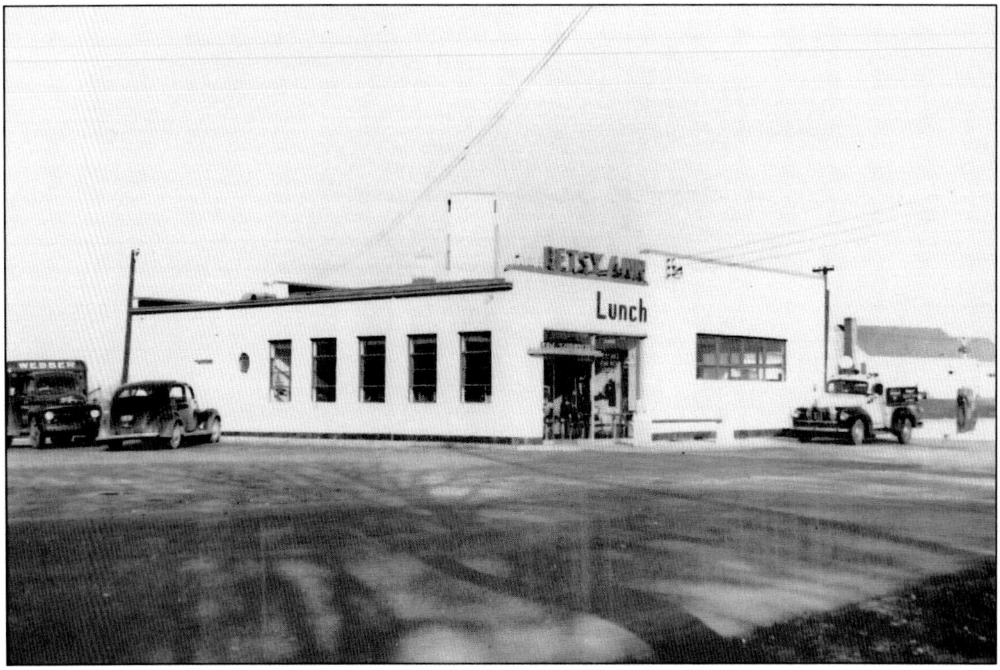

THE BETSY ANN. Bessie Lemon opened the Betsy Ann in the spring of 1948 because she felt the town needed a good place to eat. Built as a restaurant on one side (above) and a Standard Oil gas station on the other (below), it was located at the intersection of U.S. 27 and Washington Street, a prime location for all passing traffic. Maggie Rembus was the longtime lunchroom manager. At the same time, S. E. "Seilus" Bedford II and his son S. E. "Sonny" Bedford III ran the service station. The restaurant and service station remained important parts of the town until the 1970s. The rebuilding and realigning of U.S. 27 spelled the end of the line for this business.

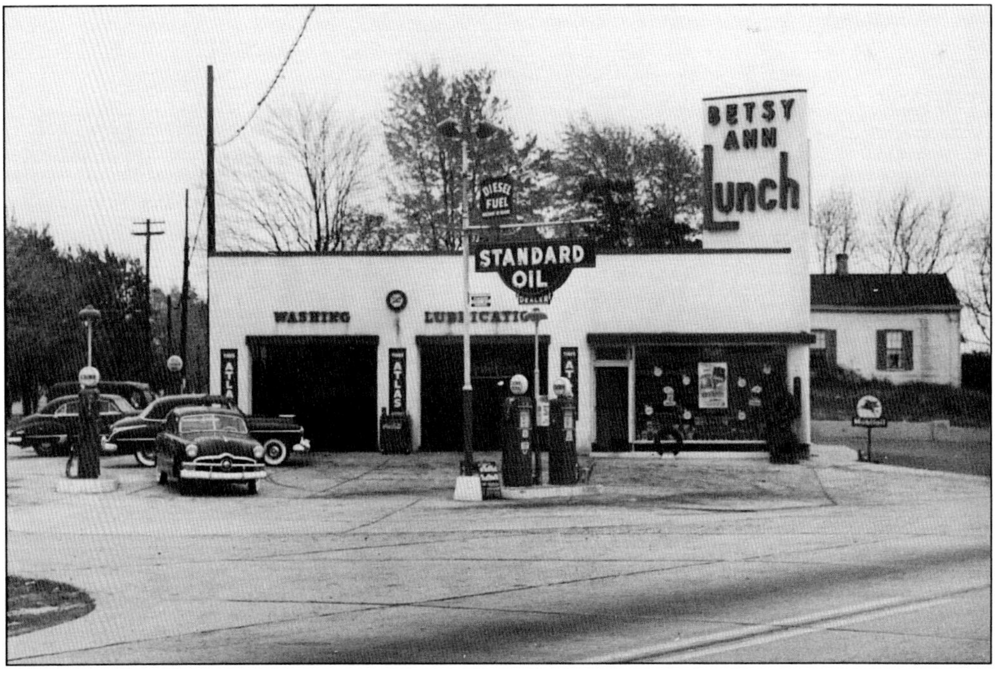

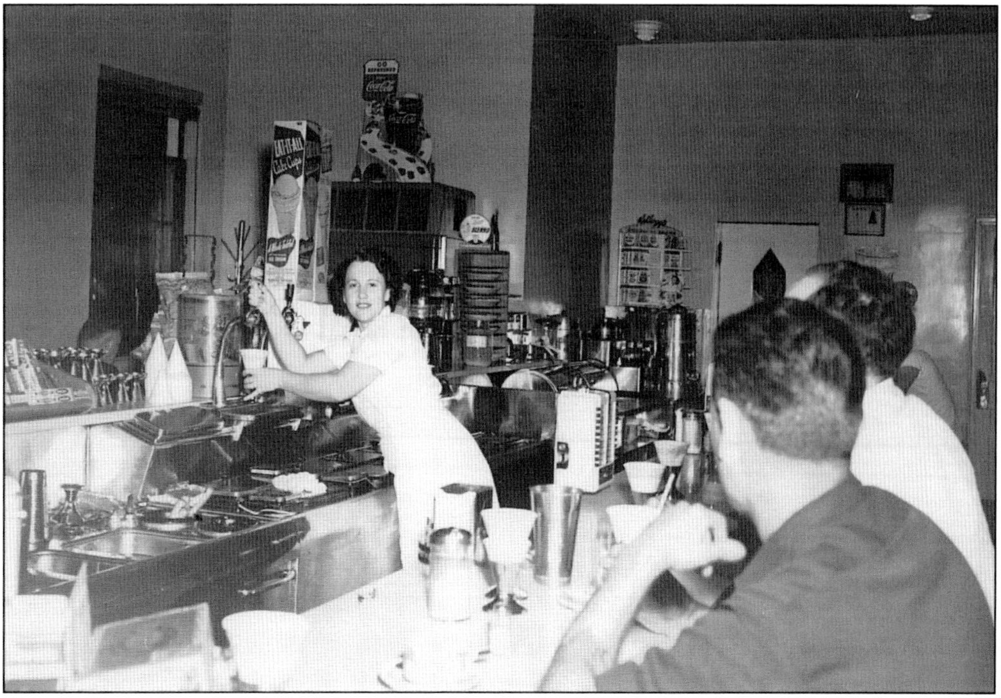

INSIDE THE BETSY ANN. A portion of this photograph was used as the cover for this book. The restaurant not only served up the favorite dishes of the day, but was also a good place to meet with friends or to conduct business in a casual environment. Many children's birthday parties were held at the diner. Along with Madeline "Maggie" Rembus (at the fountain), is Sonny Bedford (at the right) having his pie and coffee.

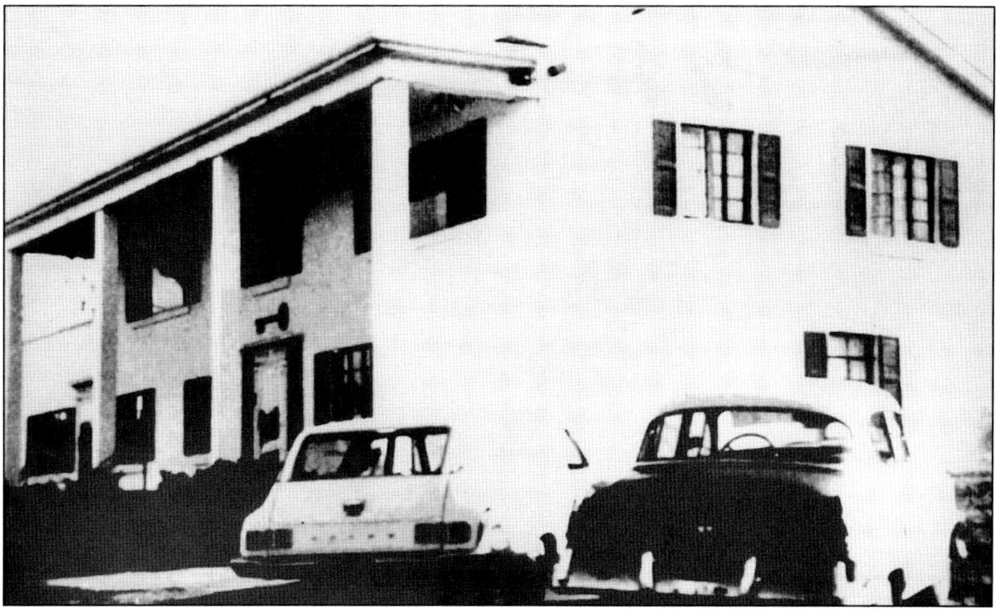

THE BRASS KEY. A popular destination near U.S. 27 and Highway 10, the Brass Key was not only a restaurant and bar, but also a family gathering spot in the summer, sporting a large public pool. It was demolished sometime in the 1970s or 1980s.

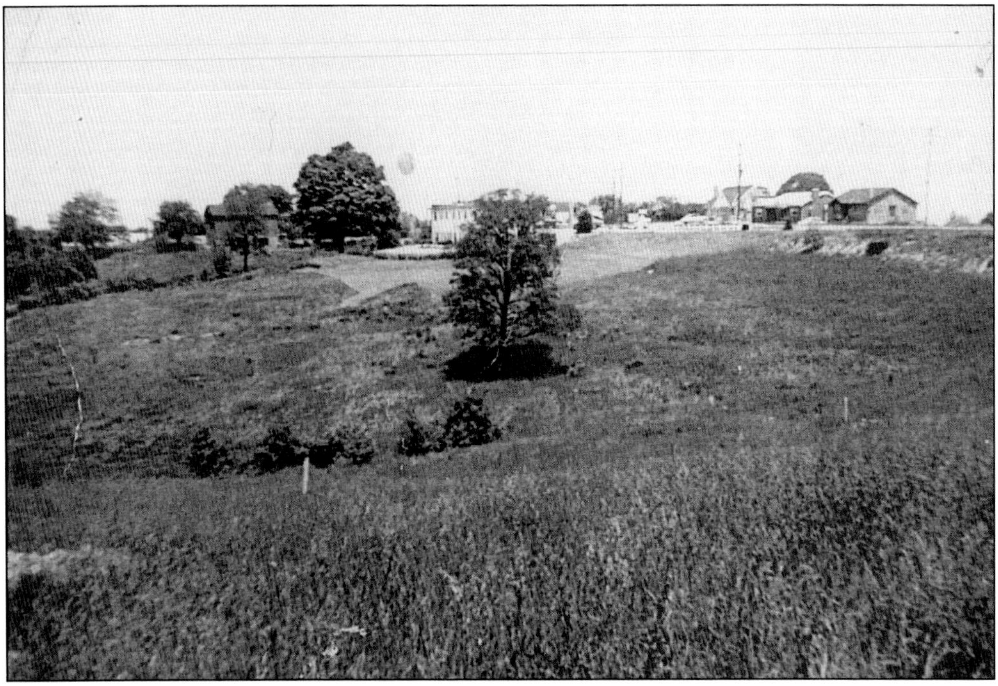

SPARE-TIME GRILL. Ask any resident about the Spare-Time Grill, and you will get a quick response. Time has changed many things in Alexandria but not this restaurant. Chester Alford operated an A&P grocery store in town and then decided to build this piece of Americana in 1958. The above photograph shows the lot before construction. Chester's son Roy later took over the business, and today his grandson Tony operates the restaurant, as pictured below.

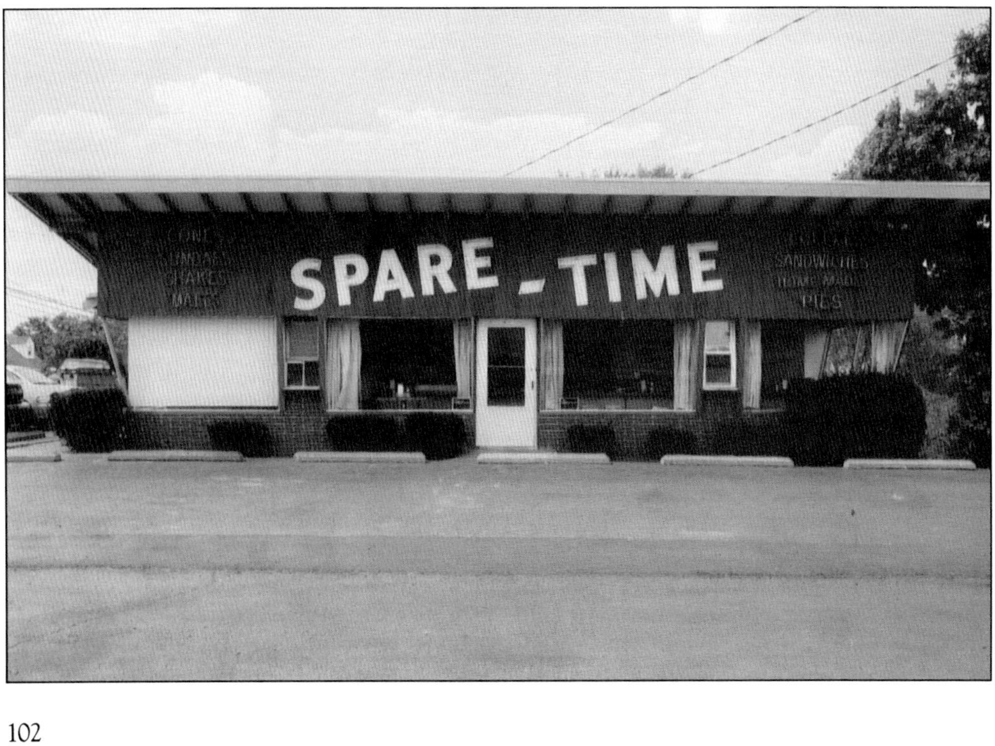

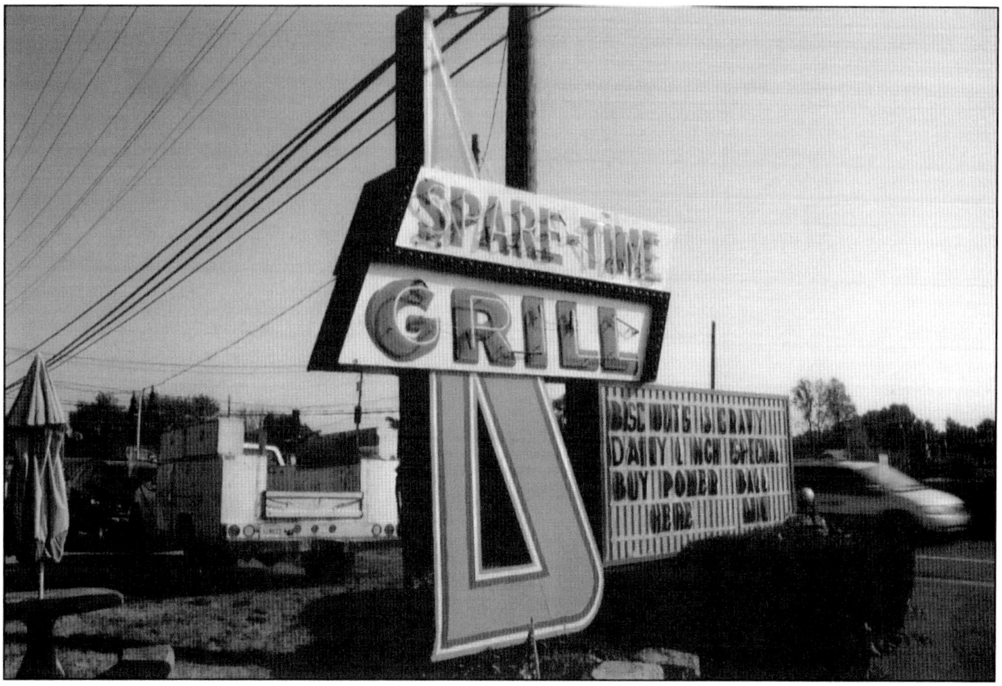

SPARE-TIME GRILL SIGN. Hollywood came knocking in 1988 when the movie *Fresh Horses* used the Spare-Time Grill (above) in one scene. For many years, workers from all around Alexandria have gathered at the grill (below) while on their way to work. All the latest news, rumors, and jokes are passed around the establishment. A good cup of coffee and an excellent breakfast plate are only part of the ritual.

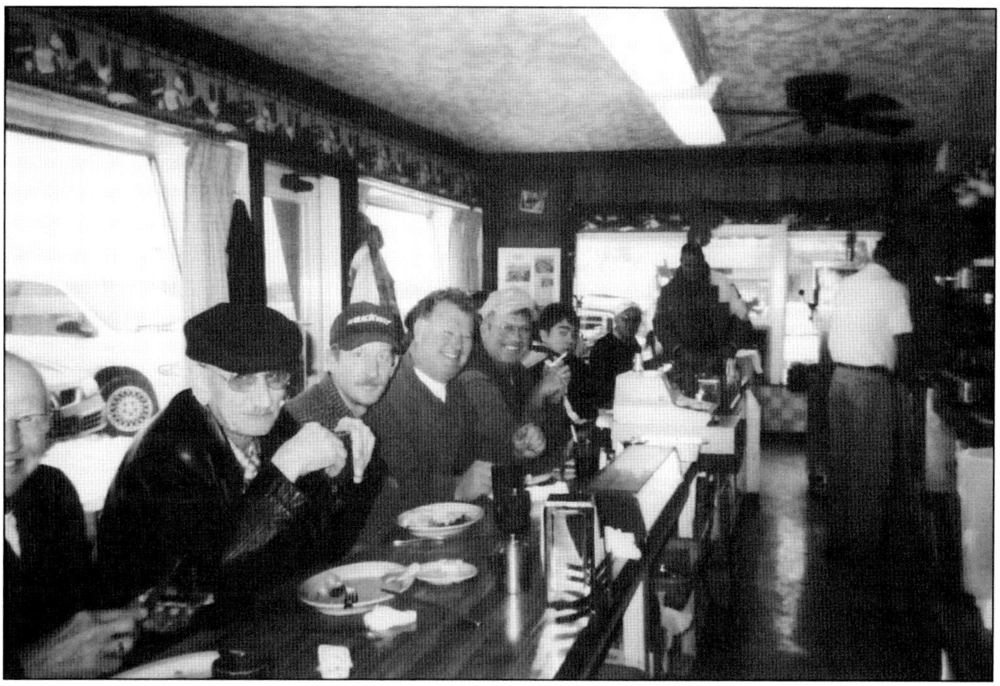

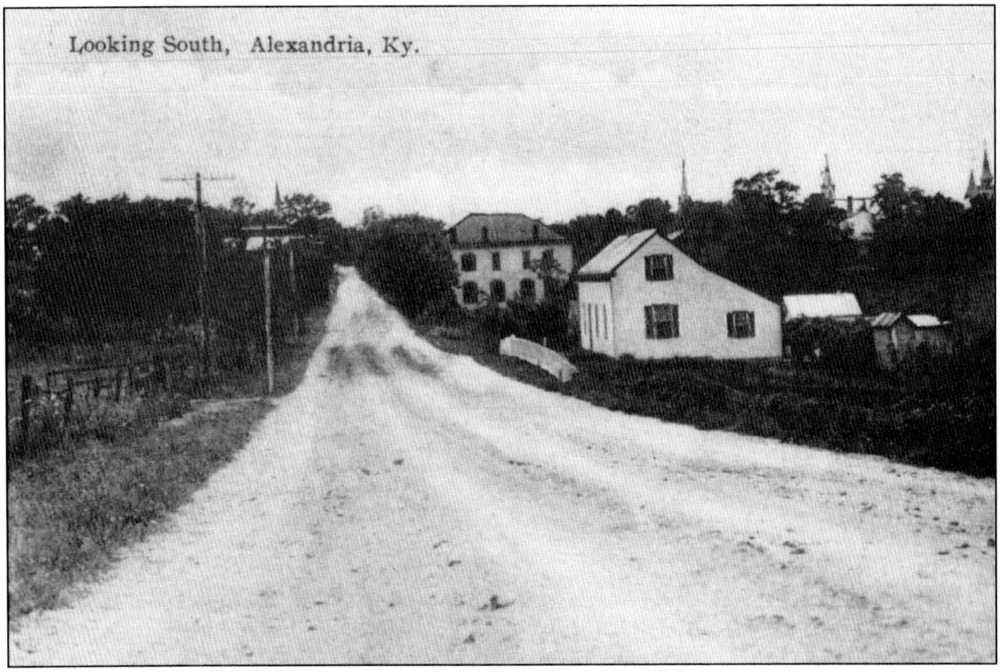

TRAVELING SOUTH ON WASHINGTON STREET. The large building on the right side of the road is the Meister Brewery. In the distance, the steeple of the Baptist church is visible on the left. To the right (from left to right) are the steeples of St. Mary Catholic Church, St. Paul's United Church of Christ, and the Methodist Episcopal church, all located on Jefferson Street.

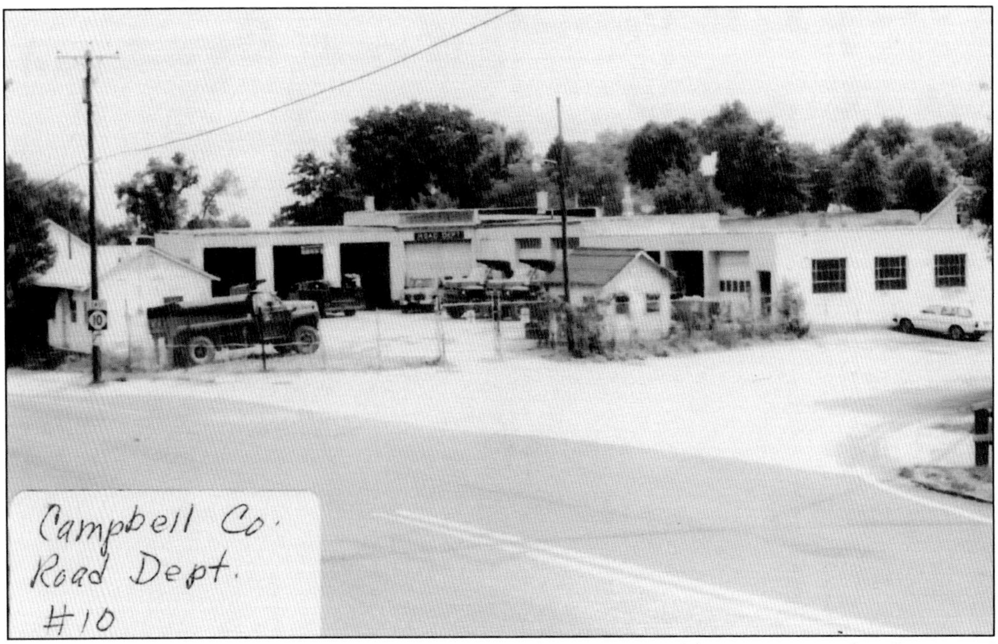

CAMPBELL COUNTY ROAD DEPARTMENT GARAGE. The county road department was headquartered in these concrete block buildings at the corner of Highway 10 and Persimmon Grove Pike. Driving by, motorists saw a road grader, dump trucks, piles of gravel, and mowing tractors. The department was later relocated with the A. J. Jolly Parks Maintenance Department on Race Track Road.

Six

LOCAL GOVERNMENT

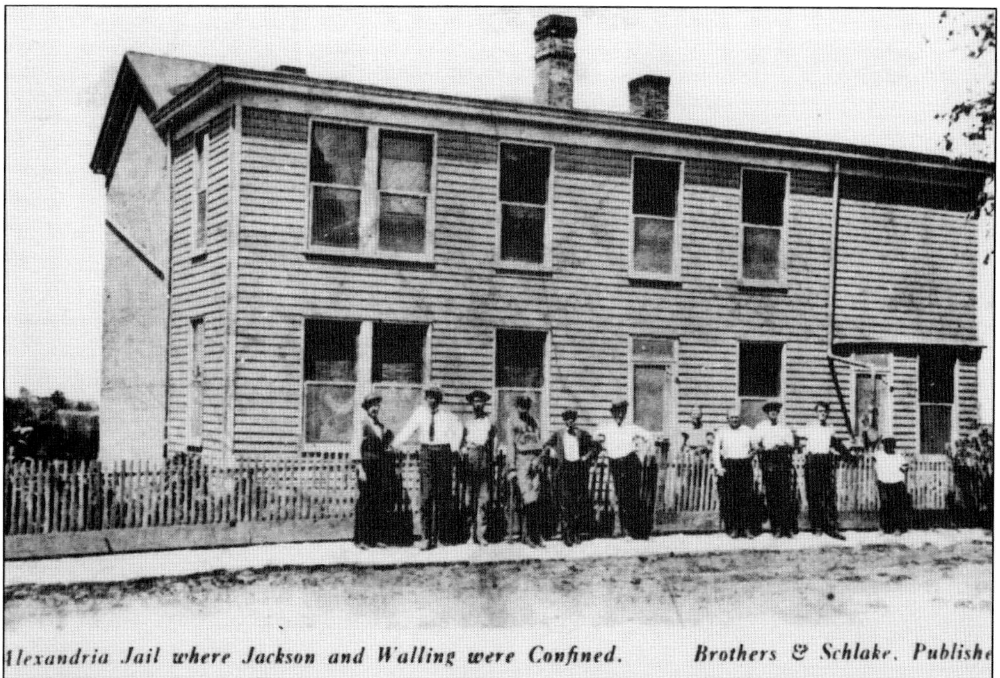

OLD JAIL. Built during the Civil War to house prisoners of war, the jail was located across Main Street from the courthouse. It was made of logs, and the walls were lined with sheet metal. At a later date, a brick exterior was added and the sheet metal was removed. A frame addition was built onto the front of the building to house the jailer and his family.

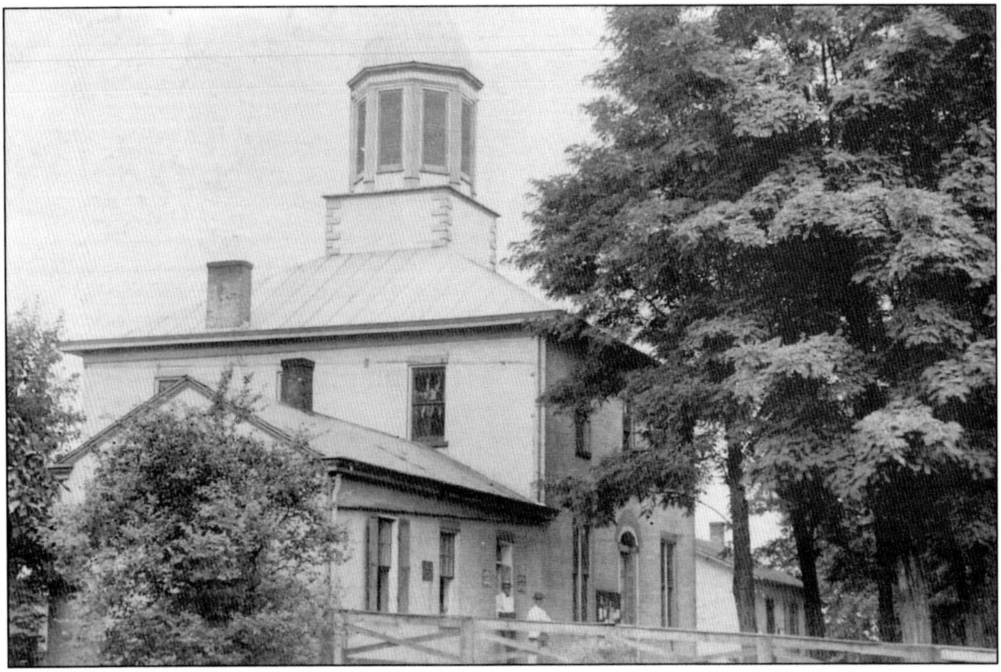

CAMPBELL COUNTY COURTHOUSE, ALEXANDRIA. The courthouse in Alexandria is situated in the heart of the old town. Beginning in 1840 and finishing two years later, brick mason and Baptist preacher Rev. James M. Jolly built the square, two-story structure. Bricks were made by hand at the nearby Spilman brick kiln. A one-floor clerk's office was housed on the left side of the original building. Pictured above, a bell tower sits atop the building, which bears no front porch or pillars. In the 1920s, a jail (pictured below) was erected to the right of the structure. The two-story brick building had a cell block on the second floor and a jailer's apartment on the first floor, both of which were closed in the 1970s.

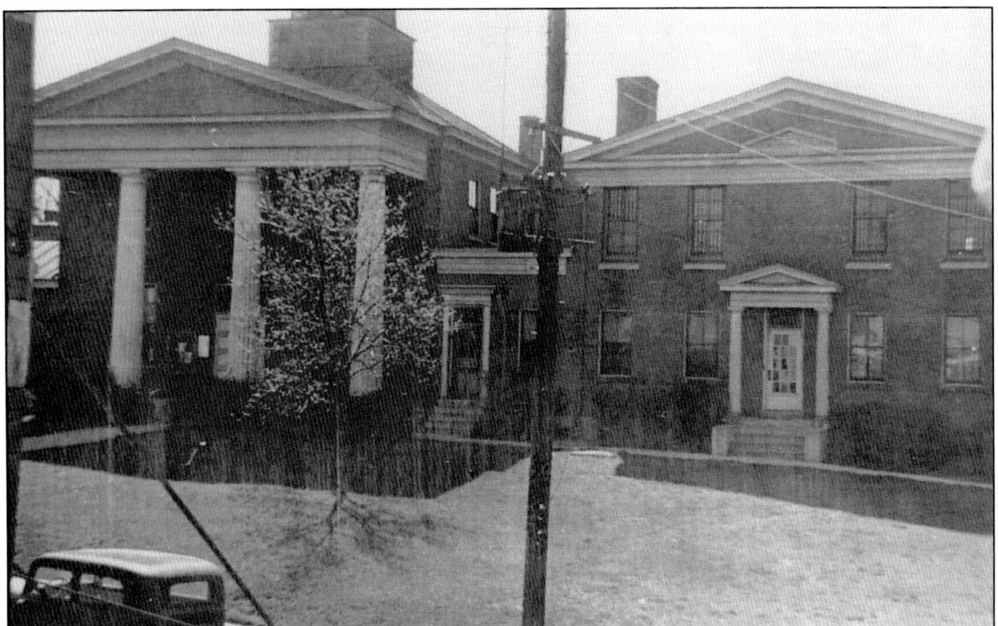

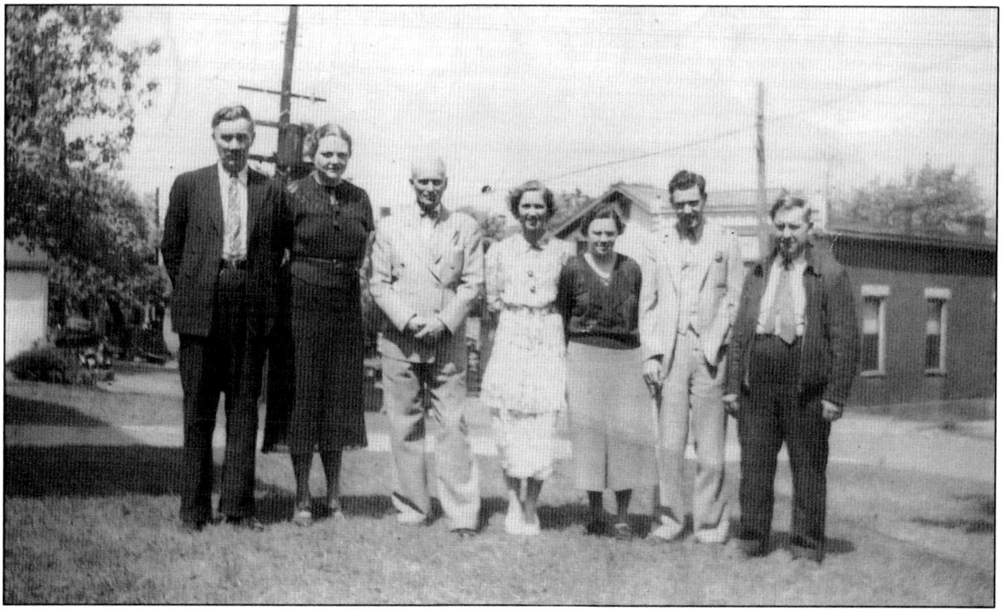

Alexandria Courthouse Personnel. In addition to the county clerk's office, the Alexandria Courthouse was also home to several other government agencies. Pictured here from left to right are Verner Reiley of the clerk's office, home demonstration agent Ruth Hunter, county auditor Charles Applegate, county agents' secretary Wilma Flora, county agents' secretary Dorothy Horosett, Carol Flora of the agriculture office, and county extension agent Sam Porter.

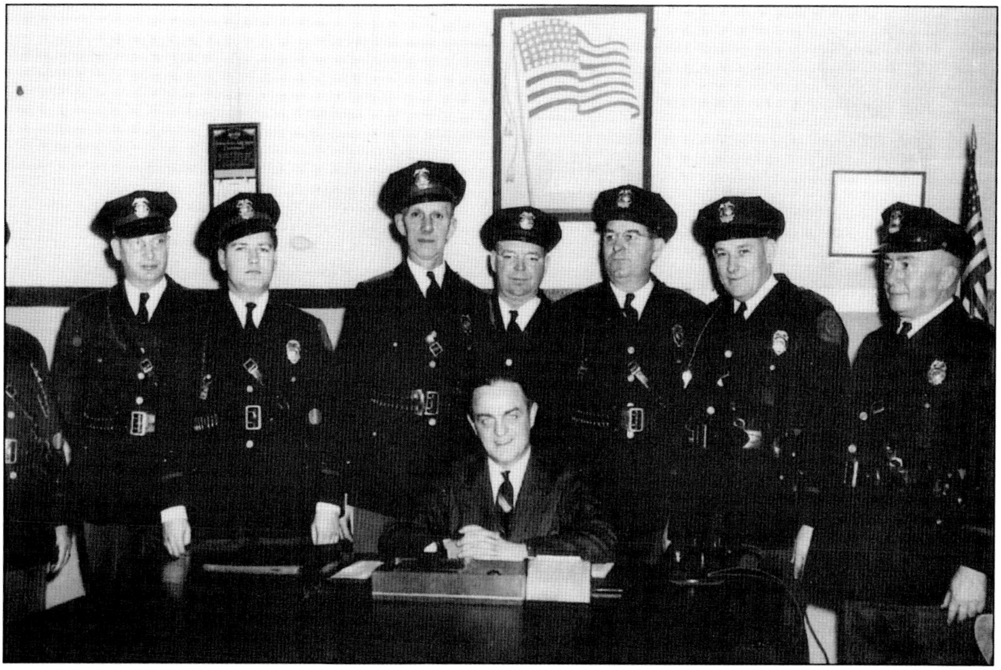

Campbell County Police Department, 1940s. Seated at the desk is county judge Odis W. Bertelsman. Shown with him, from left to right, are George Benz (partially hidden), Oscar Wells, Richard Gegan, police chief Len Plummer, Jacob Racke, Harry Stuart, Robert Rickels, and Gus Utendorfer. The police department had an office in the Alexandria Courthouse.

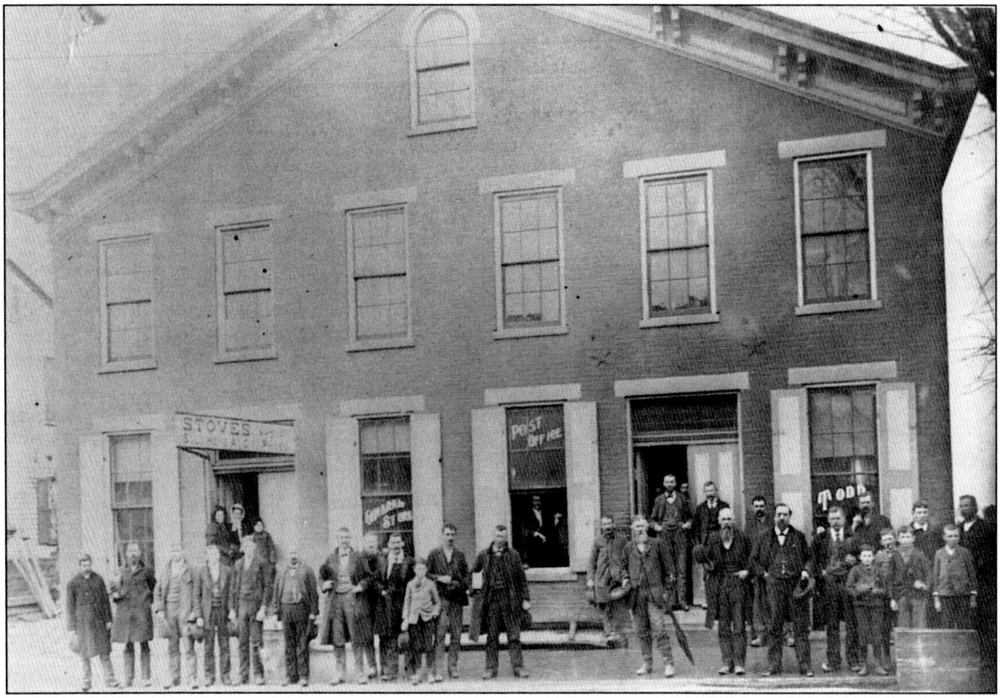

ALEXANDRIA POST OFFICE AND MAIL WAGON. This early post office (above), with its name on the window, was located in the same building as that shown on page 82. At the time, the structure also housed Todd and Boesch, written on the last window to the right. Long before e-mail, all mail was distributed by hand. One of the earliest ways to deliver mail was on horseback. As the population grew, the cart or wagon came into use, as pictured below. Robert Wheeler (below) delivers mail on Washington Street. Once cars and trucks became more affordable, carriers used their own automobiles to make their appointed rounds.

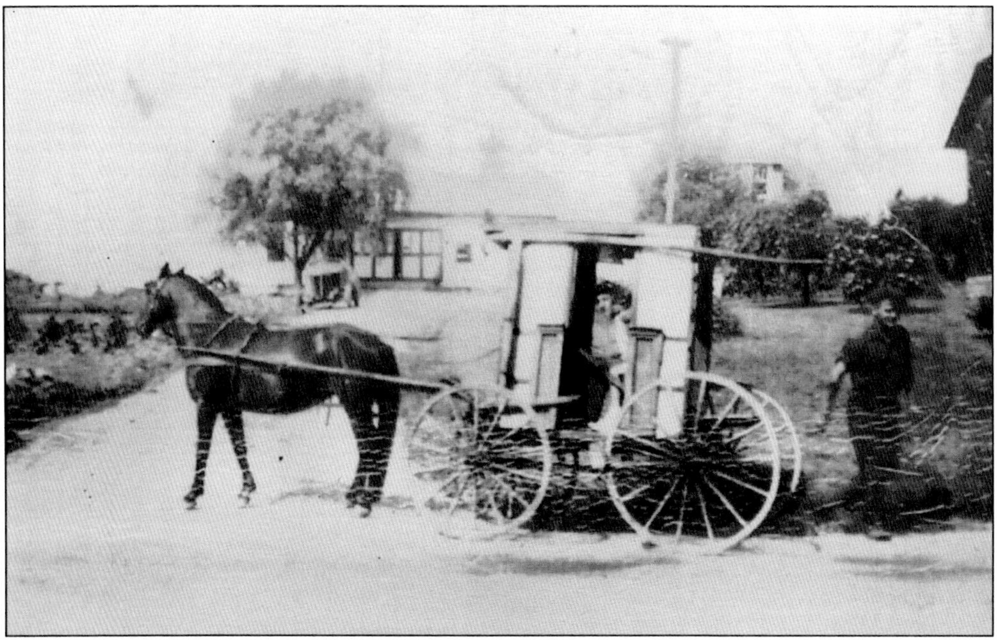

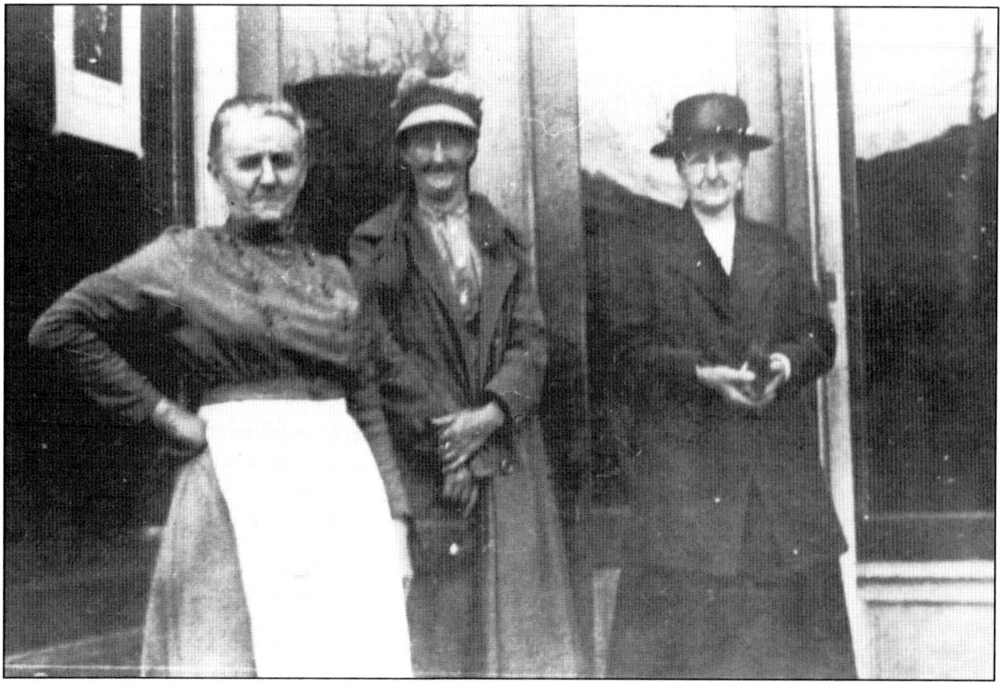

POST OFFICE PERSONNEL. With the passing of time, many things change—a sentiment especially true of the postal service. In the above photograph, postmistress ? Neal (left), Lucy Wright (center), and Bonnie Charles stand in front of the second post office in Alexandria. Over the years, Alexandria has had five different post offices in the town. The photograph below shows the fourth, located on Washington Street next to the Alexandria Funeral Home. Constructed in 1960, it operated until January 20, 1995. The dedication plaque now hangs in the Campbell County Historical and Genealogical Society's museum. Cassons Realty currently occupies the building. The fifth Alexandria Post Office is part of the Alexandria Village Green Shopping Center.

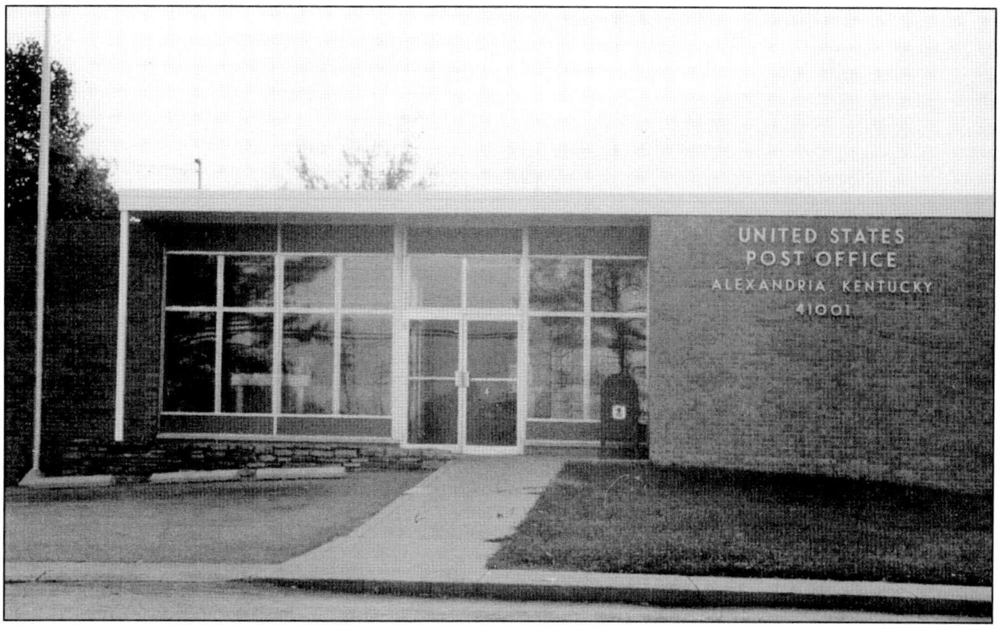

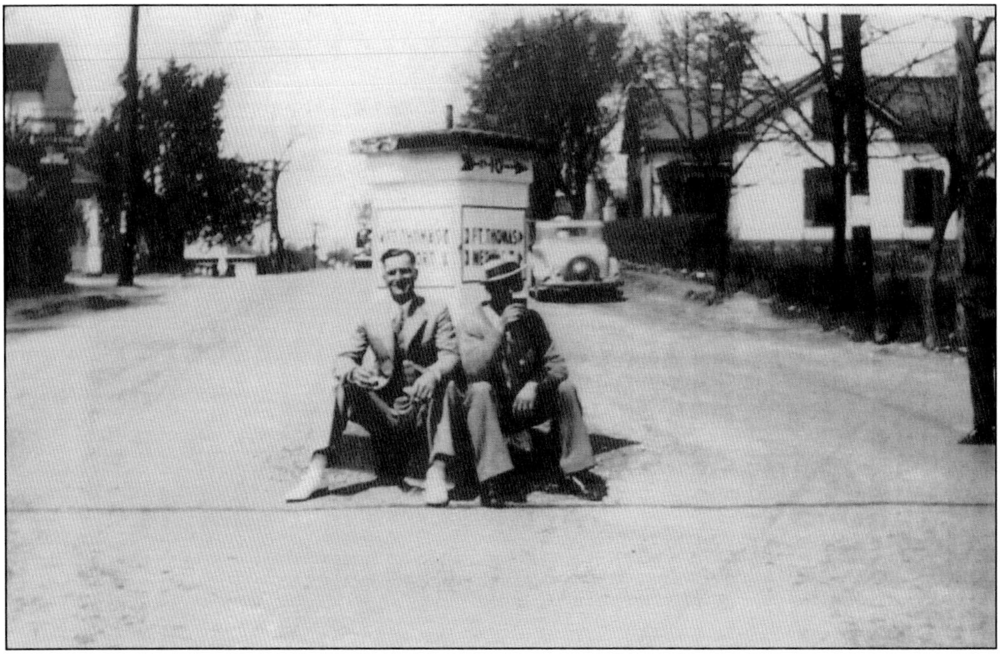

What a Parade! These unidentified gentlemen sit on the monument once located at the intersection of Main and Washington Streets. A stop sign was plastered to the reverse side. The men appear to be waiting for the homecoming parade to round the corner. The one on the right seems to have foam on his iced tea.

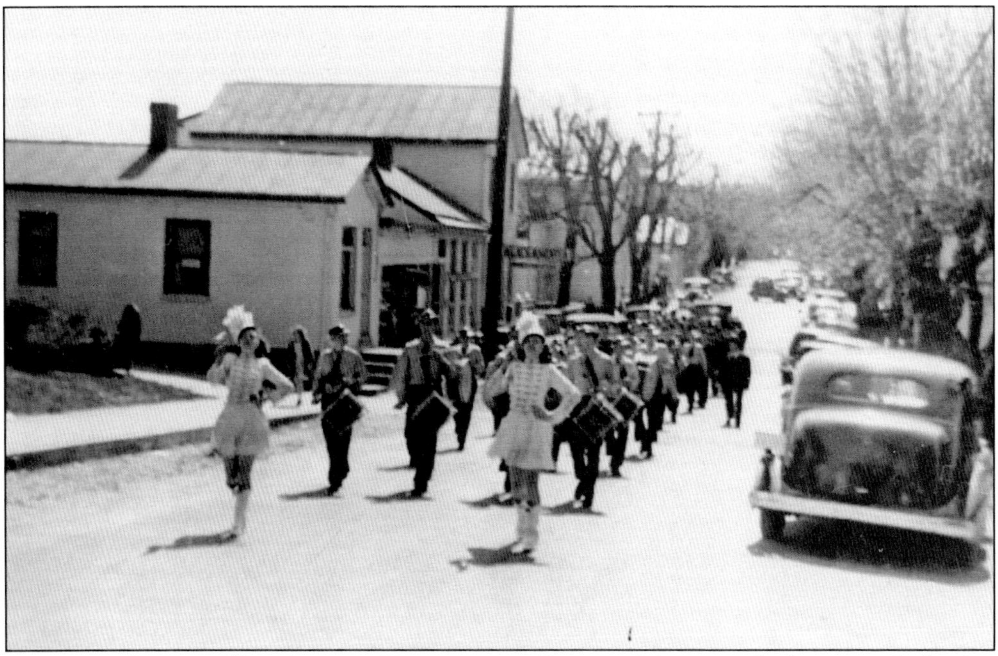

Campbell County High School Homecoming Parade. Majorettes high step in the lead as the band marches down Main Street in front of the courthouse during the late 1940s. In the left background are many of the old business establishments once lining Main Street. The tallest structure is the old post office. None of these buildings remain.

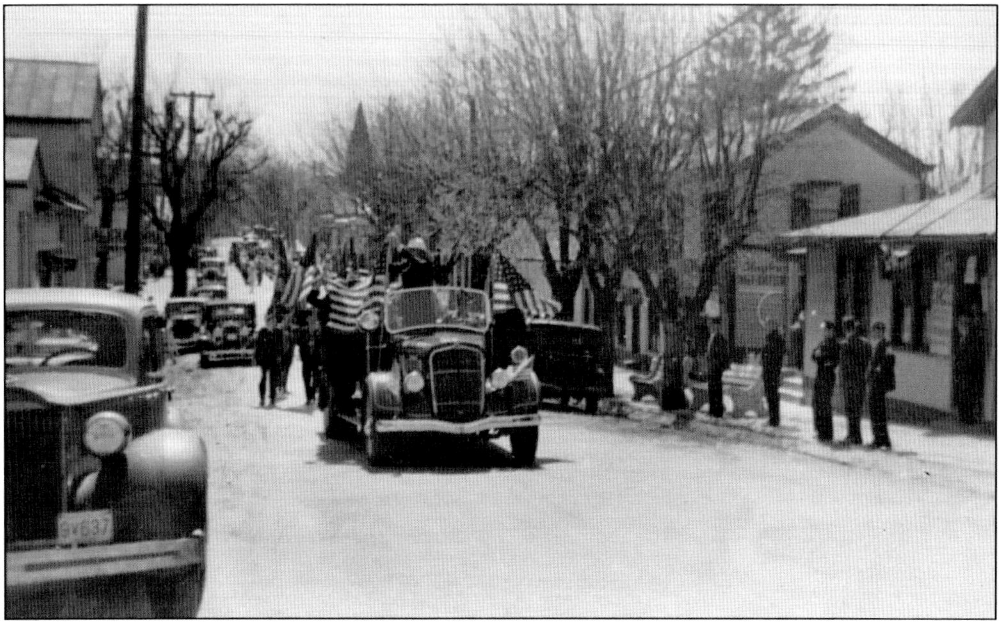

PARADE DOWN MAIN STREET, *c.* 1940. The Alexandria Volunteer Fire Department shows off its new truck in the homecoming parade. The three gentlemen to the right are standing in front of Pete Neiser's Café, which was adjacent to the bank. The benches along the tree-lined sidewalk suggest a more relaxed period in the history of the town.

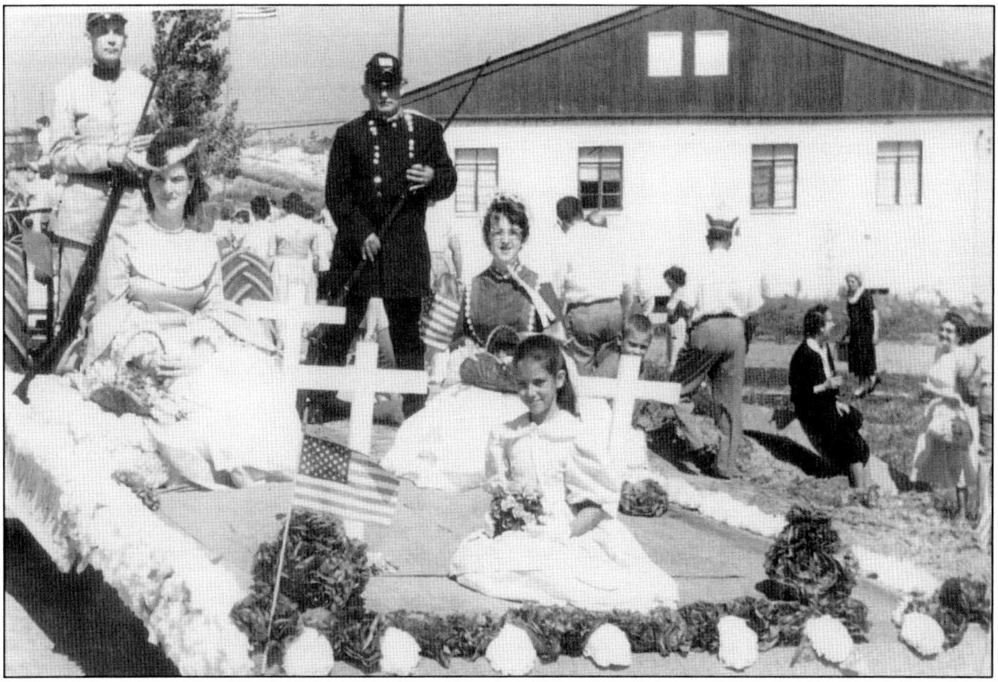

PARADE FLOAT, 1960S. VFW No. 3205 in Alexandria built this float for the annual Memorial Day Parade. Presented on the float, from left to right, are (first row) Pam Neiser (girl); (second row) Jean Neiser (left) and Sue White; (third row) Bob Steelman (Confederate soldier) and Jack Ruff (Yankee soldier). This photograph was taken on U.S. 27 near Spilman Drive.

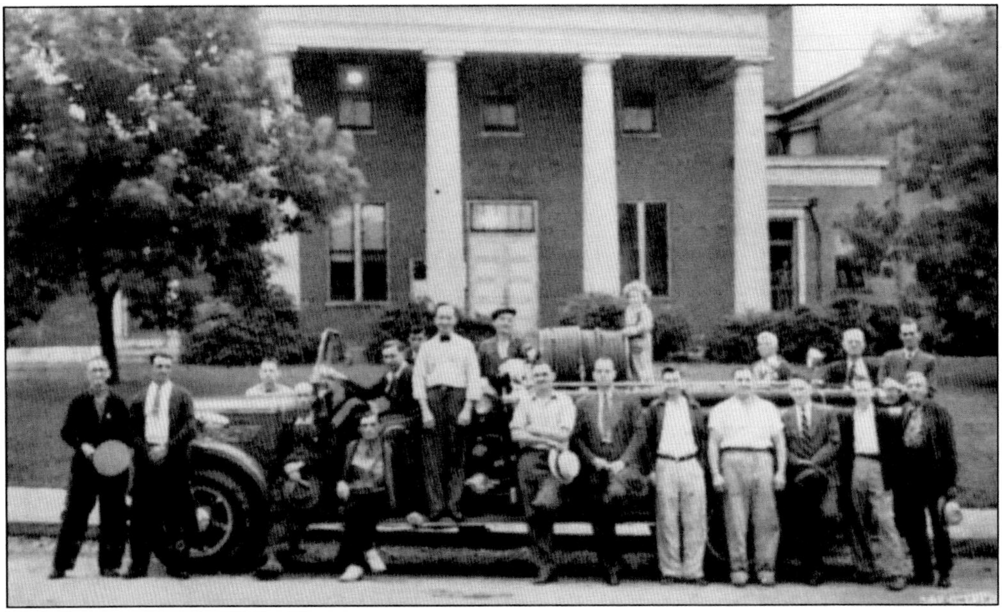

ALEXANDRIA VOLUNTEER FIRE DEPARTMENT, 1941. Volunteer firemen pose with their truck in front of the Campbell County Courthouse. Seen from left to right are (first row) Viles Rulon, George Neiser, assistant chief Thomas Schmidt, William Ampfer, chief Karl Ziegler (at the wheel), Pete Neiser, Harry McGuire, C. E. Lautewasser, Myron Hess, Bud Seibert, Grant Kees, Jack Kees, and Otto Neal; (second row) Emery Gosney, Roy Shaw, Joe Hugglow, county jailer Charles W. Kemper, county commissioner Mont D. Truesdell, W. E. Ziegler, and Douglas Gosney (standing by the hose reel).

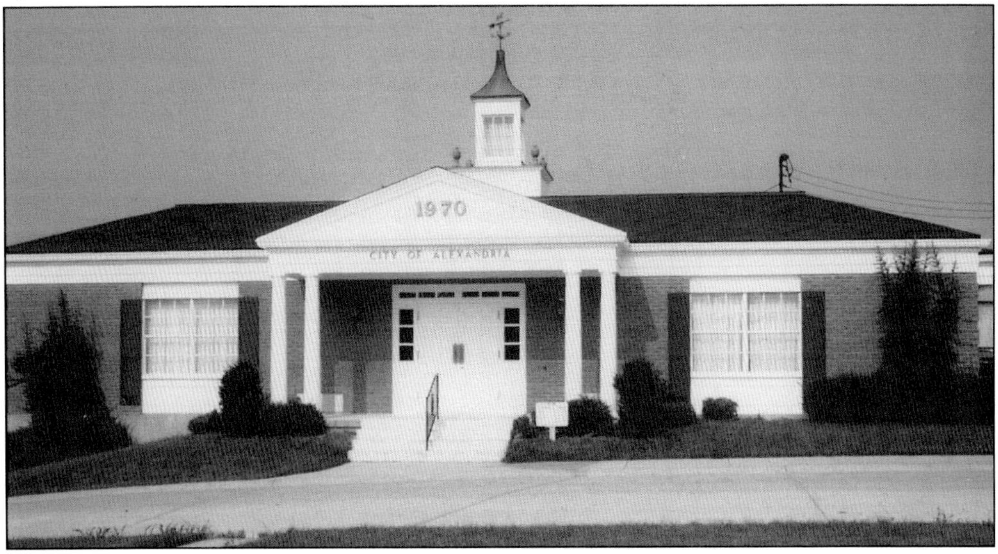

ALEXANDRIA CITY BUILDING, 1970. After experiencing a large growth period, the city built this redbrick building at the corner of Kentucky Highway 10 and Gilbert Ridge Road just across the street from the Alexandria Cemetery, where city's administration offices and police department were located. The city vacated the building and moved its operations to 8236 West Main Street in Alexandria on February 20, 2007. Today the Campbell County Clerks Office and the County License Bureau for southern Campbell County are located in the building..

Seven

ALEXANDRIA FAIR

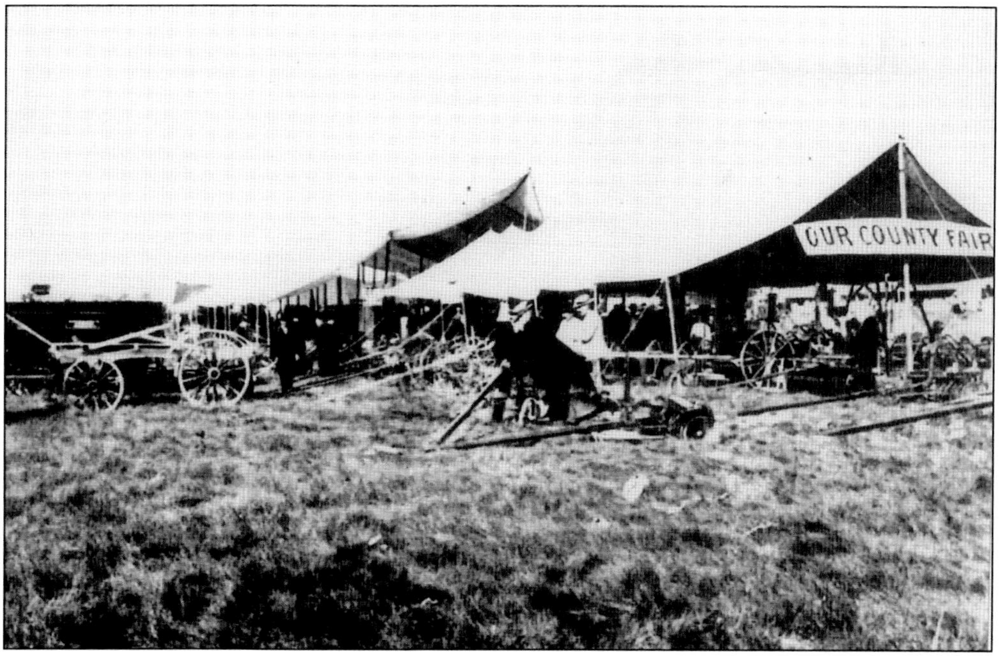

EARLY FAIR. This undated photograph reveals the beginnings of the Alexandria Fair. Once the Agricultural Society of Campbell County was formed in 1856, some 10 acres of land were purchased from John Stevens for $500, and 25,000 feet of hemlock lumber were used to build a 7-foot-tall fence around the fairgrounds. Workers constructed 75 stalls, along with the $1,000 amphitheater.

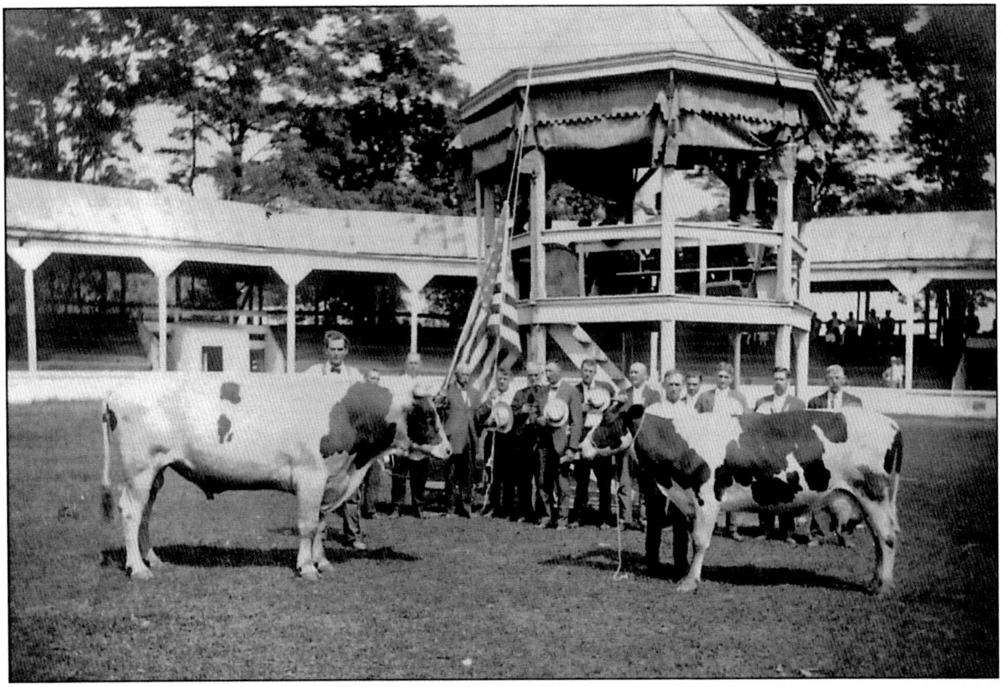

ALEXANDRIA FAIR, c. 1890. The fair was organized at the Alexandria Courthouse on June 7, 1856, and the first fair was held from October 14 to 16 of that year. The original bandstand, shown here, was used until the early 1920s, at which time it was moved to the grandstand. In 1972, the entire grandstand was destroyed by fire. In 1973, new concrete bleachers were erected and an oval-shaped ring was created to show horses and livestock.

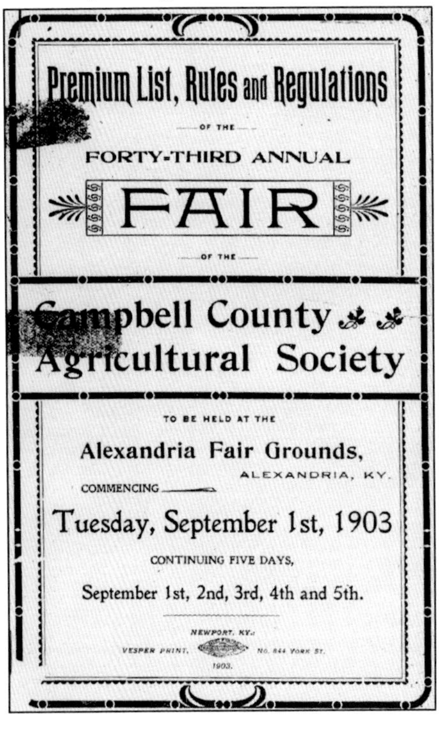

Premium List, Rules and Regulations

OF THE

FORTY-THIRD ANNUAL

FAIR

OF THE

Campbell County Agricultural Society

TO BE HELD AT THE

Alexandria Fair Grounds,

ALEXANDRIA, KY.

COMMENCING

Tuesday, September 1st, 1903

CONTINUING FIVE DAYS,

September 1st, 2nd, 3rd, 4th and 5th.

NEWPORT, KY.

VESPER PRINT. No. 844 YORK ST.

1903.

FAIR PROGRAM, 1903. The 43rd annual fair program details the rules and regulations for contestants entering the various competitions. Seemingly lost arts such as silk embroidery on various types of fabric, handmade Battenburg lace, needle- and fancywork, and willow or split baskets were contests open to all. Practical items like brooms, calico dresses and sunbonnets, preserves, jellies and canned fruits, and pickles were also part of the competition.

COMMEMORATIVE PROGRAM, 2006. Within this booklet's pages is a glimpse of the Alexandria Fair over its 150-year history. In addition to the horse and other animal competitions, Floral Hall is shown exhibiting gardening of all types. Today the fair would not be complete without the beauty pageant to determine Miss Alexandria Fair, baby contests, and mother and daughter look-a-like contests.

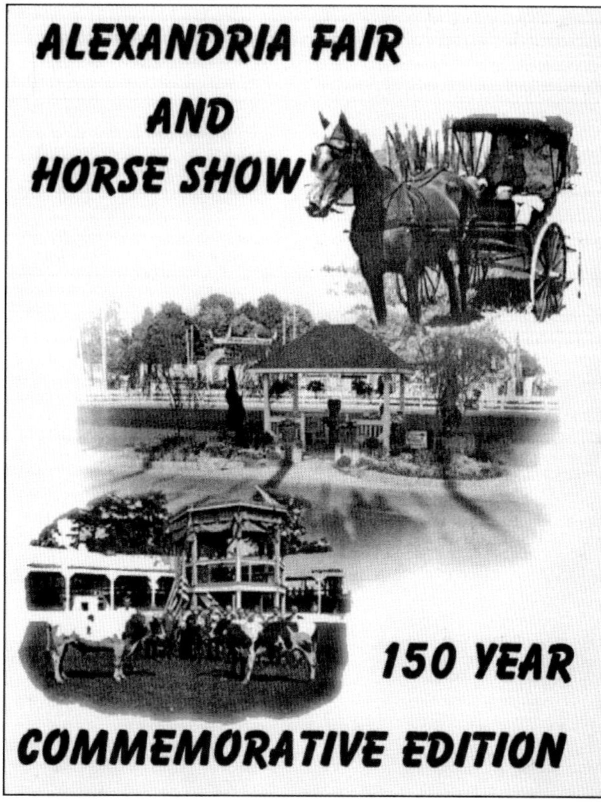

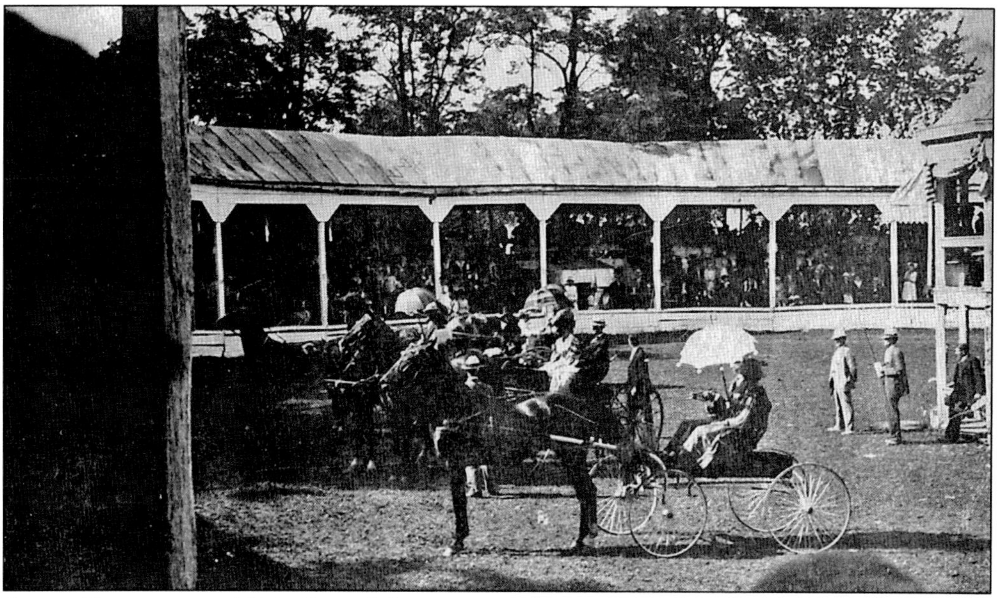

FANCY TURNOUT, c. 1890. One of the most popular events at the Alexandria Fair and Horse Show was the Fancy Turnout. Families entered the ring with their best-looking horse pulling a finely detailed buggy. The ladies and gentlemen wore their finest clothes and conducted themselves with great decorum in hopes of taking home the blue ribbon and bragging rights. These people are pictured in the ring of the original grandstand.

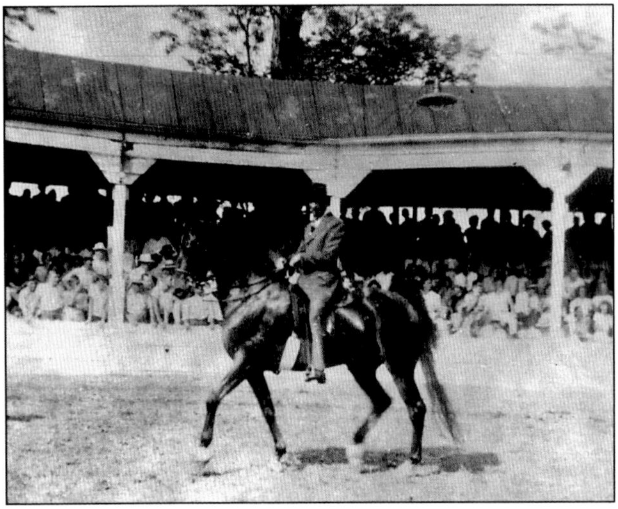

MASTER GENIUS, 1940S. Max Beederman of North Middletown, Kentucky, owned Master Genius, a five-gaited American Saddlebred champion, ridden here by Pete Deatley. The breed is a cross between its ancestor, the Narragansett Pacer, and the Thoroughbred. It inherited the ability to learn lateral gaits; the slow gait, which is the simultaneous movement of two legs on the same side, with the hind foot hitting the ground before the front foot; and the rack, with each foot hitting the ground separately in a four-beat cadence.

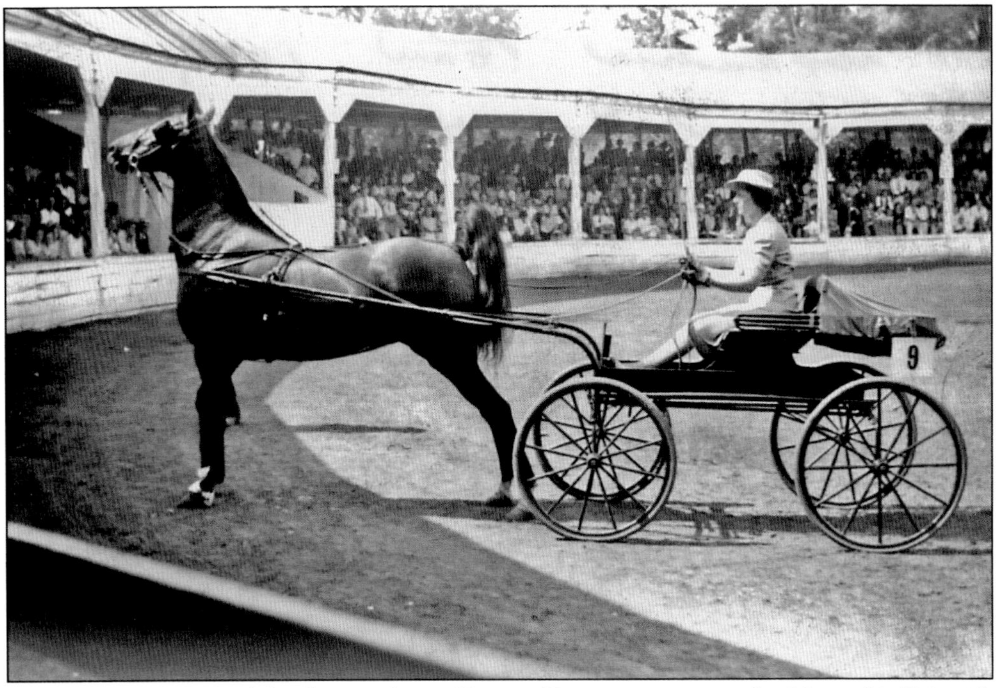

FRANCES TRUE, 1944. A fine harness horse, Frances True participates in the Alexandria Fair with Frances Gossett at the reins. The fair draws entries from all over Kentucky, as well as adjoining states, in competition for the first-place blue ribbon. Additional ribbon colors are second place, red; third place, yellow; fourth place, white; fifth place, pink; sixth place, green; seventh place, purple; eighth place, brown; ninth place, gray; and tenth place, light blue.

LEAD PONY, 1940S. This somewhat blurry photograph shows a proud young man mounted on his lead pony. The class is a crowd pleaser, as the patrons ooh and aah over the youngsters in their fine dress and the pretty ponies.

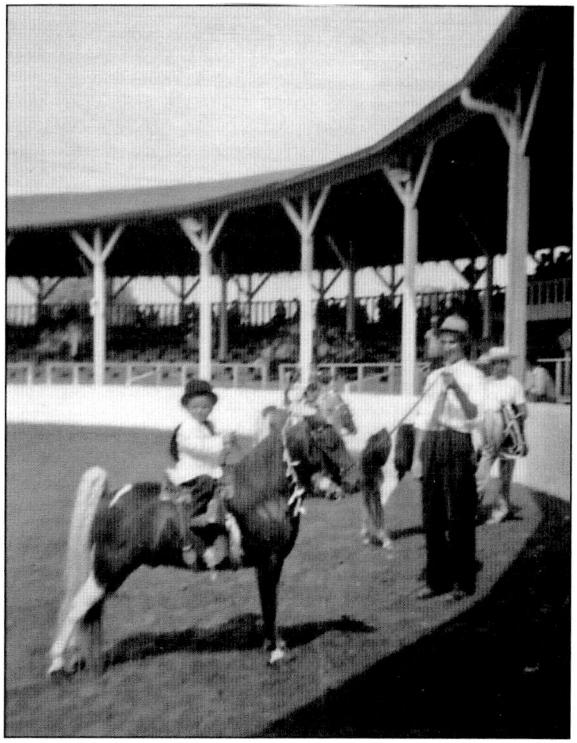

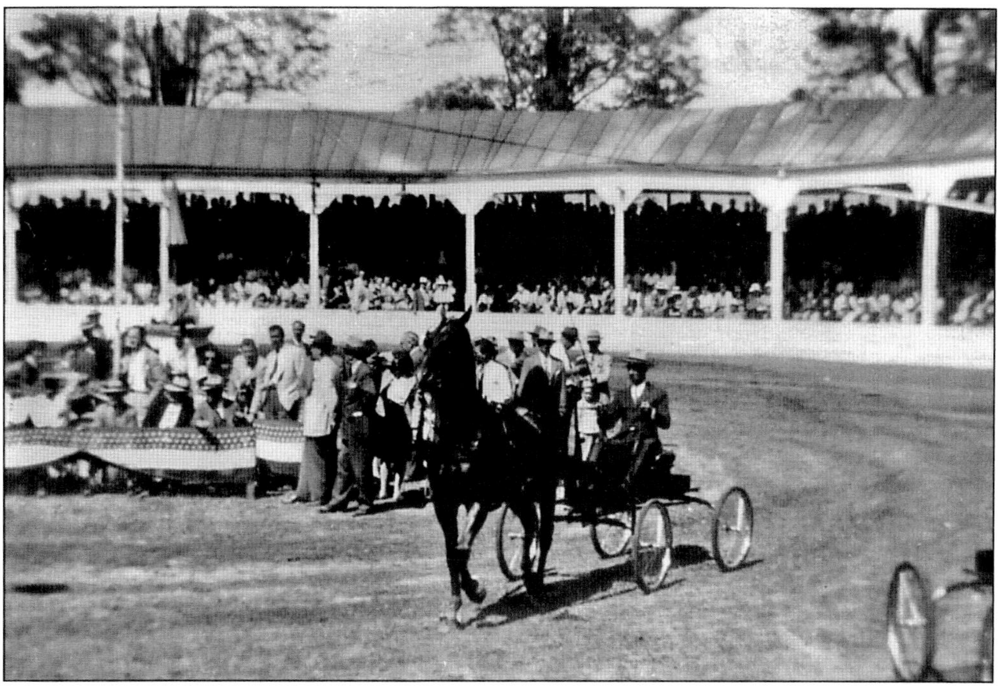

FINE HARNESS CLASS, 1940S. Here Pete Deatley competes in the Fine Harness Class. In this class of competition, the horse, hitched to a light, four-wheeled buggy, is required to perform a walk, park trot, slow trot, and flashy trot with as much animation as possible. The center ring appears to be more crowded than usual, and the bunting has a patriotic flare.

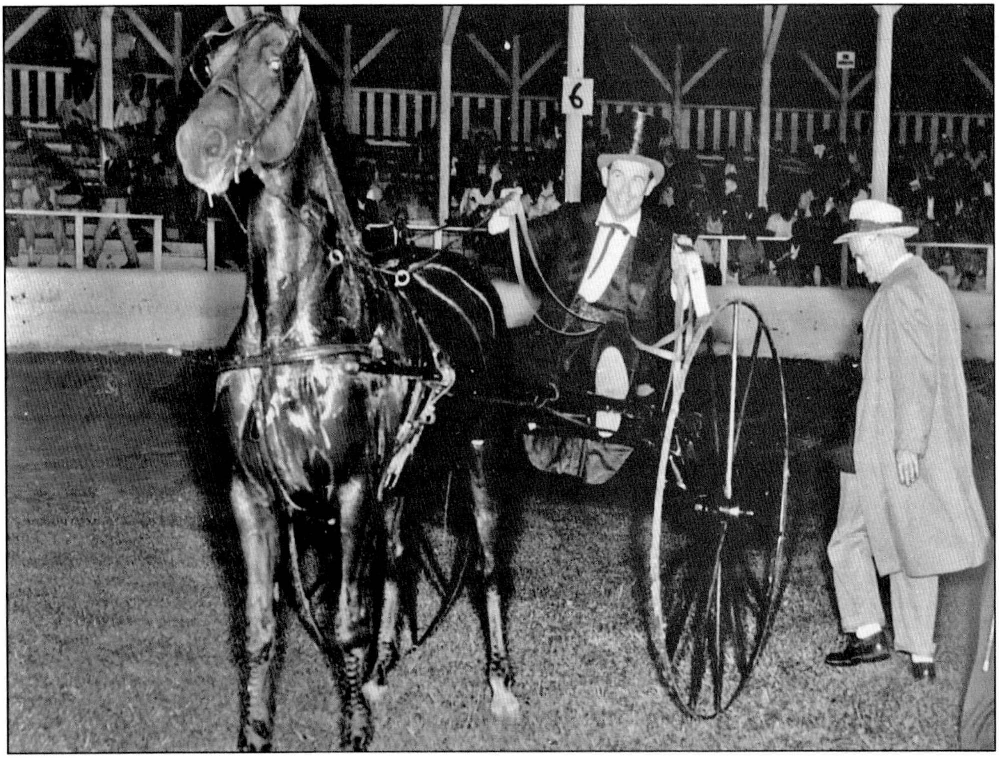

MR. TWEED AND KING OF THE BLUEGRASS. Standardbred Mr. Tweed (above) battles in the Road Horse Class at the 1956 Alexandria Fair with Edwin Sims of Harrodsburg, Kentucky, at the reins. In this class, the horse, carriage, and driver are judged for suitable turnout and neatness. Judge Sol Youtsey looks over the entry. King of the Bluegrass (below), also a Standardbred, competes in the Pleasure Class, in which the entry is judged on its walk, two speeds of trot, and manners. Jack Thatcher handles the reins while Billy Faye Redmond rides in the period buggy.

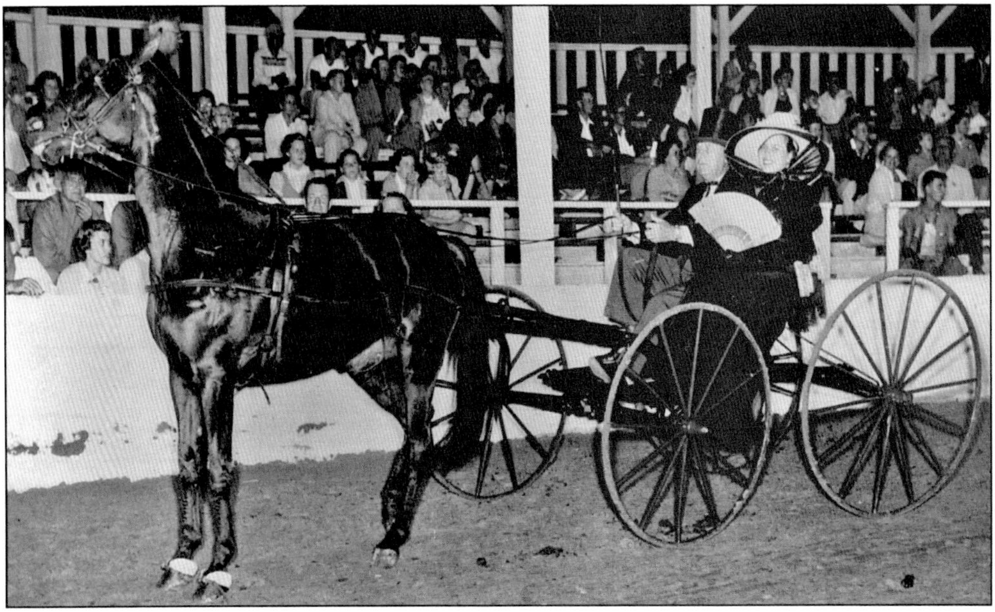

BOURBON. A young Jack Thatcher with the winning ribbon on his sleeve sits on Bourbon, a five-gaited American Saddlebred. Bourbon is a fine example of this beautiful breed. Notice its flashy look: long, straight legs with broad, flat bones, sharply defined tendons, and sloping pasterns for high stepping and jumping. This breed is strong enough for farm work and fast enough for match races.

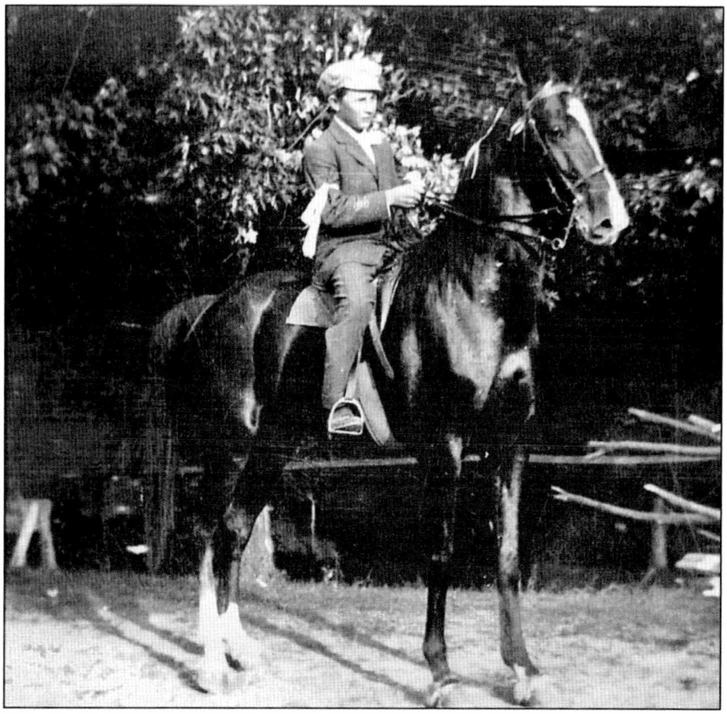

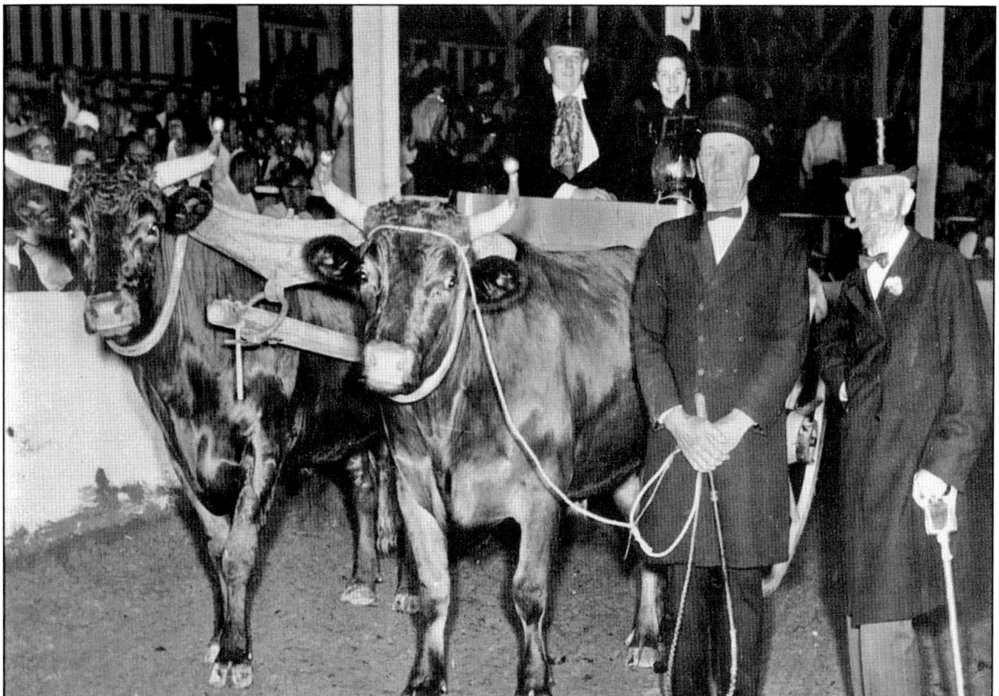

CELEBRATING 100 YEARS. Frank Brennan Jr. (left) of Augusta, Kentucky, stands with John Thatcher while holding rein on a team of oxen. In the wagon are Frank Brennan III and Shirley Dickens of Mentor, Kentucky. The Agricultural Society of Campbell County was organized in 1856 and approved by a special act of the Kentucky legislature.

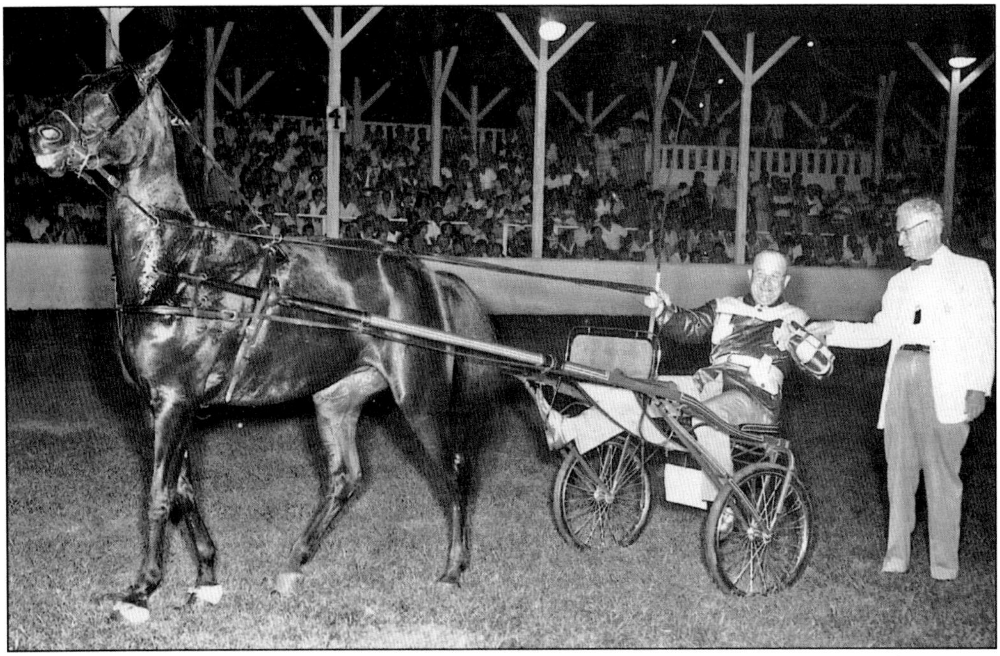

LITTLE MISS GIANT KILLER. Sol Youtsey (right), president of the Alexandria Fair Board, presents Jack Thatcher with an award. A lover of horses, Jack was a major exhibitor every year at the fair. Little Miss Giant Killer was also the Kentucky State Fair Champion and a Chicago International Horse Show Champion. She ran the Red Mile in Lexington, Kentucky, which is currently the second oldest harness track in the world.

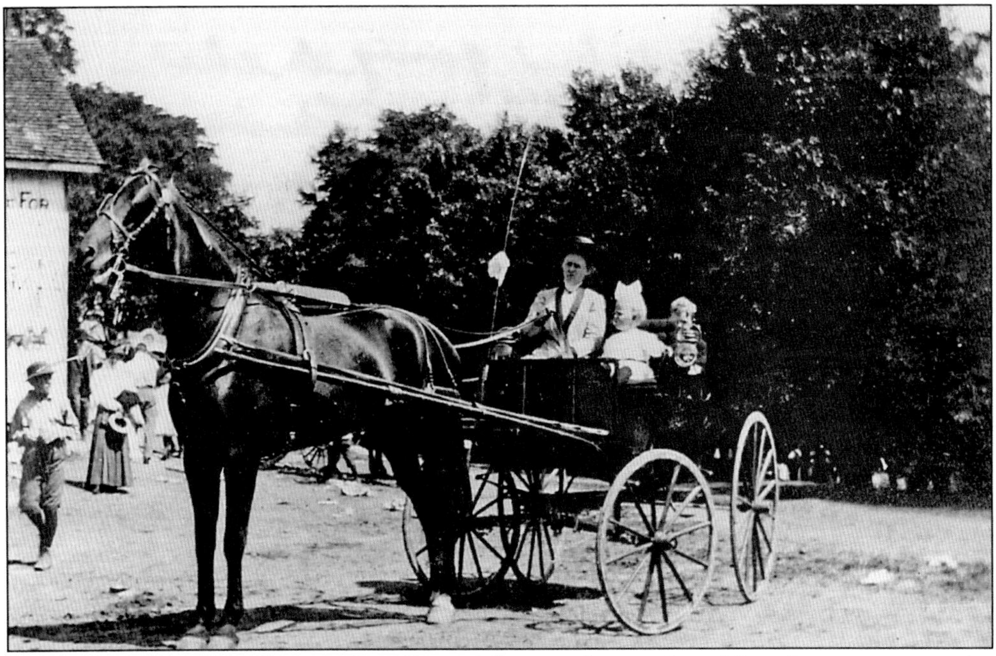

GOING TO THE FAIR. Driving her favorite harness horse, Bess Thatcher transports the children from the farm. The horses and buggies were put in the shade while families enjoyed the fair festivities.

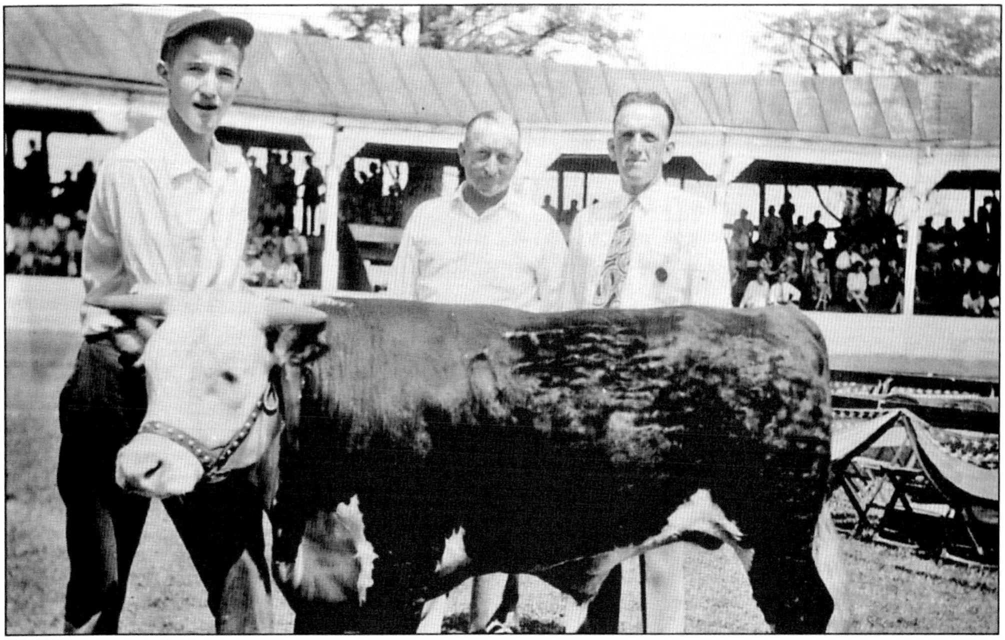

AL SCHNEIDER JR. Al Jr. (left) displays his winning Hereford entry as his proud father (center) looks on. The gentleman on the right is W. C. Dickens. The Hereford breed was founded more than two centuries ago in Hereford, Herefordshire, England, and was introduced to this country in 1817. Although it has undergone some modifications, it still remains a premier beef cattle breed.

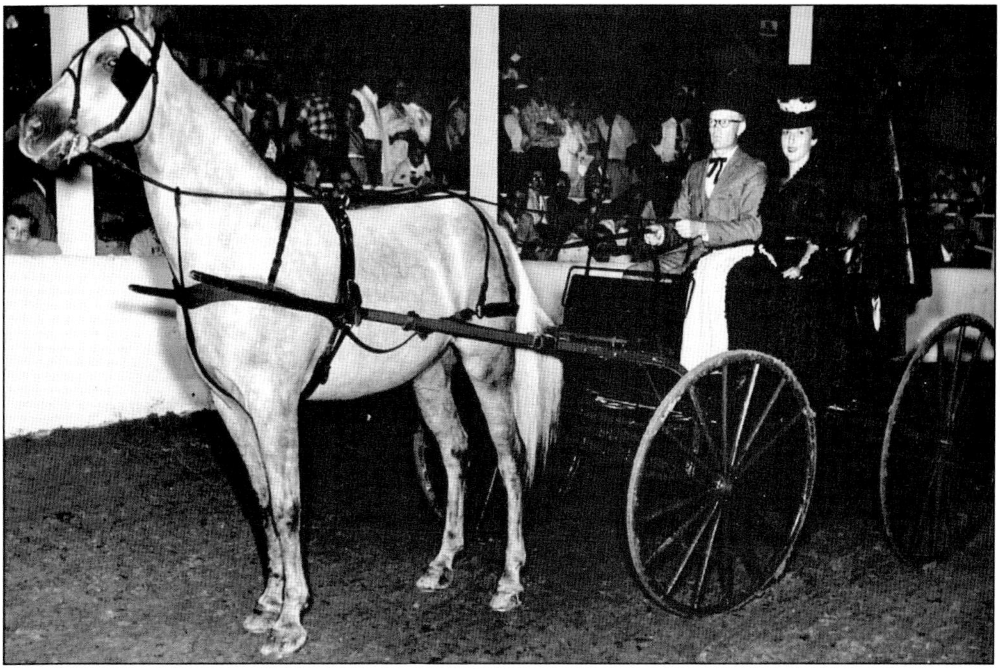

LIGHT HARNESS HORSE, 1956. The use of the harness varies greatly depending on the type of work that is at hand. For light work such as competing in a horse show, the harness, sometimes called horse tack, consists of only a breast collar. Although the harness looks light, it is strong enough to pull any passenger vehicle such as a carriage or buggy.

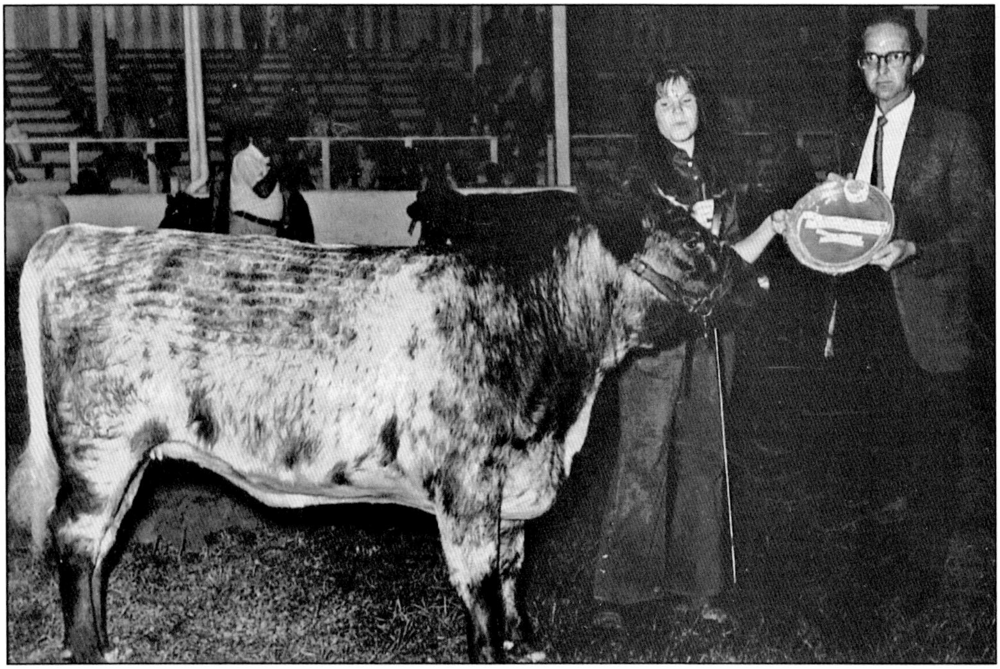

Award Presentation, 1970. Brenda Prim receives a trophy from Campbell County extension agent Bob Crouch at the Alexandria Fair. One can see the results of many hours of currycombing on the back of this animal. By definition, a currycomb is a square comb with small plastic or rubber teeth that help bring dust and dandruff to the surface. The process of brushing shines and straightens the hair.

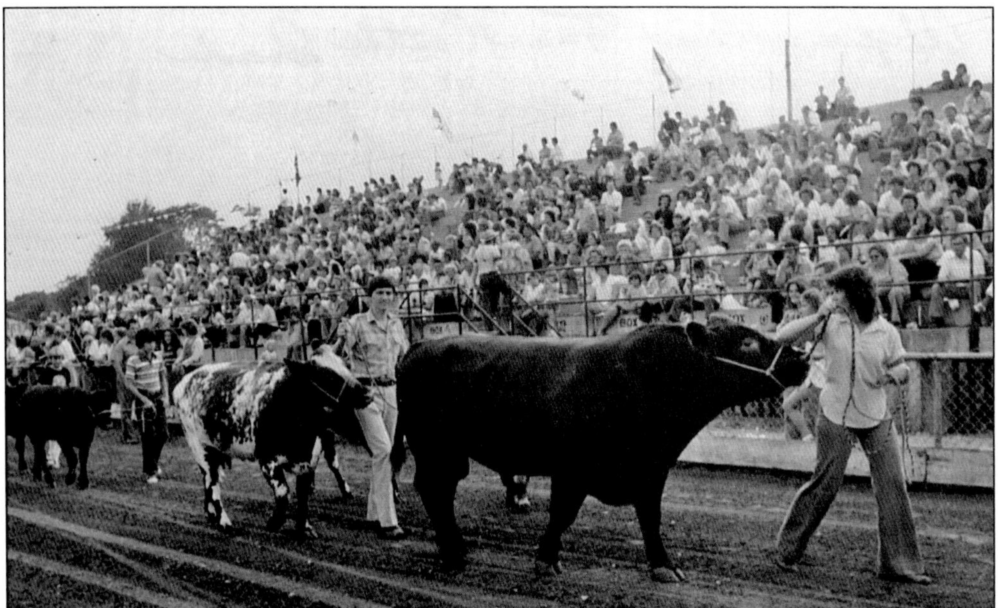

Cattle Parade, 1974. The new grandstand appears in the background as Brenda Prim leads her entry, followed by Owen Prim. A roof has been added to the grandstand since this photograph was taken.

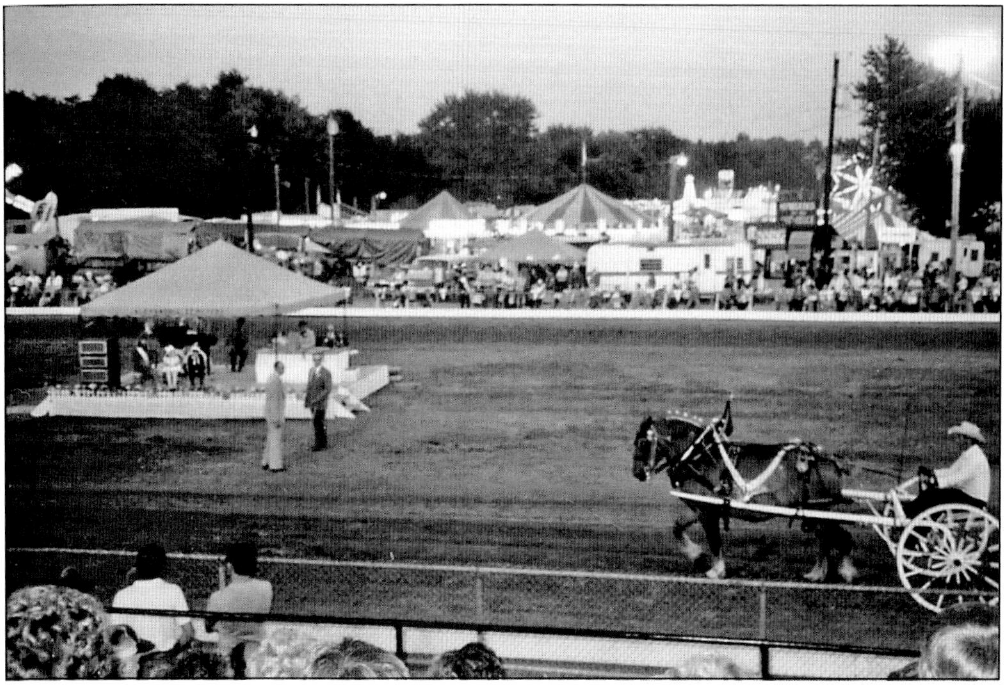

DRAFT HORSE CLASS, 2002. A gentleman passes the judges with his rig during the Alexandria Fair's Draft Horse contest. Lit brightly in the background, the midway is the place to go for entertainment, amusement rides, and foods such as corn dogs and cotton candy.

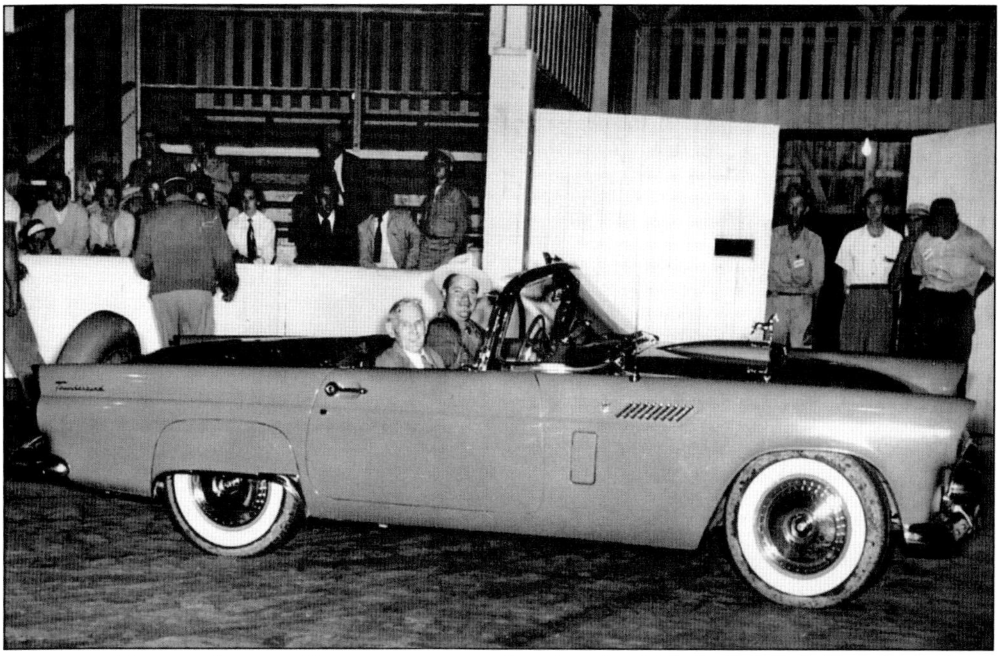

DOUGLAS NELSON. Reportedly never missing a fair, Douglas Nelson (1856–1957) is shown here riding in the ring. At the wheel of the 1956 Thunderbird is Bruce Lovins (1916–1966), who made custom show saddles at his shop in Alexandria. Note the chrome horse hood ornament. The individual in the white shirt in the doorway is Robert Crouch, the county agricultural agent.

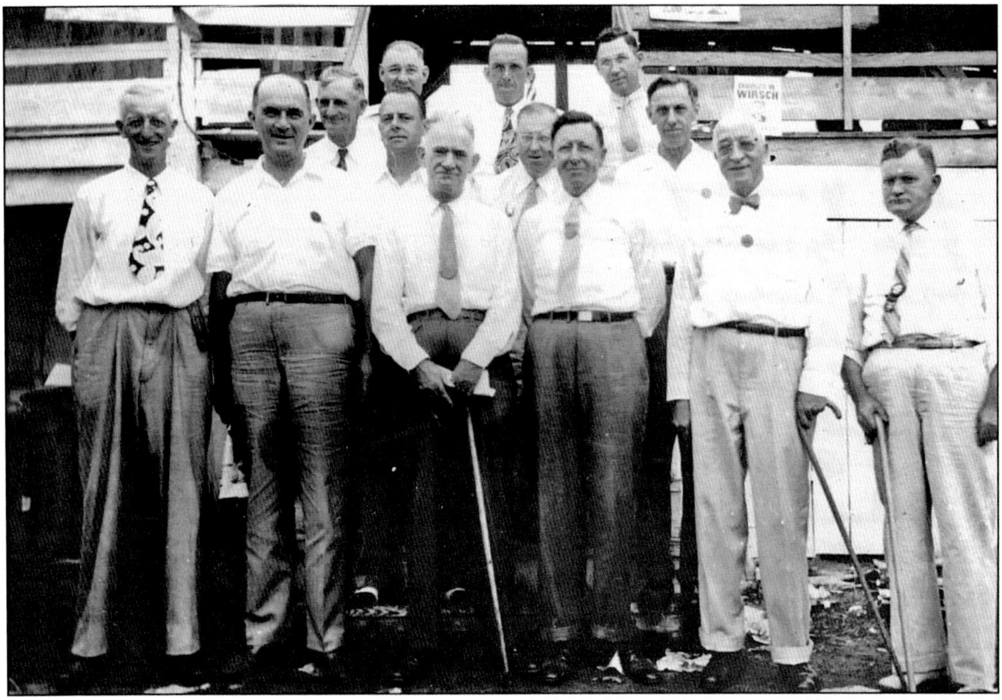

ALEXANDRIA FAIR BOARD. Board members included, from left to right, (first row) Edward Schaefer, Joseph Schmidt, Sol Youtsey, J. W. Shaw, ? Droege, and Charles Truesdale; (second row) John Thatcher, C. E. Lauterwasser, Sam A. Porter, and ? Alford; (third row) George Heringer, W. C. Dickens, and Raymond Beck. The sign in the background indicates that Charles Wirsch was running for office at this time.

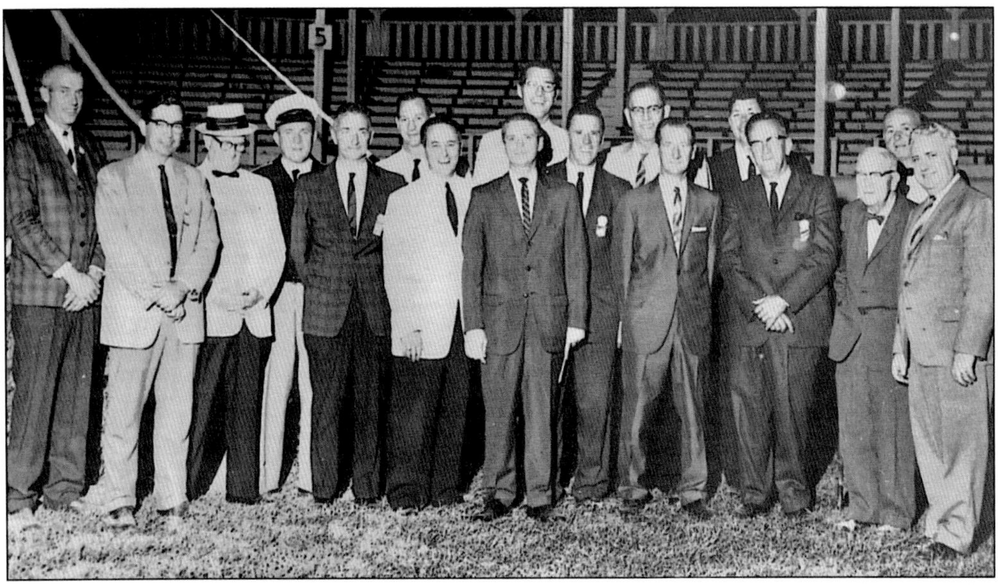

ALEXANDRIA FAIR BOARD, 1964. Pictured from left to right are: (first row) Melvin Schafer, Bruce Hutchinson, Bud Hamilton, Bill Edwards, Tom Carnes, Rodger Neiser, Art Drogue, Charles Hatcher, Jack Kees, W. C. Dickens, Sam Porter, and unidentified; (second row) Dick Schaber, Hank Schmidt, unidentified, Art Woeste, and Bob Janson.

Eight

Campbell County Historical and Genealogical Society

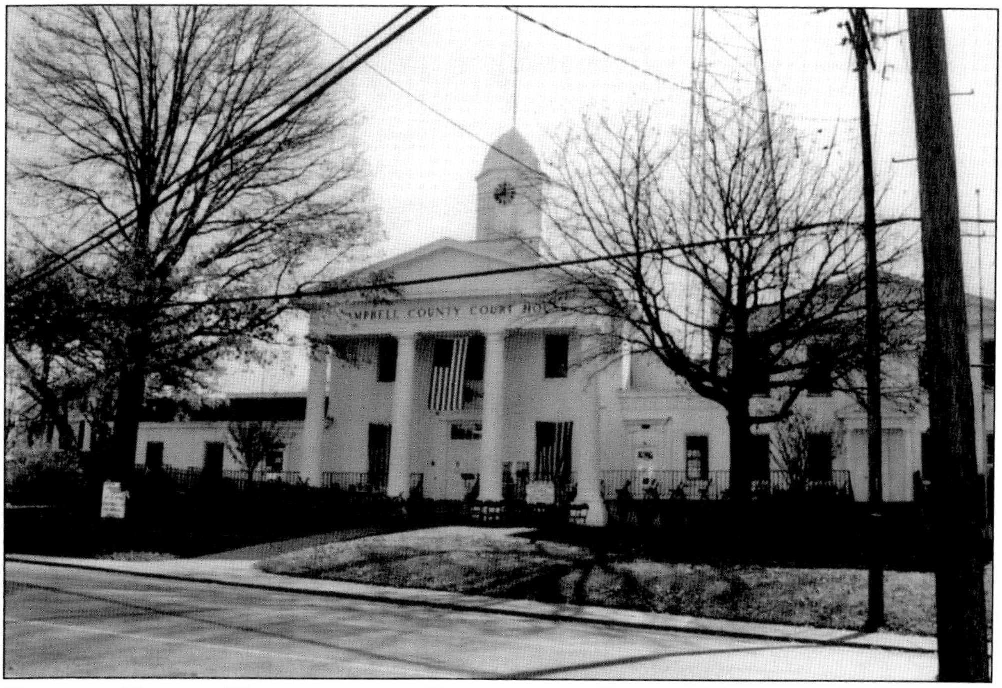

CAMPBELL COUNTY HISTORICAL AND GENEALOGICAL SOCIETY. The society was established in January 1990, and by 1994, the Campbell County Fiscal Court had asked members if they would like to locate on the second floor of the 1840s courthouse. Today Campbell County has the largest research library of any historical society in northern Kentucky.

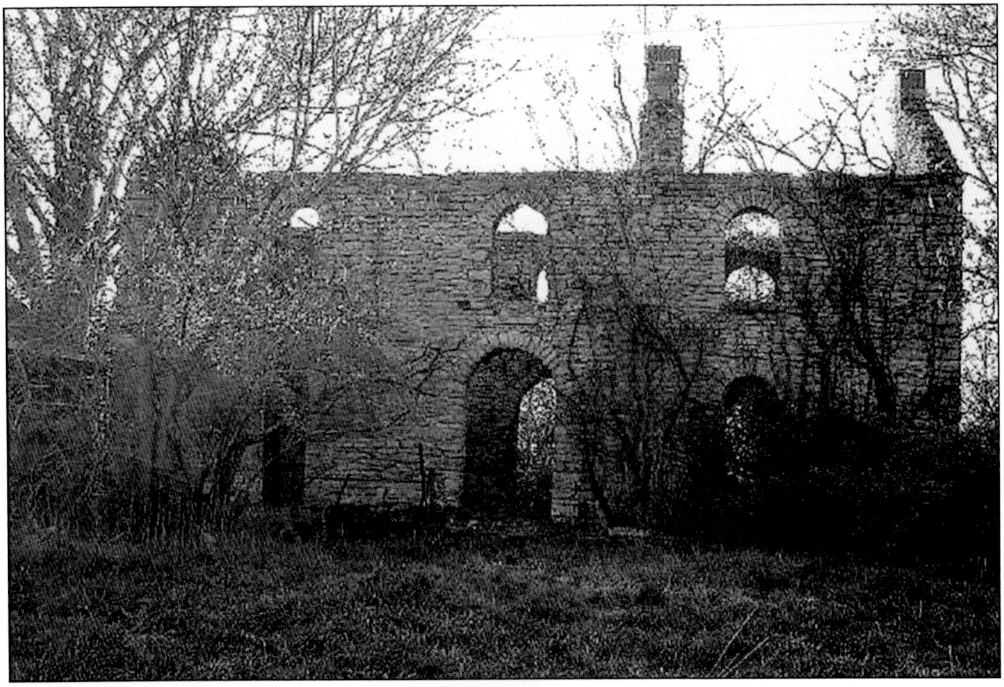

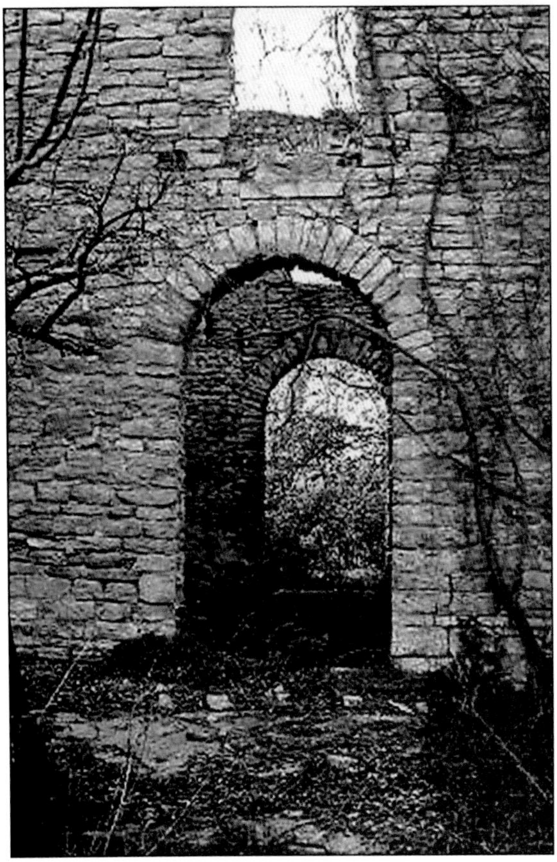

George Leonard Trapp Home. One of the missions of the Campbell County Historical and Genealogical Society is the documentation of buildings of historic significance. Recently, a little-known stone house was located within two miles of the courthouse and documented. The building pictured above was the residence of George Leonard Trapp, who was born in Oberhochstadt, Mittelfranken, Bayern, Germany, on March 21, 1841. Entering this country in 1855, Trapp married Josephine Weinel, the daughter of Thomas Mack Weinel and Elizabeth Lear, on September 15, 1863, in Newport. He died on June 15, 1905. Both Trapp and his wife are buried in the Alexandria Cemetery. The prevailing German custom at the time was to go by one's middle name; therefore, he was known as Leonard. Services were held at the Alexandria Lutheran Church. Quite wealthy, he owned the Licking Turnpike as well as considerable real estate. Shown at left is one of entrances, measuring 9 feet tall and 5 feet wide.

DETAILS OF THE HOME. The house was likely built sometime after 1870, and according to 1888 Alexandria tax records, Leonard Trapp owned 266 acres valued at $7,800 and $830 in improvements or personal property. Because of the fine stone construction, the walls are still standing, although now resembling the old ruins seen in Europe. The house—with two stories, an attic, and a full basement—had several fireplaces on each floor. Its construction details reportedly reflect the English rather than the German style. The farm had numerous outbuildings, including a circular stone structure believed to be a smokehouse, pictured below. A smokehouse was an enclosed structure in which a fire could be kept smoldering for a few weeks, the smoke slowly curing the meat and adding flavor. After curing, meat would keep for a long time. The house burned in the 1970s.

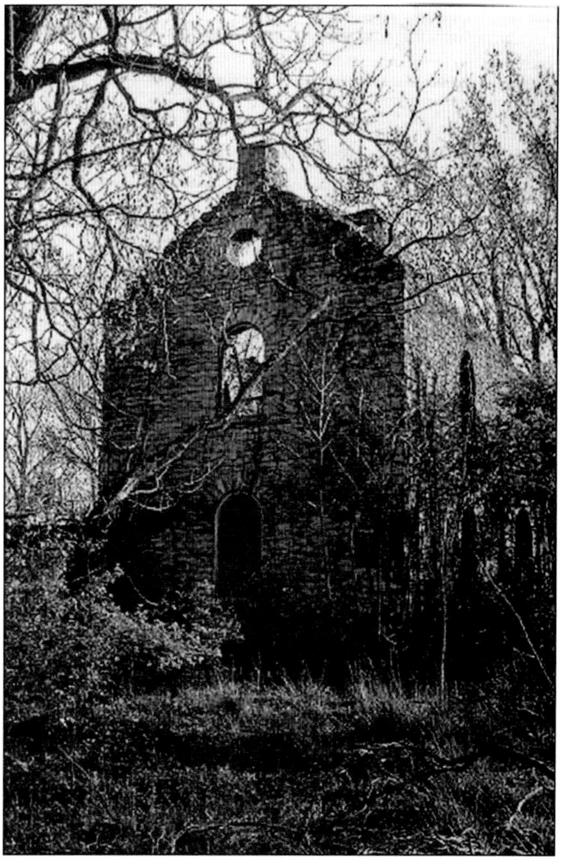

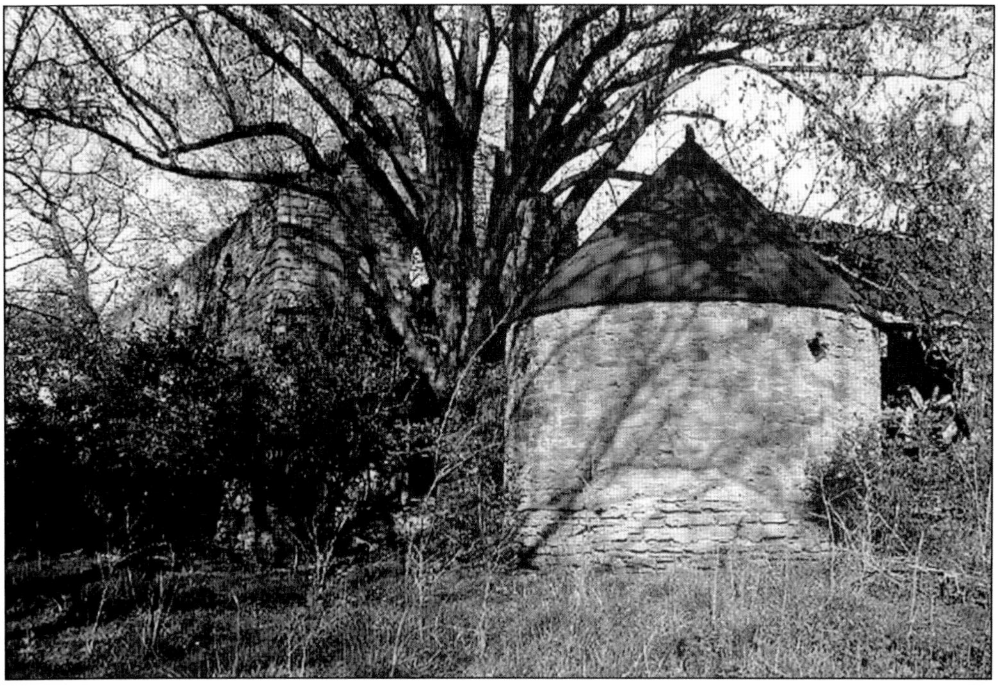